The Neighborhoods of New York City

KENNETH T. JACKSON, GENERAL EDITOR

Although outsiders often regard New York City as an undifferentiated mass of 7 million rude, indifferent people, Gotham is in fact a collection of more than 400 individual neighborhoods, each containing its fill of involved and friendly residents and each cherishing a unique sense of identity and place. Here, as elsewhere in America, locally owned haberdasheries, hardware stores, delicatessens, greengroceries, and bakeries along main streets compete with shopping centers and malls, but it is still a fact that New York is almost the last place in the nation where neighbors routinely pass one another on the sidewalk or exchange greetings at a corner store, in the local park, or at a community center. From stoops and front porches they discuss news of their block, or of the world. Indeed, New York has become the best place in the United States to experience what was once the essence of small-town America.

THE   NEIGHBORHOODS   OF

Brooklyn

Second Edition

Introduction by Kenneth T. Jackson

John B. Manbeck, Consulting Editor

CITIZENS for NYC
Your Partner For Better Neighborhoods

Yale University Press ■ New Haven and London

PROJECT STAFF

Zella Jones, Project Coordinator

Michelle LeMay-Santiago,
  Development Coordinator

Judy Metro, Sponsoring Editor

Julie Carlson, Manuscript Editor

Susan Laity, Production Editor

Anne Ellen Geller, Research Editor

Alexie Waters, Research Associate

Matthew Savino, Research Associate

Ed Grazda, Photographer

William L. Nelson, Cartographer

Martha Hostetter, Photo Researcher

Timothy Calabrese, Demographer

Nancy Ovedovitz, Designer

Sonia Scanlon, Designer

Paul Royster, Production Manager

Cele Syrotiak, Production Controller

First published 1998 by Yale University Press.
Second Edition published 2004 by Yale University
Press.

Copyright © 1998 by Yale University.
Second Edition © 2004 by Yale University.

Photographs by Ed Grazda unless otherwise
identified.

Set in Bodoni type by BW&A Books, Inc. Printed
and bound by R. R. Donnelly, Willard, Ohio.
Manufactured in the United States of America.

Library of Congress Control Number: 2004101455

ISBN 0-300-10310-7 (pbk. : alk. paper)

A catalogue record for this book is available from
the British Library.

The paper in this book meets the guidelines for
permanence and durability of the Committee on
Production Guidelines for Book Longevity of the
Council on Library Resources.

10 9 8 7 6 5 4 3 2 1

Major support for *The Neighborhoods of Brooklyn* was provided by
J.P. Morgan Chase & Co.

Additional support was provided by

- The Jill and Marshall Rose Foundation
- Furthermore, the publication program of the J.M. Kaplan Foundation
- Jeanette and Bernard Workman

Contents

Foreword

Brooklyn's greatness comes from its rich and diverse neighborhoods—each with its own history, architecture, people, ethnicity, languages, and cuisine. You can travel the world from China to the Caribbean, Poland to Pakistan without ever leaving Brooklyn.

We are—and always have been—a city of immigrants. The American dream is made up of stories of immigrants who created successful businesses; in Brooklyn, entrepreneurs built neighborhoods with their dreams. Junior's Restaurant in downtown Brooklyn, Nathan's in Coney Island, Peter Luger's in Williamsburg, Kleinfeld's Bridal Shop in Bay Ridge—these are just a few of the long-standing businesses that are inseparable from the neighborhoods that grew up around them.

To tour our communities is to set out on one of the world's greatest treasure hunts. There are international fashions, music, culture, and a movable feast of foods, from kielbasa and pierogis in Greenpoint to cannoli in Bensonhurst and roti in Flatbush. There are sounds—of Creole and Yiddish in Crown Heights, Chinese and Spanish in Sunset Park, and Russian along the boardwalk in Brighton Beach.

History is made all over Brooklyn. The Battle of Brooklyn, during the American Revolution, laid the cornerstone for our fierce pride and independent spirit. Erasmus Hall High School in Flatbush is the second-oldest public school in the United States. In 1838 Weeksville became one of the first free African-American communities in the country. And Coney Island is the home of the world's first roller coaster.

Brooklyn is an economic powerhouse, currently experiencing major capital investment, development, and urban renewal. Businesses are attracted by our can-do attitude, our vast resources and opportunities, and our world-class cultural institutions, breathtaking natural settings, incredible community spirit, strong faith communities, and educational institutions.

Part of our strength is what I call Brooklyn's "big town, small town" qualities. While we offer everything you'd find in a world-class city, Brooklyn is still a place where people know their neighbors, often went to the same schools their children do, and greet their dry cleaner by name.

Here we live together peacefully and with respect—people of every faith, creed, and color, from every nation and walk of life. Brooklyn today is America's tomorrow.

Marty Markowitz
President, Borough of Brooklyn

Preface

A neighborhood is more than a physical space: it is a social, cultural, and emotional home, an arena of civic engagement, a place people organize around—that they work to preserve and improve. New York City has more than 400 neighborhoods, each with its own individuality and character. Ask a New Yorker "Where are you from?" and the answer is as likely to be "Flatbush" as "New York." So before you can understand the city, you must first come to know its neighborhoods. For nearly 30 years Citizens for NYC (formerly known as the Citizens Committee for New York City) has been dealing with the people of New York at this basic level. Citizens for NYC supports neighborhood volunteer organizations, working with them to improve the quality of life in every neighborhood and thus the city as a whole.

In 1996 Citizens for NYC joined forces with Kenneth T. Jackson and Yale University Press, editor and publisher of the highly regarded *Encyclopedia of New York City,* to create a series that will celebrate the history and spirit of every neighborhood in the city. Organized by borough, the five-volume Neighborhoods of New York City will tell the story of the world's greatest city from an intimate and unusual perspective.

We began our research for the series by surveying the 1,000 largest neighborhood and civic associations of the more than 12,000 we serve. In interviews and questionnaires, we asked residents to tell us about their neighborhood: what its boundaries are, who their neighbors are, and how they spend their time. The neighborhood groups spend thousands of hours every year on local initiatives, coming together for meetings, festivals, and community improvement projects. Their understanding of, their pride and investment in these neighborhoods uniquely qualified them to introduce us to their homes. With their help, we began to construct our neighborhood portraits.

Why begin with Brooklyn? Because everyone, everywhere has heard of Brooklyn: as Professor Jackson notes in his introduction, Brooklyn is one of the best-known place names in the United States. In addition, it is one of the city's oldest settlements: many of its neighborhoods date back to before the beginning of our nation. Indeed, Brooklyn was present at the creation of the nation, the site of the Revolutionary War's Battle of Brooklyn. And for millions of immigrants it was—and is—their first home in America. If we are a nation of immigrants, Brooklyn, which boasts residents of 200 nationalities, is America's quintessential hometown.

This volume identifies 90 individual neighborhoods. These neighborhoods are discussed in 45 chapters that further delineate what we describe as subneighborhoods—areas that are now merged within larger entities by virtue of physical expansion or social evolution but that still exhibit distinct features such as architectural similarities (many began as housing developments) or a shared history or ethnic background. Flatbush, for example, boasts 11 such subneighborhoods. Some chapters also cite "ghost neighborhoods"—areas that were, at the borough's beginning, the center of a community's activity but that are no longer distinct neighborhoods as such. Each neighborhood portrait seeks to convey the "feel" of the area through an examination of its people, history, architecture, landmarks, points of interest, curiosities, and what might be called vital statistics. Each chapter contains a street map.

A word about the maps. No one has ever before attempted to map all 400-plus of the city's neighborhoods, although local maps have identified a number of the largest. This caution is understandable. There are no official government boundaries, and not every boundary is agreed upon by every resident of a particular area. Yet neighborhoods are "real" social entities. We identified boundaries on the basis of hundreds of hours of research and consultation with local civic and neighborhood associations. In the course of these interviews, we were delighted to discover strong agreement among resident groups concerning their own neighborhood's boundaries as well as those of the neighborhoods around them. Surprisingly few Brooklyn neighborhoods seem to overlap, and very few blocks lie unclaimed. In cases where a subneighborhood could be said to belong to either of two larger neighborhoods—City Line, say, which has ties to both East New York and Cypress Hills—we obtained a consensus of residents and official groups. (One neighborhood, Ridgewood, actually claimed ties to more than one borough. Because Ridgewood straddles the Brooklyn-Queens line and has a Queens zip code, it will be discussed in our forthcoming volume on the neighborhoods of Queens.) The maps are therefore meant as tools in understanding each neighborhood in its current social as well as political context. A composite map on page xxxii situates each neighborhood geographically within the borough.

We are very pleased to include 2000 census numbers, compiled by Timothy Calabrese, research associate for the Population Division of the New York City Department of City Planning. The Neighborhood Profiles found within each chapter provide quick reference to essential places and services. Because some services, like fire departments and hospitals, cross neighborhood boundaries, we have generally listed only those that actually sit in the neighborhood. Similarly, a comprehensive list of schools or services like senior or day-care centers provided difficulties both in terms of length and because new entities are constantly springing up to accommodate growing communities and changing populations. Famous schools and longstanding neighbor-hood associations are discussed in the text of the chapter.

Our team was large and the details were daunting. Michael Clark of Citizens for NYC and Tina Weiner of Yale University Press independently conceived this project as an overdue recognition of the primacy of neighborhoods in the lives of New Yorkers. Citizens for NYC and the Press were brought together by their mutual friend Thomas H. Guinzburg. Michelle LeMay-Santiago next introduced the project to its funders: J.P. Morgan & Co. Incorporated; the Jill and Marshall Rose Foundation; the Furthermore program of the J.M. Kaplan Foundation; and Jeanette and Bernard Workman.

Kenneth T. Jackson's *Encyclopedia of New York City* provided the basic source material on Brooklyn, while his introduction gives an overview of the borough. Building on this, in consultation with former Brooklyn Borough Historian John Manbeck—who knows Brooklyn as only a Brooklyn-born historian can—Anne Ellen Geller began collecting a base of data and interviews, overseeing preliminary mapping and researching numerous sources of Brooklyn information, after which Julie Carlson turned research and recollections into intimate neighborhood portraits. Susan Laity of Yale University Press oversaw the inclusion of an endless stream of facts and deftly orchestrated the editing. Ed Grazda, another Brooklynite, roamed the borough for nine months giving life to more than 2,000 photographic images from which we could select only a small portion for this volume.

Richard Heaps and Michell Hackwelder of the Brooklyn Historical Society generously unpacked archive photo treasures they were preparing to relocate for a year of building restoration. Many others also offered invaluable assistance: Robert Macdonald, director of the Museum of the City of New York; Ken Cobb, director, and Leonora Gidlund, assistant director, of the Municipal Archives; Judy Walsh, Julie Moffat, and Joy Holland of the Brooklyn Public Library's Brooklyn Collection; Leon Goldstein, president of Kingsborough Community College; Angelo DeCandia of the Kingsborough Historical Society; Tim Tomkins, director, and Ras Kirmani, Brooklyn outreach coordinator, Partnership for Parks; and Joseph Salvo and Frank Vardy of the New York City Planning Commission.

Brian Merlis helped us fill in the photographic gaps from his peerless collection of early Brooklyn photographs. Mike Armstrong, Judith Blahnik, Robert Cohen, Charles Denson, Daniel Fingerer, John Gallagher, Mary Kay Gallagher, Tony Giordano, Dennis Holt, Julie Houston, Ira Kluger, Liz Koch, Margaret Latimer, Barbara Millstein, Joyce Mulvaney, Greg O'Connell, David Sharps, Peter Spanakos, Claudette J. Spence, Janine St. Germaine, Craig

Steven Wilder, and Jack Wolkenfeld all lent expertise in finding primary data.

The entire enterprise would have been impossible without the ceaseless efforts of Zella Jones of Citizens for NYC and Judy Metro of Yale University Press, who kept the whole group focused, on schedule, and motivated.

In the end, this volume is a tribute to the countless committed, enthusiastic residents of the 90 (yes, 90!) neighborhoods in the borough of Brooklyn. For it is the people of Brooklyn who ultimately created this wondrous tapestry called *The Neighborhoods of Brooklyn.*

Osborn Elliott   Michael E. Clark
Founding Chairman   President

Citizens for NYC

Introduction

Kenneth T. Jackson, Jacques Barzun Professor of History
and the Social Sciences, Columbia University

Brooklyn is an enigma. On the one hand, it is New York City's most populous
and arguably its most colorful borough. It is one of the best-known place
names in the United States and has long been one of America's greatest liter-
ary landscapes. It has nurtured Woody Allen, Isaac Asimov, Mel Brooks,
Aaron Copland, Shirley Chisholm, Neil Diamond, Milton Friedman, George
Gershwin, Jackie Gleason, Joseph Heller, Lena Horne, Robert Maynard
Hutchins, Alfred Kazin, Sandy Koufax, Spike Lee, Vince Lombardi, Norman
Mailer, Wynton and Branford Marsalis, Mary Tyler Moore, Zero Mostel,
Joseph Papp, S. J. Perelman, I. I. Rabi, Max Roach, Maurice Sendak, Beverly
Sills, Barbra Streisand, Walt Whitman, and hundreds of other distinguished
writers, musicians, actors, artists, politicians, scientists, and sports figures.
As many as a quarter of all Americans can trace their ancestry to people who
once lived in its 81 square miles. Brooklyn has been featured in dozens of
songs, movies, books, photographs, and television programs. It had legendary
Ebbets Field and the famous Dodgers. It has miles of beach front, scores of
vibrant neighborhoods, spectacular cultural institutions, and numerous architectural treasures. And it has the Brooklyn Bridge, celebrated as the eighth
wonder of the world when it opened in 1883. In its structure and design, wrote
the distinguished urban critic Lewis Mumford, "the architecture of the past,
massive and protective, meets the architecture of the future, light, aerial,
open to sunlight, an architecture of voids rather than solids."

Yet Brooklyn remains a mystery. Few of the 30 million tourists who annually visit Manhattan's glittering attractions venture across the East River;
not until 1998 did New York's largest sightseeing company begin scheduling
buses to Brooklyn. Even the residents of New York's four other boroughs and
its 26 suburban counties rarely sample the pleasures of Brooklyn. Too often
they see only its aging industrial buildings or curse at its poor highway system. And for too many, Brooklyn appears either boring and out-of-date or,
more ominously, torn by racial strife and violence.

This book aims to change the popular perception: to remind New Yorkers
that Brooklyn is an urban delight and to convince skeptics that the borough is
a center of culture, the starting point for immigrants from around the world.
At the same time, we hope to give current and former Brooklynites new reasons to explore their home ground and to visit neighborhoods that are just a
few miles distant. I hope that *The Neighborhoods of Brooklyn,* with its marvel-

ous illustrations and intimate community portraits, will give readers hours of pleasure. For in its pages they will learn what makes Brooklyn special.

First, it is huge. Located on the southwestern tip of Long Island and situated across the Upper Bay and the East River from Manhattan, Brooklyn had 2,465,326 inhabitants in 2000, or more than any independent city in the United States except New York, Los Angeles, and Chicago. One need only remember that Brooklyn currently is as populous as Boston, San Francisco, St. Louis, and Atlanta *combined* to get a sense of its immensity.

Second, Brooklyn is diverse even by the standards of a multicultural nation. From the time of its initial European settlement more than three and a half centuries ago, Brooklyn has been heterogeneous. In 1855, for example, nearly half the 205,000 residents of Brooklyn were foreign born, more than half of them Irish and almost a quarter each from Germany and Britain. And it has been for centuries the home of a large and energetic black population. In 2004 Brooklyn remains *the* center in the United States for Caribbeans, for Russians, and for Orthodox Jews, and it contains in Bedford-Stuyvesant the largest African American community on the continent. At the same time, thousands of Irish, Arabs, Scandinavians, West Indians, Chinese, and Italians, to take only the more obvious examples, make Brooklyn's demographic pattern unusual in its variety.

In addition, while many urban centers have a fine museum or library, Brooklyn boasts some of the foremost cultural institutions in the world, most notably the Brooklyn Academy of Music, the Brooklyn Museum, and the Brooklyn Botanic Garden. It also possesses in Prospect Park an urban open space of matchless quality and in Coney Island an amusement park of matchless fame.

But Brooklyn is more than just a great city masquerading as a borough. Brooklyn is a collection of neighborhoods, many of them centuries old and all of them with a distinct feel and character. They differ architecturally, economically, demographically, ethnically, and sociologically, but all are alike in that each is uniquely Brooklyn.

Colonial History

Before 1524, when Giovanni da Verrazano became the first known white man to sail up the Narrows into the lower bay, the place now known as Brooklyn was home to Munsee-speaking Indians called Lenapes or Delawareans. The Canarsees, one of several subgroups, were especially prominent in Brooklyn. Many thousands in number, they had settlements in what are presently Gowanus, Sheepshead Bay, Flatlands, and Canarsie, as well as on Governors Island and Staten Island.

None of these local Indian groups had as advanced a civilization as the Mayans, Incas, or Aztecs, who lived farther south in the Western Hemisphere. But these early inhabitants of Brooklyn did cultivate wheat, maize, beans, and squash, which they combined with fish, shellfish, and assorted wild animals to provide a varied diet. Their homes were long bark houses, topped by thatched domes of substantial size, which accommodated many families at one time.

In 1624 these first Americans were perhaps startled when the Dutch West India Company established a permanent settlement of Europeans on Governors Island in the harbor. In 1625 the Dutch moved their tiny community to the island of Manhattan, which they "bought" from the Indians in 1626. In 1636 the newcomers turned their attention to Brooklyn and made several land purchases from the natives, who probably did not understand that to Europeans land once bought could not be used again by the former owners. By the 1640s the Dutch had established regular ferry service across the East River between Brooklyn and Manhattan. Ultimately, they created five towns in what is now Kings County (the borough of Brooklyn): Breuckelen (Brooklyn) in 1646, New Amersfoort (Flatlands) in 1647, Midwout (Flatbush) in 1652, New Utrecht in 1657, and Boswijck (Bushwick) in 1661. A sixth town was founded in 1645 by an Englishwoman, Lady Deborah Moody, who was in search of a place where she and her Anabaptist followers could worship in peace. They called it Gravesend.

The De Hart, or Bergen, House once stood in the original Dutch town of Flatlands (Brooklyn Historical Society)

The Dutch period ended in 1664. On August 18 a fleet of four British warships and 500 professional soldiers arrived in the harbor. The Dutch governor, Peter Stuyvesant, wanted to fight the invaders. But his citizens lacked the stomach for a contest with the powerful guns of the Royal Navy. So on September 8, with drums beating and flags flying, Stuyvesant surrendered Fort Amsterdam in lower Manhattan. The English renamed the community New York, after the duke of York (later James II). The city subsequently gave its name to the entire colony.

In 1683 Kings County became an administrative subdivision of the province of New York, but otherwise English rule affected Brooklyn only slightly. The six, predominantly agricultural towns grew slowly, even as the remaining Indian population almost died out because of disease and the loss of traditional hunting and farming lands. By the eighteenth century, perhaps a third of the population was black, a larger proportion of blacks than in any other county of what became New York State. Most of these were slaves and indentured servants brought to Brooklyn from Africa who worked the large landholdings of the Schencks, the Van Nuyses, and the Wyckoffs, among others. (Although gradual emancipation began around 1799, it wasn't until 1827, when New York State abolished slavery, that all Brooklynites were finally free.)

When revolutionary fervor swept the colonies in the 1770s, Brooklyn remained mostly outside the debate—if anything, its white population was loyal to the British monarchy. When war did break out, Kings County became the site of the first major battle in the American Revolution. In July and August 1776, the Royal Navy concentrated 400 ships and 30,000 soldiers, the greatest display of military might the Western Hemisphere had yet seen, in the harbor adjacent to Brooklyn. George Washington, who had moved the Continental Army south from Boston in an attempt to protect New York City, was in an unenviable position. If he chose to defend Brooklyn, the British might move their ships into the East River and thus trap the American army on Long Island. On the other hand, if he abandoned the nearby high ground of Brooklyn Heights, strategically significant New York City would surely fall to the redcoats. Washington chose to fight, with disastrous results. On August 22 the British shifted their main force from Staten Island to Brooklyn, near present-day Gravesend. On August 27, a great battle began. Although many of the Americans fought bravely (especially 400 volunteers from Maryland, only nine of whom escaped death or capture), the redcoats and their Hessian mercenaries swept the patriots from the field and nearly ended the war then and there. More than 1,200 Americans were killed and another 1,500 wounded or taken prisoner. The British, by contrast, lost about 60 dead and 300 wounded.

So complete was the rout that contemporaries reported that even British camp followers took prisoners. More soberly, an anonymous observer remarked: "The Declaration of Independence that was signed in ink in Philadelphia was signed in blood in Brooklyn."

Fortunately for the Americans, however, neither Gen. William Howe nor his brother Adm. Richard Howe had the good sense to place British warships in the East River to block the retreat of the Continental Army. Thus the Americans were able to sneak across the water under cover of fog in the early morning hours of August 30 and regroup in Manhattan. England had lost its golden opportunity to win the war quickly.

The Battle of Brooklyn (also called the Battle of Long Island) taught George Washington that his ragtag forces could not stand up against British and Hessian regular troops. So in the manner of Ho Chi Minh in Vietnam two centuries later, Washington adopted a strategy of avoiding confrontation with the main body of the enemy, choosing instead to protect his army and prolong the conflict, with the aim of encouraging the stronger nation eventually to despair of a military solution and sail away.

Before they left, however, the British made Brooklyn the scene of the greatest American tragedy of the eighteenth century: the horrors of the infamous prison ships. These ghastly vessels, which held American prisoners of war, lay at anchor in Wallabout Bay between 1776 and 1783, near the future site of the Brooklyn Navy Yard, and they caused more deaths than all the battles and campaigns on land and sea in all the years of the war combined. The 6,824 American fatalities in actual combat represented only about a third of American deaths. Most of the rest were people who lost their lives in captivity, about half of them in Brooklyn. Because careful records were probably never kept—at least, they have never been found—exact numbers cannot be known. But enough bones later washed up in the muddy flats of the Brooklyn shore to indicate that as many as 11,000 Americans may have died there. (More conservative estimates place the number at 4,000.)

After 1776 quiet returned to Brooklyn. The area remained agricultural, and its economic ties to the booming city across the river were slight. As late as 1810, it was occupied mostly by farms, and its population was less than 5,000.

The Nineteenth Century
In the next four decades the town of Brooklyn was transformed. Regular steam ferry service to New York City (then consisting only of Manhattan) began in 1814, and a year later the *Brooklyn Star* predicted that the town "must necessarily become a favorite residence for gentlemen of taste and fortune,

for merchants and shopkeepers of every description, for artists, merchants, laborers, and persons of every trade in society." The accuracy of this prophecy soon became apparent. With its tree-shaded streets, pleasant homes, access to Manhattan, and general middle-class ambiance, Brooklyn attracted those who sought respite from the bustle and congestion of Gotham. Walt Whitman, whose office at the *Brooklyn Eagle* overlooked the Fulton Ferry slip, frequently commented on the area's phenomenal growth. In Brooklyn, he said, "men of moderate means may find homes at a moderate rent, whereas in New York City there is no median between a palatial mansion and a dilapidated hovel."

Additional ferry lines soon expanded the commuting possibilities. In 1836 the South Ferry began regular runs between Atlantic Street in Brooklyn and Whitehall Street in Manhattan, and in 1846 the Hamilton Ferry began connecting Hamilton Avenue with the Battery. By 1860 the various East River ferries were carrying 33 million passengers a year (about 100,000 each working day), and by 1870 the patronage had increased to 50 million. Indeed, the folk wisdom of the day held that when there was fog in the harbor, half the business population of Manhattan would be late for work.

As the ferry districts became distinct from the more rural areas that comprised the rest of Kings County, the political form began to change. In 1834 Brooklyn leaders won city status from the state legislature over the opposition of Manhattan representatives. By that time, suburban landowners and speculators were anxious to subdivide their farms into city lots, and they perceived that a stronger government would provide the streets and services that would aid the rapid development of the periphery.

Whether the attraction was easy access to Manhattan, pleasant surroundings, cheap land, or low taxes, Brooklyn was growing faster than New York City by 1820, and in almost every decade until the Civil War its population doubled. One wag noted that Brooklyn "sold nature wholesale" to real-estate developers for sale to homeowners at retail. In 1853, 360 lots were sold in single sales in Bushwick, 150 in Fort Hamilton, and 600 in Brooklyn proper. Even on the farthest outskirts of the built-up region, the influx of middle-class families soon became apparent. Newspaper advertisements in New York offered a home in Brooklyn no farther from Wall Street offices than many Manhattan tenements, for 10 to 40 percent down and payments spread over three to five years. Soon Brooklyn developers were not only advertising elegant mansions for the wealthy that boasted "clean sea breezes and a glorious view of greater New York and its harbor" but touting less expensive dwellings for the middle classes.

The Brooklyn Bridge, which opened in 1883, was a major contributor to the

Fireworks mark the completion of the Brooklyn Bridge, seen from the Brooklyn side
(Library of Congress; ink drawing by Charles Graham)

area's growth, and every year thousands of families, many of them immigrants, moved across the river, drawn by Brooklyn's open spaces, relatively affordable housing, and reputation for safety. As the century wore on, Brooklyn was gradually transformed from a suburb into a major city in its own right, the third largest in the country in the latter part of the nineteenth century. In 1890 Brooklyn counted more than 261,000 foreign-born residents, equal to its entire population 30 years earlier. With this increase in size, the decay, noise, and hectic way of life so many had fled Manhattan to avoid followed the immigrants across the river.

The newcomers also brought their cultures and religions with them, however. By mid-century, Brooklyn had so many houses of worship that it was known as "the city of churches." One of the most famous was the Plymouth Church of the Pilgrims, where abolitionist Henry Ward Beecher held the pulpit for 40 years. Meanwhile, local residents were pioneering in a number of fields: Brooklyn had the nation's most widely read afternoon newspaper (the *Brooklyn Eagle*, founded 1841); the first use of gas in an urban area (1848); the first recruiting office in the Civil War; the largest contribution to the Union cause raised during 1864; and the first birth-control clinic in the United States (Margaret Sanger's, in Brownsville, in 1916).

Even though Brooklyn's initial budding was due to a quiet environment that was easily accessible to the central business district of the world's busiest seaport, the city grew later as the result of its own commerce and industry. After the Civil War, it became a major center of the "five black arts": glassmaking, porcelain manufacture, printing, petroleum and gas refining, and iron making. In 1875, for example, there were 50 oil refineries in Brooklyn, and Charles Pratt's Astral Oil Company had about the same capacity as John D. Rockefeller's Standard Oil Company of Ohio. By 1890 Brooklyn possessed large factories, chemical works, foundries and iron mills, candy companies, coffee and syrup mills, and especially breweries. Only Chicago had a bigger dressed-meat operation, and no city in the world had larger sugar refining or grain-depot operations.

Far from seeing the growth of Brooklyn as an advantage, however, as early as 1850 New York newspapers, politicians, and land developers were brooding over the intense competition and expressing concern about the "desertion of the city by its men of wealth." At the same time, the residential and industrial growth of Brooklyn required funds for roads, sewers, schools, and mass transportation systems. By the 1890s the city had nearly reached its allowable debt limit and had exhausted its ability to issue bonds. The solution to the problem was consolidation with New York City and its massive tax base. After a close advisory vote in 1895, the City of Brooklyn ceased to exist on January 1, 1898, and in the most important municipal consolidation ever, Brooklyn became a borough of New York City.

The Twentieth Century

The loss of political independence did not slow Brooklyn's transformation. The new borough grew from 1.2 million people in 1890 to 2.7 million a half-century later. The first subway to Brooklyn opened in 1908, and over the next two decades tens of thousands of new homes and apartments went up in Flatbush, Gravesend, Flatlands, and New Utrecht. Large-scale development in Sheepshead Bay began after the Brighton Beach line of the Brooklyn-Manhattan Transit was opened to the district in 1920. Throughout the giant borough, speculators were active in petitioning for transit routes near their housing ventures. The trolley extension along Nostrand Avenue from Avenue Q to Avenue U, for example, was completed as a result of vigorous campaigning by realtors, who paid $10,000 of the $30,000 needed to complete the line.

The developers' enthusiasm was contagious, and Brooklyn grew by 540,000 residents in the single decade of the 1920s. Indeed, in 1922 and 1923 Brooklyn led the nation in housing construction. Sometimes new roads were as important as new subways or trolleys in stimulating development. In southeastern Brooklyn, promoters stressed that paved streets would soon be extended to their "conveniently situated lots," making commuting to Manhattan possible even in the absence of mass transit. They promised that the city would upgrade Kings Highway—which would then run for 17 miles across Brooklyn—

that Flatbush Avenue would become a direct artery to Rockaway Beach and Downtown Brooklyn, and that Nostrand and Bedford Avenues would be connected with the proposed Marine Park on Jamaica Bay. As it happened, these promises were yet to be fulfilled when the Depression hit in 1930, but by that time the developers had sold their houses and moved on to other areas.

Meanwhile, Brooklyn was a borough of big shoulders and ceaseless industrial activity. Newcomers were awed by the waterfront and by the vast number of tramp steamers, sailing vessels, barges, and ferries that filled the nearby waterways. Ramshackle docks and piers loomed mile after mile from Greenpoint to Red Hook. Behind the docks stretched acres of warehouses and storage tanks, coal dumps and stoneyards, sugar mills and breweries, dry docks and ship chandlers. By 1930 Brooklyn had become, along with Chicago and Pittsburgh, one of the greatest manufacturing centers on earth. It handled 55 percent of all the freight in the Port of New York, and it had the largest docking and terminal station in the world.

Throughout the first half of the twentieth century, the most potent symbol of Brooklyn's industrial muscle was the Navy Yard. First opened in 1801, it became famous in the 1850s for the construction of fast clipper ships, which sped prospectors and merchants to California during the Gold Rush, and in the Civil War for the outfitting of the Union ironclad *Monitor,* which defeated the Confederate warship *Merrimac* in the world's first battle between steel-hulled vessels. Later the source of dozens of America's most famous warships, the facility reached its employment peak during World War II, when 70,000 men and women worked around the clock to produce more ships than all of Japan between 1942 and 1945. (The USS *Missouri,* on which the Japanese surrender was signed in 1945, was built at the Navy Yard.) Meanwhile, the Brooklyn Army Terminal was the point of departure for many of the men as

Fourth Avenue between St. Marks Place and Warren Street, Park Slope, 1959 (Brooklyn Historical Society)

well as most of the military hardware destined for Europe and combat with Hitler's armies.

But human and industrial muscle were often accompanied by other kinds of muscle as well: the might of organized crime. Along with Chicago, Brooklyn was one of the centers of organized crime in the 1920s and especially in the 1930s. Chicago had Al Capone; Brooklyn had "Murder, Inc." (For a while Brooklyn even had Capone; he began his criminal career in Red Hook and was married at St. Mary's Star of the Sea Church in Carroll Gardens.) For a few years in the 1930s, Lucky Luciano, Meyer Lansky, Joe Adonis, Frank Costello, Louis (Lepke) Buchalter, and Albert Anastasia made Brownsville synonymous with contract killing, until Abe (Kid Twist) Reles turned stool pigeon in 1940. In a peculiarly Brooklyn development, the testimony that brought the mob down was first delivered in a Coney Island hotel room.

Before Disneyland, there was Coney Island, the most famous fantasy space in the world until 1954. Between 1897 and 1904, three separate amusement parks—Steeplechase, Luna Park, and Dreamland—opened on Coney Island, and their elaborate mechanical rides and sideshows helped workers forget the drudgery of the factory and the shop floor. The "Nickel Empire," so called because everything—the subway, the hot dogs, and the rides themselves— was priced at five cents, sometimes drew a million holiday makers in a single day to its beaches and its midways.

More sophisticated cultural tastes were also being served in Brooklyn. The Brooklyn Art Museum, built in 1897, boasted (and still does) one of the finest collections of African, Egyptian, and American holdings in the world. Behind it, the Botanic Garden, which opened in 1911, stressed education along with beauty, establishing the world's first gardening program for children in 1914 and emphasizing plant physiology and genetics. The Brooklyn Public Library, created in 1897 and envisioned as a network of small libraries that would better serve the borough than a single large structure, was one of the first libraries that allowed readers to browse. Its grand Central Library is one of the architectural wonders of Grand Army Plaza. All three institutions are adjacent to Prospect Park (1873), considered their masterpiece by designers Frederick Law Olmsted and Calvert Vaux, who had already created Manhattan's Central Park. And Brooklynites of all tastes jammed Ebbets Field to cheer on the hapless Dodgers, who made baseball history when they signed Jackie Robinson in 1947 and won the World Series for Brooklyn in 1955 (after seven losses)—only to be sold and transplanted to Los Angeles two years later.

The loss of the Dodgers mirrored other changes. After World War II, Brooklyn began to decline both in population and in industrial employment. Spurred by new roadways to the suburbs and by federal mortgage programs that made new homes on the periphery available to young families for little or no down payment, hundreds of thousands of white, middle-class

On the Parachute Jump at Steeplechase Park, 1940s (Worldwide Photos, Kingsborough Historical Society)

residents abandoned Brooklyn for Nassau County, Staten Island, New Jersey, or the American South. Once-vibrant neighborhoods fell quiet. Manufacturing employment dropped from more than 235,000 in 1954 to less than half that by the 1990s, as older firms took advantage of federal tax credits for new capital investment and built new facilities elsewhere. And the Brooklyn docks, once as busy as any on earth, were largely quiet and abandoned by 1990.

The history of Brooklyn's brewing industry illustrates the problem. In 1900 Brooklyn was so important in the production of beer that the borough alone had 45 breweries, more than Chicago, Milwaukee, St. Louis, Pittsburgh, Louisville, and Cincinnati combined. In the single neighborhood of Bushwick, there were never fewer than ten breweries along a single street between 1850 and 1890. As late as 1960, one-fifth of American beer production took place in the New York area, and half of that was in Brooklyn.

Twenty years later, New York's breweries were all gone. No one factor was responsible for the shutdown of this vital local industry; rather, at least four reasons were behind the change. First, Prohibition reduced the number of New York breweries from 70 in 1918 to 23 in 1935. Afterward, a series of strikes for two-man trucks and a 35-hour work week stopped local breweries in 1948 and 1949 (although they did not affect deliveries from outside the metropolitan region). At the same time, the introduction of easily transport-

Schaefer Brewery, Kent Avenue, 1948
(Library of Congress; photo Gottscho-Schleisner, Inc.)

able beer cans in the late 1940s meant that it was cheaper for a large company like Schlitz, for example, to ship beer from Winston-Salem, North Carolina, than to produce the beverage locally. Finally, the last two Brooklyn breweries to close, Rheingold in 1974 and Schaefer in 1976, noted that the cost of energy was so prohibitive in Brooklyn that they could cut their power costs in half simply by moving a hundred miles to the west.

Brooklyn Today

By the 1960s and 1970s the Dodgers had long since left town, and Brooklyn was losing both jobs and people to the nearby suburbs and the more distant Sunbelt at an alarming rate. After 165 years, the Brooklyn Navy Yard closed. Rioting became a constant threat, arson was on the rise, and poverty, labor strikes, and racial tensions seemed to be the only stories the outside press reported about Brooklyn.

But if the borough was down, it was not out. By the 1990s there were signs of renaissance from Williamsburg to Brighton Beach, Carroll Gardens to New Lots. And much of this growth was the result of small-scale, community-based initiatives.

Brooklyn, the home of neighborhoods, has long hosted a conglomerate of neighborhood associations. Some of the oldest such groups in the United States began in Brooklyn Heights, Lefferts Manor, and Prospect Park South. But it was in 1967, with the Bedford-Stuyvesant Restoration Corporation, that Brooklyn showed the nation what a few concerned citizens could do—even in one of the biggest cities in the world. Following the interest in historic preservation that swept through Brooklyn Heights, Park Slope, Fort Greene, and Boerum Hill in the 1950s and 1960s, the Bedford-Stuyvesant Restoration Corporation hired unemployed residents to renovate and restore historic structures in the neighborhood. So successful was their initiative—economically, artistically, and socially—that soon groups all over Brooklyn were fixing up their row houses and brownstones, preserving their past while ensuring their future. Brooklyn's new look brought in new businesses and new housing, and with them, new optimism.

It also brought new residents. Immigration from the Caribbean, the Middle East, and the Soviet Union (before and after its demise) rose dramatically. And in addition to transplanting their families and cultures to Brooklyn, the immigrants—as immigrants have always done—brought their energy, enthusiasm, and talent to their new home. Enclaves of West Indians, Pakistanis, Chinese, Orthodox Jews, and Arabs, among others, brought the world to Brooklyn. New cuisine, new arts and crafts, and new festivals crowded the

Worshiper outside a Brooklyn mosque
(Photo Jeffery A. Salter. © 1989 *Newsday*,
November 26, 1989)

streets. The city of churches added Santeria, Bahai, Buddhist, Hindu, Muslim, Hasidic, Eastern Orthodox, and Mormon houses of worship to its older Dutch Reformed, Methodist, Baptist, Episcopalian, Catholic, and Congregational churches.

And even as racial and ethnic diversity have led to tensions, they have also led to coalitions. Caribbean and Hasidic neighbors who once fought each other in Crown Heights now host an annual Unity Day celebration. Meanwhile, neighborhoods that have long been integrated, like Prospect-Lefferts Gardens, avoided much of the turbulence of the 1960s and 1970s because they had learned to live together in harmony.

Equally important in the public view has been the spectacular decline in crime in Brooklyn in the 1990s. Although neither the borough nor New York City as a whole ever led the nation in homicide, robbery, or rape, those violent acts were once part of the image the region projected to the world. More recently, Brooklyn has been a leader in new methods of policing, and despite a few tragic breakdowns, the borough has seen a 75 percent drop in major crime in the past dozen years. Indeed, in 2004, Brooklyn ranks as one of the safest urban centers in the Western Hemisphere.

And it is growing. New government programs at every level are successfully encouraging private investment. The two most visible results of new initiatives are the Nehemiah Houses, built in cooperation with black churches, and the 5-million-square-foot MetroTech business center in Downtown Brooklyn. Even a few old industries are reviving. In 1995 the Brooklyn Brewery moved into Williamsburg, resurrecting a neighborhood tradition that began in 1819.

As Brooklyn prepares to enter the third millennium, it is recapturing the optimism and confidence that characterized it a century ago. Then, as now, its strength lies in its people and its neighborhoods. This book will provide exciting clues to treasures that have been so near yet lain so long hidden.

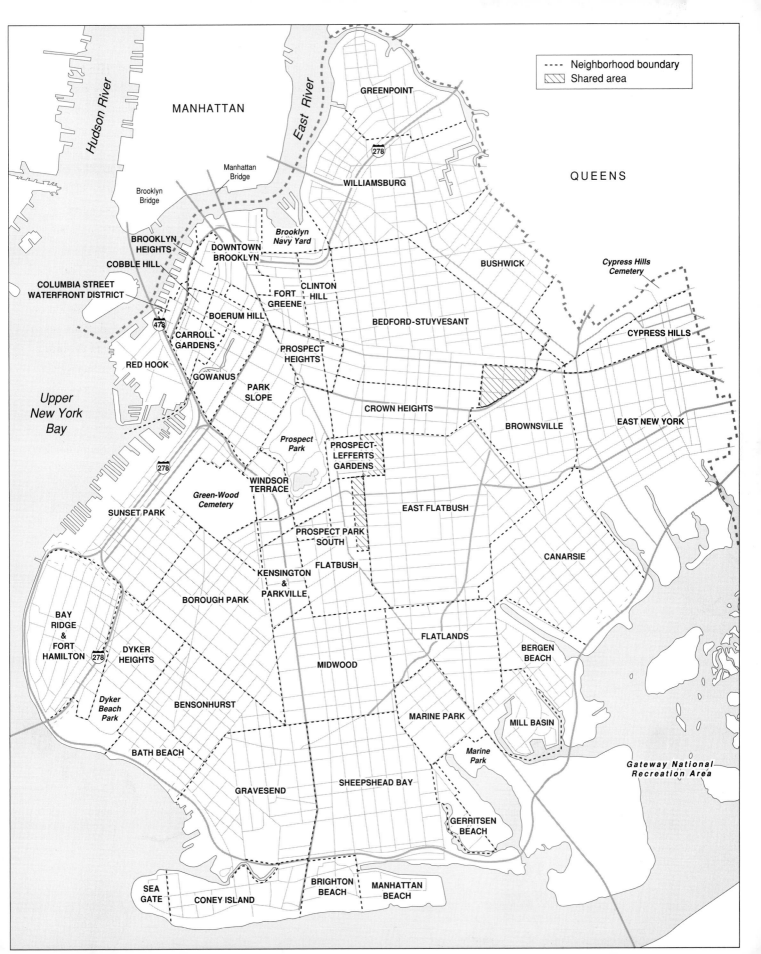

MANHATTAN

Hudson River

East River

QUEENS

Brooklyn Bridge

Manhattan Bridge

GREENPOINT

WILLIAMSBURG

Brooklyn Navy Yard

BROOKLYN HEIGHTS

DOWNTOWN BROOKLYN

COBBLE HILL

CLINTON HILL

FORT GREENE

BUSHWICK

Cypress Hills Cemetery

COLUMBIA STREET WATERFRONT DISTRICT

BOERUM HILL

BEDFORD-STUYVESANT

CYPRESS HILLS

CARROLL GARDENS

PROSPECT HEIGHTS

RED HOOK

GOWANUS

PARK SLOPE

CROWN HEIGHTS

BROWNSVILLE

EAST NEW YORK

Upper New York Bay

Prospect Park

PROSPECT-LEFFERTS GARDENS

WINDSOR TERRACE

Green-Wood Cemetery

EAST FLATBUSH

SUNSET PARK

PROSPECT PARK SOUTH

CANARSIE

FLATBUSH

KENSINGTON & PARKVILLE

BOROUGH PARK

FLATLANDS

BERGEN BEACH

BAY RIDGE & FORT HAMILTON

DYKER HEIGHTS

MIDWOOD

MILL BASIN

Dyker Beach Park

BENSONHURST

MARINE PARK

BATH BEACH

Marine Park

Gateway National Recreation Area

GRAVESEND

SHEEPSHEAD BAY

GERRITSEN BEACH

SEA GATE

CONEY ISLAND

BRIGHTON BEACH

MANHATTAN BEACH

278

478

278

278

Chess game at Bensonhurst Park

■ One of Brooklyn's earliest African American settlements is in Bath Beach. Around the middle of the nineteenth century, after being given a parcel of land on which to settle, a group of freed slaves made their home near what is today a four-block area around Bath Avenue. The church that was once located at the heart of that community, Mount Zion Baptist, has moved to Bedford-Stuyvesant.

■ Over the years, Bath Beach has been the reputed home of Brooklyn's Mafia, including in the 1930s some hit men connected to "Murder, Inc.," an organization of criminals who carried out contract killings. In 1927 Frankie Yale was living in Bath Beach when he was shot to death "Mafia style." And in the 1980s, Frank DeCiccio, the reputed underboss to John Gotti, head of the Gambino crime family, was killed when a car bomb exploded in Bath Beach.

■ The actor Vincent Gardenia lived in Bath Beach for 37 years.

Ocean breezes drying lines of clothing, backyard rosebushes, hanging chimes —all evoke the feel of today's Bath Beach, a small, quiet seaside neighborhood tucked between Fort Hamilton and Gravesend. Bath Beach, named for the English spa of Bath, was developed as a retreat for well-to-do families who escaped the city on weekends to sail, sunbathe, and swim.

Bath Beach was a part of the original Brooklyn town of New Utrecht, and before its heyday it was rural and sleepy. By the turn of the twentieth century, however, New York's elite had learned of its beautiful shore. Fashionable villas and yacht clubs soon dotted the coast, and mansions sprawled on inland lawns. For fun, residents could wander down to the Captain's Pier at the end of Bay 19th Street to dine at a restaurant of the same name, watch daredevil high divers, or swim. They could also hop on the Brooklyn, Bath, and Coney Island Line (opened in 1862) and head for the beach. Nearby

Bath Beach

NEIGHBORHOOD PROFILE

Boundaries: from 14th Avenue on the west to Bay Parkway on the east, from the south side of 86th Street on the north to Gravesend Bay on the south.

Subway: <u>BMT 4th Avenue B</u>: 18th Ave., 20th Ave., Bay Parkway, 25th Ave. <u>Local M</u>: 18th Ave., 20th Ave., Bay Pkwy.

Bus: <u>B1</u>: 86th St. <u>B64</u>: Bath Ave./Harway Ave./Stillwell Ave. <u>B8</u>: Cropsey Ave./18th Ave. <u>Bx28</u>: Cropsey Ave. <u>B6</u>: Shore Pkwy./Bay Pkwy. <u>B82</u>: Cropsey Ave./Bay Pkwy. <u>B3</u>: 25th Ave.

Libraries: Brooklyn Public Library New Utrecht Branch (86th St. at Bay 17th St.), Ulmer Park Branch (2602 Bath Ave.)

Community Board: No. 11

Police Precinct: 62nd Precinct (1925 Bath Ave.)

Fire Department: Engine 243 Ladder 168 (8653 18th Ave.), Engine 253 (2429 86th St.)

Hospitals and Clinics: Sephardic Home for the Aged (2266 Cropsey Ave.)

Family housing on Bay 26th Street and Cropsey Avenue

Coney Island entertainments beckoned, but Bath Beach also had its own amusement park. Opened in 1893 by the Ulmer Brewery of Brooklyn and advertised as a "family resort," Ulmer Park offered rides, a dance hall, and swimming. A residential community grew up around it that remained after the park closed in 1899.

With more rapid rail transit in 1916 and 1917, Jewish and Italian families from the Lower East Side of Manhattan began to settle in Bath Beach. The stock market crash of 1929 acceler- ated this shift in population and caused Bath Beach to change focus. As mansions were abandoned and the condition of other grand houses declined, smaller homes and apartment buildings were constructed to match the housing needs of immigrants from Italy and elsewhere. The completion of the Belt Parkway in 1939 stimulated even greater neighborhood growth, as did landfill development along the shore of Bath Beach. The Shore Haven Apartments, at 21st Avenue near the Belt Parkway, were built in 1949 as part of Bensonhurst-by-the-Sea but are now considered part of Bath Beach. The Contello Towers, three high-rise apartment buildings opened in 1960, 1963, and 1967, are situated on this reclaimed land. But residents do not feel hemmed in by the new developments: Bath Beach still offers a sense of space with its 19-acre Bensonhurst Park and the nearby 73-acre Dreier-Offerman Park.

Apartment house at Cropsey Avenue and Bay 29th Street

Game in progress at Bensonhurst Park

Among residents of other nationalities, many generations of Italian Americans have made Bath Beach their home. Services at the Catholic churches of St. Finbars and St. Frances Cabrini attract large crowds each Sunday. More recently, Russian Jews and Asian immigrant families have contributed to the area's rich history.

3

Bay Ridge &

The history of Bay Ridge and Fort Hamilton, two neighborhoods overlooking New York Bay, illustrates how innovations in transportation have reshaped Brooklyn and underlines the importance of preserving vital landmarks. Both Bay Ridge and Fort Hamilton were transformed by the building of the Verrazano Narrows Bridge, an experience that has inspired residents to develop a shared, positive vision of their area's future.

The colonial history of Bay Ridge began in 1652, when the Dutch West India Company acquired the land from the Nyack Indians. The Dutch settlers originally referred to the area, which was part of the town of New Utrecht, as Yellow Hook (and sometimes Yellow Ridge) for the color of the clay found there. But after the yellow-fever epidemic of 1848–49, residents chose to rename their community to evoke instead the beautiful surrounding bay and the glacial ridge that runs along what is now Ridge Boulevard.

Wealthy industrialists and businessmen were drawn to the area as a summer retreat and built mansions on the Bay Ridge bluffs. Two examples of these extraordinary homes remain. The Howard E. and Jessie Jones House, nicknamed the Gingerbread House by

Brownstones along Senator Street

local residents, is a landmarked stone building with a pseudo-thatched roof on Narrows Avenue and 83rd Street. Built in 1916–17 in the Arts and Crafts style rarely seen in New York City, the house offers a glimpse of the fanciful summer cottages that filled Bay Ridge during those years. The second mansion that remains, the current home of the Fontbonne Academy, a private girls' school, is a relic of Bay Ridge's heyday as a summer rendezvous for members of high society. Local legend

has it that this house was once purchased for the actress Lillian Russell by the high-living financier "Diamond Jim" Brady.

Bay Ridge has given new life to other unusual buildings of this early era. What is today Fort Hamilton High School, for example, was once the site of the Crescent Athletic Club, a posh retreat that brought together the richest Bay Ridge residents.

NEIGHBORHOOD PROFILE

Boundaries: <u>Bay Ridge</u>: from the Narrows on the west to the Gowanus Expressway and 7th Avenue on the east, from 65th Street on the north to the Verrazano Narrows Bridge and Poly Place on the south. <u>Fort Hamilton</u>: the area inside Bay Ridge boundaries south of 86th Street.

Subway: <u>BMT 4th Avenue R</u>: Bay Ridge Ave., 77th St., 86th St., 95th St./ Fort Hamilton.

Bus: <u>B1</u>: Bay Ridge Ave. <u>B9</u>: Bay Ridge Ave./Ovington Ave. <u>B4</u>: 77th St./ 78th St. <u>B16</u>: 86th St./Shore Rd. <u>B64</u>: 86th St. <u>B8</u>: VA Hospital <u>B63</u>: 5th Ave. <u>Bs53</u>: Verrazano Bridge <u>Bs79</u>: Verrazano Bridge/4th Ave. <u>B37</u>: 3rd Ave. <u>Bx27</u>: Shore Rd.

Libraries: Brooklyn Public Library Bay Ridge Branch (Ridge Blvd. at 73rd St.), Fort Hamilton Branch (4th Ave. at 95th St.)

Museums: Harbor Defense Museum (Fort Hamilton)

Community Board: No. 10

Police Precinct: 68th Precinct (333 65th St.)

Fire Department: Engine 241 Ladder 109 (6630 3rd Ave.), Engine 242 (9219 5th Ave.)

Hospitals and Clinics: Veterans Administration Hospital (800 Poly Pl.), Victory Memorial Hospital (9036 7th Ave.)

Perhaps the greatest challenge to residents' conception of their community was the building of the Verrazano Narrows Bridge to Staten Island. Robert Moses, chairman of the Triborough Bridge and Tunnel Authority, pushed the project through over strong opposition by Bay Ridge residents, 8,000 of whom were displaced to make room for the bridge. Many claim that the Bay Ridge community's unsuccessful opposition to the construction fueled the activism that remains strong today. The results of this community involvement are impressive. Bay Ridge has preserved the 16-acre Leif Ericson Park, which is popular for soccer, and the 27-acre Owl's Head Park, a favorite picnic area that was once the estate of Brooklyn mayor and senator Henry C. Murphy. The 58-acre Shore Road Park —which connects Owl's Head Park at the northern end of Bay Ridge to the south-ernmost Fort Hamilton area—boasts a two-and-a-half mile winding path on which walkers, joggers, and roller-bladers enjoy breathtakingly clear views of the New York City harbor.

Today, Bay Ridge has its own motel, and its tree-lined streets are filled with one- and two-family homes. Unlike many other Brooklyn neighborhoods, these houses have garages, basements, and lawns, which make certain streets of Bay Ridge look like those in the outer suburbs. Ethnic diversity is a strength of the community. Generations of original Scandinavian and Italian residents have welcomed more recent Chinese, Russian, Greek, Korean, Lebanese, Egyptian, Syrian, and Jordanian immigrants. In the 1980s, Chinese entrepreneurs who had settled in nearby Sunset Park transformed some of Bay Ridge's abandoned warehouses into bustling garment factories. The most prevalent settlers in the 1990s have been newcomers from China and the former Soviet Union.

The ethnic foods served in 3rd and 5th Avenue restaurants and sold in specialty stores now represent the full diversity of the neighborhood's residents, and the shopping area from 4th to 6th Avenues is vibrant and diverse. One of the most famous stores in Bay Ridge is Kleinfeld's, which opened

Fort Hamilton

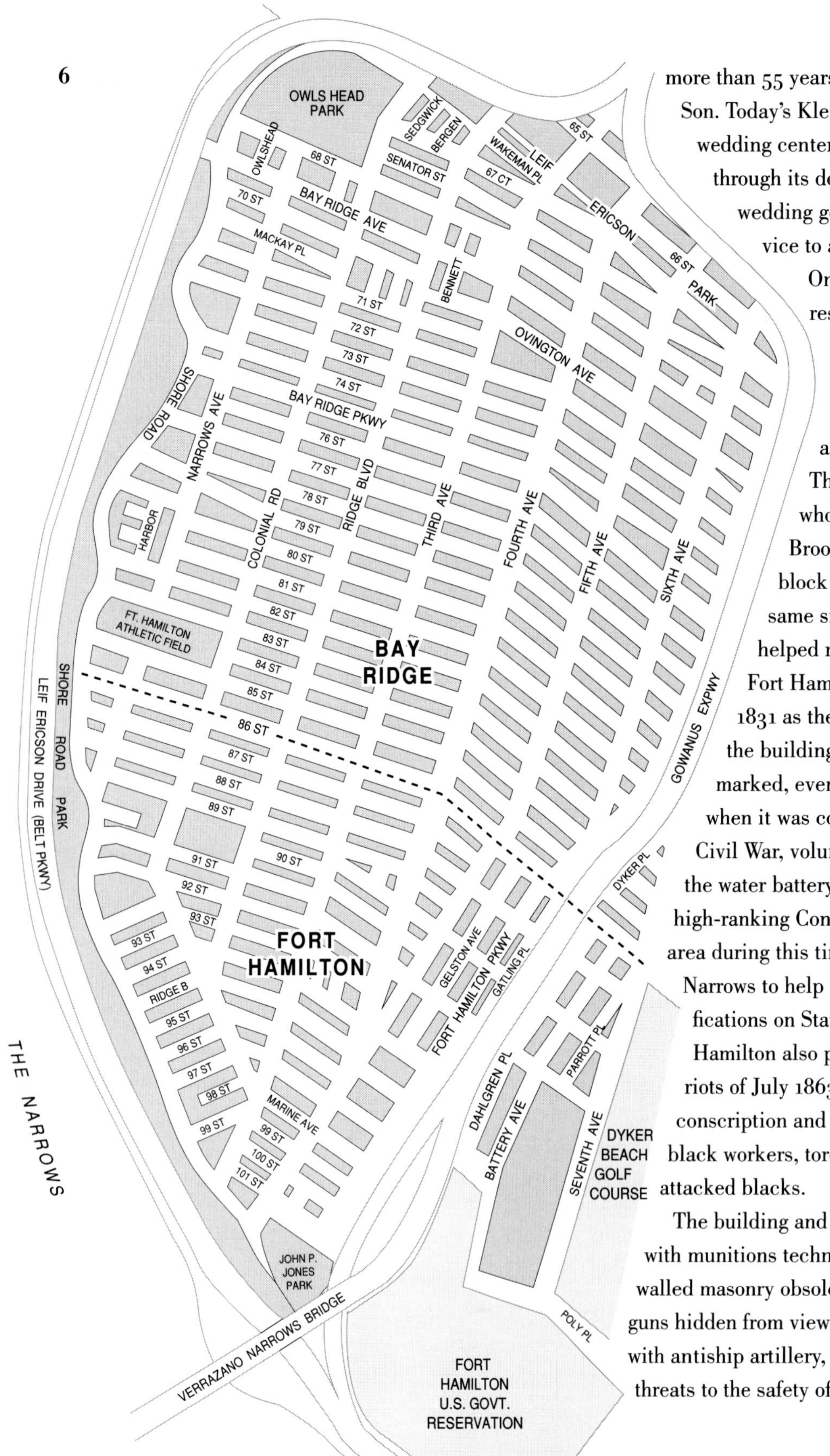

Map labels: OWLS HEAD PARK · SEDGWICK · BERGEN · SENATOR ST · WAKEMAN PL · LEIF · 65 ST · 68 ST · 67 CT · OWLSHEAD · BAY RIDGE AVE · 70 ST · MACKAY PL · ERICSON · 66 ST · PARK · 71 ST · 72 ST · 73 ST · 74 ST · BENNETT · OVINGTON AVE · SHORE ROAD · NARROWS AVE · BAY RIDGE PKWY · 76 ST · 77 ST · 78 ST · RIDGE BLVD · THIRD AVE · FOURTH AVE · FIFTH AVE · SIXTH AVE · COLONIAL RD · 79 ST · 80 ST · 81 ST · 82 ST · HARBOR · GOWANUS EXPWY · FT. HAMILTON ATHLETIC FIELD · 83 ST · 84 ST · 85 ST · BAY RIDGE · 86 ST · 87 ST · 88 ST · 89 ST · SHORE ROAD PARK · LEIF ERICSON DRIVE (BELT PKWY) · 90 ST · 91 ST · 92 ST · 93 ST · FORT HAMILTON · 93 ST · 94 ST · RIDGE B · 95 ST · 96 ST · 97 ST · 98 ST · MARINE AVE · 99 ST · 100 ST · 101 ST · GELSTON AVE · FORT HAMILTON PKWY · GATLING PL · DAHLGREN PL · PARROTT PL · SEVENTH AVE · DYKER PL · DYKER BEACH GOLF COURSE · BATTERY AVE · POLY PL · THE NARROWS · JOHN P. JONES PARK · VERRAZANO NARROWS BRIDGE · FORT HAMILTON U.S. GOVT. RESERVATION

more than 55 years ago as a furrier named I. Kleinfeld and Son. Today's Kleinfeld's, the nucleus of Bay Ridge's retail wedding center, welcomes more than 18,000 brides through its doors each year, sells more than 8,000 wedding gowns annually, and offers a shuttle service to and from Manhattan.

One foot of the Verrazano Narrows Bridge rests in Fort Hamilton, which is listed in the National Register of Historic Places as the second oldest continuously garrisoned federal post in the United States, although in 1997 it was severely reduced. The fort is named for Alexander Hamilton, who fought with the colonials in the Battle of Brooklyn, and is on the site of an early Dutch block house. Fort Lewis, an earlier fort on the same site, was made of earth and timber and helped repel the British during the War of 1812. Fort Hamilton itself was built between 1825 and 1831 as the first granite fort in New York harbor, and the building in the center of today's fort is landmarked, even though it was altered in 1937 and 1938 when it was converted to an officers' club. During the Civil War, volunteer regiments trained at the fort, and the water battery, Fort Lafayette, became a prison for high-ranking Confederate captives. Brooklynites in the area during this time could see ships lined up across the Narrows to help defend Fort Hamilton and other fortifications on Staten Island from Confederate raiders. Fort Hamilton also provided troops to help put down the draft riots of July 1863, when New Yorkers, resenting enforced conscription and a perceived threat to their jobs from black workers, tore up railroad tracks, burned hotels, and attacked blacks.

The building and armaments of Fort Hamilton kept pace with munitions technology. When rifled cannon made vertical-walled masonry obsolete, the fort was refitted with long-range guns hidden from view. These guns in turn were replaced, first with antiship artillery, then with anti-aircraft defenses as the threats to the safety of the harbor changed. The guns were re-

Verrazano Narrows Bridge from Fort Hamilton army base

Robert Moses kept a close eye on his bridge, the Verrazano Narrows (Brooklyn Historical Society)

● **Verrazano Narrows Bridge**

"The bridge began as bridges always begin—silently . . . when the noise finally started, on January 16, 1959, nobody in Brooklyn or Staten Island heard it."—Gay Talese, The Bridge, *1964*

The Verrazano Narrows Bridge was the longest suspension bridge in the world when it opened in 1964, five years after construction began. Named for Giovanni da Verrazano, the first European to sail into New York harbor, it was the sixty-sixth built in New York City and the eighth designed by Othmar H. Ammann. The doubledecker roadway is suspended by four steel wire cables, each three feet in diameter.

The Verrazano Narrows Bridge has sparked contemporary interest as well. In the movie *Saturday Night Fever* (1978), John Travolta and his friends play dare games on the bridge, with ultimately tragic consequences. And every year since 1976, runners competing in the New York City Marathon have started their race at the Staten Island toll booths and have entered Brooklyn to the cheers and applause of onlookers in Bay Ridge and Fort Hamilton.

8

NEIGHBORHOOD FACTS

■ In July 1776, General Henry Knox, American Revolutionary War officer and adviser to General George Washington, shelled the approaching British HMS *Asia* from the site of Fort Hamilton. During the encounter, one British sailor was killed and several were wounded. The *Asia* returned fire, but missed.

■ Abner Doubleday, long-credited with being the inventor of modern-day baseball's diamond-shaped field and playing positions, was the post commander of Fort Hamilton in 1861. He was later a commander of I Corps at Gettysburg.

■ St. John's Episcopal Church, at Fort Hamilton Parkway and 99th Street, is often called the "church of the generals." During the nineteenth century, military personnel joined the church because the fort had no chapel of its own. Lieutenant Thomas (later "Stonewall") Jackson was baptized there, and Robert E. Lee was a vestryman. Another place of worship that benefited from the involvement of servicemen was St. Patrick's. Its first church building was completed in 1921 with the help of Catholic Irish and German volunteers who were stationed at the fort.

■ During 1944 and 1945, Sergeant Joe Louis, the "Brown Bomber," heavyweight champion of the world from 1937 to 1949, taught boxing at Fort Hamilton.

the area in a small museum founded in 1980.

The civilian area named Fort Hamilton features more high-rise housing than does its neighbor, Bay Ridge, but it also includes one- and two-family homes. Many who live in the area consider themselves a part of Bay Ridge as well as of their own neighborhood, in a fitting testament to how both early and more recent residents have shared common assets and have united to preserve them.

moved altogether in 1954 when Nike missiles began a 20-year term of protecting New York City. But Fort Hamilton remained active. During both world wars, the base was used as a major embarkation and separation center. And more recently, in the mid-1990s, it was used as a recruiting command post and as the military entrance and processing station for New York City. The 26th Army Band is in residence there, and the Veteran's Administration Hospital serves the needs of veterans and families of military personnel from all over New York. Visitors to the fort will discover an extensive collection of military paraphernalia and old maps of

Apartment houses surround a small neighborhood park with its reminder of nearby Fort Hamilton

Bedford-

Bedford-Stuyvesant is the largest black neighborhood in New York City, and the community's many landmarks and its beauty reflect grassroots leadership and civic pride. Originally settled by freed slaves who were among the first to purchase land for homes, Bedford-Stuyvesant is an area where Brooklynites have effectively negotiated the difficult balance between protecting meaningful, historic places and developing and reshaping public resources.

The Magnolia Grandiflora perhaps best symbolizes the relationship of old and new in Bedford-Stuyvesant. Brought to Brooklyn from North Carolina as a slip in 1885, the huge landmarked tree is now the heart of a four-building, landmarked environmental and cultural center built between 1880

Restored wood-frame houses on Chauncey Street

Stuyvesant

and 1883. The center is located at Lafayette Avenue between Marcy and Tompkins Avenues, and its creation was inspired by Hattie Carthan, a grassroots organizer who helped revitalize the area in the late 1960s.

Over the years, many of Bedford-Stuyvesant's residents have transplanted their own cultures and experiences to the historically rich community. The Dutch were the first among the colonial settlers. In the 1630s and 1640s, the Dutch West India Company acquired woodlands from the Canarsee Indians and named the site **Bedford**. The area was officially recognized by English governor Edmund Andros in 1677. Important early figures include Thomas Lambertse, a farmer who built Bedford's first inn, and Leffert Lefferts, who bought the land from Lambertse, and was a judge and town clerk.

Bedford was used primarily for farming throughout the eighteenth century, although it was occupied by British troops after the Revolutionary War's Battle of Brooklyn. As early as 1790, more than a quarter of the residents were of African descent, and the area was occasionally referred to as **Bedford Corners.**

Slavery was abolished in New York State in 1827, but racism continued to be pervasive; in particular, it was very difficult for blacks to purchase land. The former slaves' persistence and ingenuity, however, made them dramatically successful at doing just that. In the 1830s, William Thomas and James Weeks, both African Americans, bought land that eventually became Carrville and Weeksville. These first two black settlements encompassed a region nearly as large as contemporary Bedford-Stuyvesant.

Restoration at 152 MacDonough Street in the 1970s

Innovations in transportation accelerated a growth in population. In 1836 the Brooklyn and Jamaica Railroad traversed Atlantic Street, which is now Atlantic Avenue. By 1873 the population had reached 14,000 and included Irish, German, Jewish, Scottish, Dutch American, and African American residents. Institutions were founded to attend to the needs of these many ethnicities. The Jewish Hospital (now Interfaith Medical Center),

Howard Colored Orphan Asylum (in Weeksville), St. John's Episcopal Church, and St. Mary's Hospital are prominent examples.

Bedford-Stuyvesant became more accessible from Manhattan upon completion of the Brooklyn Bridge (1883) and the elevated railroad (1885). New clusters of brownstone apartments created such small enclaves as East Brooklyn, New Brooklyn, and St. Marks. The Renaissance Apartments, on Nostrand Avenue and Hancock Street, and the Imperial Apartments, on Pacific Street and Bedford Avenue (both 1892), light-colored brick buildings that feature terracotta trim and bay windows, are two landmarked examples of these beautiful, late nineteenth-century, prestigious Brooklyn apartment buildings. Another is the landmarked Alhambra Apartments on Nostrand and Macon Streets. Built in 1889–90, they are considered a model of apartments designed for affluent middle-class tenants of the period.

During this period two other buildings were erected that became New York City landmarks: St. Bartholomew's Episcopal Church (1893) at 1227 Pacific Street and the 23rd Regiment Armory (1895) at 1322 Bedford Avenue, which was designed to resemble a medieval fortress.

Given Bedford-Stuyvesant's appreciation of beautiful, significant buildings, it is fitting that residents responded to the growing population's need for additional classrooms with two schools that have since been des-

NEIGHBORHOOD PROFILE

Boundaries: Bedford-Stuyvesant: from Classon Avenue on the west to Williams Place on the east, from Flushing Avenue on the north to approximately Park Place on the south. Stuyvesant Heights: from Tompkins Avenue on the west to Stuyvesant Avenue on the east, from Macon Street on the north to Fulton and Chauncey Streets on the south.

Subway: IND Crosstown G: Flushing Ave., Myrtle-Willoughby Ave., Bedford-Nostrand Aves., Classon Ave. BMT Jamaica M: Flushing Ave., Myrtle Ave. BMT Jamaica J: Flushing Ave., Myrtle Ave., Kosciusko St., Gates Ave., Halsey St., Chauncey St. IND A and C: Franklin Ave., Nostrand Ave., Kingston-Throop Aves., Utica Ave., Ralph Ave., Rockaway Ave., Broadway–East New York Ave. Franklin Avenue Shuttle S: Franklin Ave.

Bus: B57: Flushing Ave. B54: Myrtle Ave. B38: DeKalb Ave./Lafayette Ave. B52: Gates Ave. B26: Halsey St. B25: Fulton St. B65: Dean St./Bergen St. B45: St. John's Pl. B71: Eastern Pkwy. B17: Eastern Pkwy. B14: Eastern Pkwy. B40: Eastern Pkwy./Ralph Ave. B48: Classon Ave./Franklin Ave. B44: Bedford Ave./Nostrand Ave. B43: Tompkins Ave./Throop Ave. B15: Marcus Garvey Blvd./Lewis Ave. B46: Malcolm X Blvd. B7: Saratoga Ave./Thomas S. Boyland St. B60: Rockaway Ave.

Libraries: Brooklyn Public Library Bedford Branch (Franklin Ave. at Hancock St.), Eastern Parkway Branch (Eastern Pkwy. at Schenectady Ave.), Macon Branch (Lewis Ave. at Macon St.), Marcy Branch (DeKalb Ave. near Nostrand Ave.), Saratoga Branch (Thomas S. Boyland St. at Macon St.)

Museums: Weeksville Houses (1638–1708 Bergen St.)

Theaters: Billie Holiday Theater (Fulton St.)

Community Board: No. 3

Police Precinct: 79th Precinct (263 Tompkins Ave.), 81st Precinct (30 Ralph Ave.), Housing Police Service Area 3A (492 Marcy Ave.)

Fire Department: Engine 214 Ladder 111 (495 Hancock St.), Engine 217 (940 DeKalb Ave.), Engine 222 (32 Ralph Ave.), Engine 230 (701 Park Ave.), Engine 235 (206 Monroe St.), Engine 234 Ladder 123 (1352 St. John's Pl.), Rescue Co. 2 (1472 Bergen St.)

Hospitals and Clinics: Woodhull Hospital (Flushing Ave.), Interfaith Medical Center (555 Prospect Place), Brookdale Family Care Center (1873 Eastern Pkwy.), Catholic Medical Center of Brooklyn and Queens/St. Mary's Hospital of Brooklyn (170 Buffalo Ave.), Lola Cuffee Family Health Center (485 Throop Ave.), Ralph Avenue Medical Center (38 Ralph Ave.), Eastern Parkway Family Health Clinic (391 Eastern Pkwy.), CNR Healthcare Network/Center for Nursing and Rehabilitation (520 Prospect Pl.), Lowenstein Adult Day Care Center (520 Prospect Pl.), Adult Day Health Care (707 Franklin), St. John's Episcopal Homes for the Aged and the Blind (452 Herkimer St.)

ignated New York City historic landmarks. When Central Grammar School (1878) at Court and Livingston became inadequate for teaching the many new schoolchildren, the Girls High School (1886) on Nostrand Avenue and Boys High School (1892) on Marcy Avenue were designed by James W. Naughton, the architect for many of Brooklyn's public schools. The boys' school was considered such an important educational institution at the time that the designers also wanted it to be a major architectural monument: today, its majestic roof and towers can be seen from much of central Brooklyn. The building for Girls High School is also distinctive, but the school closed in 1964. As the schools expanded, they remained sex segregated. Notable gradu-

---

Tintype found in a 1968 archaeological dig (Courtesy of the Society for the Preservation of Weeksville and Bedford-Stuyvesant)

● **Carrville and Weeksville**

In the 1830s two of the earliest African American communities in Brooklyn were created, in part by freed slaves, within what are today Bedford-Stuyvesant and Crown Heights. William Thomas purchased a parcel of land in 1832 on which he developed **Carrville**, a community for free black farmers, laborers, and craftsmen. James Weeks, a settler from Virginia, bought the land in 1838 from the Lefferts family estate that became **Weeksville**, another such community.

Susan McKinney-Steward, who became the first African American female physician in New York State and the third in the United States, was born in Weeksville in 1847. Moses P. Cobb, the first African American policeman in the City of Brooklyn, is said to have walked to Weeksville from North Carolina. Weeksville first appeared on a local map in 1849; Schenectady Avenue was designated its main street. By the 1870s both Carrville and Weeksville had their own schools, churches, and an orphanage, the Howard Colored Orphan Asylum. One of the earliest schools was an African American free school established in Carrville that was taken over by white school district trustees in 1841 and renamed Colored School No. 2; it later moved to Weeksville and still serves the area as Public School 243 (the Weeksville School).

Eastern Parkway separated and destroyed the two communities. The large street was completed in 1869 and 1870, and immediately thereafter new side streets and homes were created. The neighborhoods were all but lost until the late 1960s, when in the process of clearing a site to make way for city housing, historians recognized the significance of four small wooden houses from Weeksville on Hunterfly Road—a small street from the seventeenth century situated off Bergen Street that predates Brooklyn's current street grid. Residents of the homes had been aware of the Weeksville connection; they often gave their address as "Weeksville, near the Hunterfly Road." The Weeksville Houses, as they are now called, have become city and national landmarks. They house the Society for the Preservation of Weeksville and Bedford-Stuyvesant, as well as a museum of African American history and culture, which features artifacts and memorabilia derived from interviews and a 1968 archaeological dig.

---

ates from the two schools include Lena Horne, Shirley Chisholm, Isaac Asimov, Norman Mailer, Aaron Copland, and Connie Hawkins. In 1976 Boys and Girls High School reopened with its new name at 1700 Fulton Street.

Public School 73 is another example of residents adding graceful touches to an otherwise functional building. The landmark, which still stands on MacDougal Street, was built in 1888 and expanded in 1895, when population growth continued to surge and additional classrooms were needed.

The grandeur of the area around Bedford Corners and its thoroughfare, Stuyvesant Avenue, lured middle- and upper-class residents—most notably, F. W. Woolworth of the five-and-ten-cent stores and Abraham Abraham of

Abraham & Straus. By 1920 the population overall had reached 45,000, and during the next decade the numbers of residents in the area rose dramatically, with an especially large increase after the subway reached the area in 1936. (The area to the east where the elevated lines met in a complex, stilted, steel subway station, surrounded by subway yards and trolley barns, took on the name Broadway Junction during the 1920s.) New immigrants poured into the neighborhood from Europe, the southern United States, and the Caribbean. (Novelist and essayist Paule Marshall often includes descriptions of her family's Caribbean American lifestyle and the brownstones of Bedford-Stuyvesant in her writing.) At

this time many began referring to Bedford and Stuyvesant Heights by their current, combined name.

By 1940 Bedford-Stuyvesant had more than 65,000 African American residents, who came to dominate the local civic scene. In the 1950s,

Bedford-Stuyvesant was one of the few Brooklyn neighborhoods where blacks could buy houses.

African American churches were at the forefront of the civil rights movement as it emerged in Brooklyn. The churches moved to Bedford-Stuyvesant from other parts of Brooklyn and joined forces with the National Urban League, the National Association for the Advancement of Colored People, and other organizations, like the Bedford-Stuyvesant Restoration Corporation, to rally against racial discrimination, segregation, and poverty. The challenge of poverty was difficult to overcome in Bedford-Stuyvesant. At the time, housing was insufficient for its many residents, and unemployment was prevalent. Landlords and owners had little extra money to improve their

Transplanted cultures along Fulton Street

The landmarked Magnolia Grandiflora tree traveled as a slip from North Carolina to Brooklyn in 1885 (Brooklyn Historical Society)

buildings, and many fell into disrepair. Today the New York City Housing Authority manages a number of large apartment developments, including the Albany, Brevoort, Kingsborough, Marcy, Summer, and Tompkins Houses.

The work of the Bedford-Stuyvesant Restoration Corporation, as well as other concerned and vocal advocates, has created a vibrant legacy of landmarked historical sites. The corporation, the first nonprofit community development corporation in the country, was the result of intensive grassroots organization in the 1960s and the bipartisan efforts of Senators Robert F. Kennedy and Jacob K. Javits. In response to the deteriorating condition of homes and businesses in their community, residents joined together to hire unemployed residents to renovate the exteriors of neighborhood homes. Among these were the houses of **Stuyvesant Heights,** designated a historic district in 1971, which boasts some of the longest sections of historically significant brick and limestone houses in the borough, most of which were built in the 1890s. On such streets as Chauncey, Bainbridge, Mac-Donough, and Decatur, the restored homes are reminiscent of Brooklyn Heights or Park Slope. Fine French Second Empire, neo-Grec, Romanesque Revival, and neo-Renaissance homes, many designed by local architects, grace the area. The John and Elizabeth Truslow House on Brooklyn Avenue has also been made a New York City historic landmark.

The corporation also organized the building of the Bedford-Stuyvesant Restoration Plaza, a complex on the site of a former milk-bottling plant that now features offices, stores, a supermarket, banks, an art gallery, and the Billie Holiday Theater. In 1967 Senator Robert F. Kennedy visited Bedford-Stuyvesant. He was so impressed with the work of the corporation he had helped to launch that he introduced federal legislation to encourage the formation of similar local restoration groups across the country.

Green space and churches have

■ In the 1940s, American Merri-Lei, located on Halsey Street, produced more leis than any other manufacturer in the world. Most were shipped from the factory directly to Hawaii.

■ Boxer Floyd Patterson, musician Eubie Blake, and baseball legend Jackie Robinson all lived in Bedford-Stuyvesant.

■ Bridge Street African Wesleyan Methodist Episcopal Church, the oldest African American church in the borough, was started in Brooklyn in 1818 and was reputed to have been a stop on the Underground Railroad. In 1938 the church moved to 311 Bridge Street, a landmarked building. It has since resided in a series of locations on Stuyvesant Avenue and continues to have an active congregation.

■ The African Street Festival, formerly the Afrikan Street Carnival, is the largest Afrocentric festival in the United States. A five-day cultural event, it began as part of the commencement exercises of the Uhuru Sasa School, but by 1976 it was too large for the school grounds and moved to its current location at the Boys and Girls High School. In 1986 it became a nonprofit organization and adopted its present name. The festival, which has included performances by regulars Russell D. Clown, Mama Kuumba, Sun Ra, the Weusi Kuumba Troupe, and the Dinizulu African Drummers, Dancers, and Singers, attracts some 60,000 people to enjoy the sights and sounds and such African goods as food, clothing, and crafts on display from more than 300 vendors.

Church (1887–92) on Greene Avenue, Berean Missionary Baptist Church (1894) on Bergen Street, Bethany Baptist Church on Marcus Garvey Boulevard (1883), Bethel Tabernacle African Methodist Episcopal Church (1847) on Dean Street, the landmarked Bridge Street African Methodist Episcopal Zion Church (1819) on Stuyvesant Avenue, Concord Baptist Church on Marcy Avenue (1847), Our Lady of Good Counsel on Putnam Street (1886), the landmarked St. George's Episcopal Church (1887–88) on Marcy Avenue, and St. Phillips Protestant Episcopal Church on Decatur Street (1899).

been preserved as well. Neighborhood parks include Brower Park, Saratoga Square Park, and Herbert Von King Park, and playgrounds throughout the neighborhood help bring young families together. Bedford-Stuyvesant is filled with houses of worship, some of which were built as early as the nineteenth century. These churches include the landmarked Antioch Baptist

Raphael Sanders (left), a West African percussionist, and friends

towns. Although Bensonhurst includes families of many different ethnicities—in particular, those of Greek, Korean, Israeli, Polish, Arab, and Russian descent—as well as African Americans, it is best known for the Italian traditions and cuisine that give the neighborhood its unique character.

Bensonhurst was settled as a small section of New Utrecht, one of the six original towns of Brooklyn. (When New Utrecht was annexed to the City of Brooklyn in 1894, it lost its identity; now New Utrecht is considered a small section of Bensonhurst whose name is kept alive by the New Utrecht branch of the Brooklyn Public Library, the New Utrecht Reformed Church, and New Utrecht High School.) The area was primarily used for farming and had fewer than 4,000 residents until the Brooklyn, Bath, and West End Railroad was built in 1885. Soon thereafter, developer James Lynch bought large parcels of land from members of the Benson family to build his suburb, Bensonhurst-by-the-Sea. Within the development's 350 acres—land that stretched from 20th Avenue on the west to 23rd Avenue on the east and from 78th Street on the north to Gravesend Bay on the south—Lynch built villas for a thousand families and planted 5,000 shade trees.

The parklike setting of Bensonhurst-by-the-Sea, as well as its proximity to Manhattan and Downtown Brooklyn, enticed middle-class families; wealthier weekend visitors were attracted by upscale sailing facilities at Bensonhurst Yacht Club and the Atlantic Yacht Club (see Sea Gate). Until at least 1894, when the

Along Cristoforo Colombo Boulevard —Bensonhurst's 18th Avenue, between 68th and 77th Streets—Italian shops entice passersby with fresh pastries, pasta, and focaccia. There are large pizza parlors, more reminiscent of Brooklyn than Italy, and small local social clubs, more evocative of Italy than Brooklyn, where Italian men gather to drink espresso, play cards, and trade memories of their home-

Bensonhurst

to the area. Seemingly overnight, two- and three-family homes were built, and by the 1920s new walk-up apartment buildings with four to six stories were appearing each week. Italian American and Jewish residents from Manhattan's Lower East Side discovered Bensonhurst during this period, adding to the population boom. By 1930 Bensonhurst had almost 150,000 residents.

After World War II, Bensonhurst's residential growth continued. In 1949

Italian delicatessen at 74th Street and 15th Avenue

area was annexed to the City of Brooklyn, Bensonhurst retained an expansive, suburban charm. At that time, there were still fewer than 10,000 residents.

In 1915 the 4th Avenue subway line reached Bensonhurst, which had shortened its name that same year when it lost its status as a "gated" community. Subway cars ran along the former Sea Beach and West End steam railway tracks and brought many new residents

NEIGHBORHOOD FACTS

■ The New Utrecht Reformed Church (1828), a New York City landmark on 18th Avenue and 83rd Street, stands on the same site as did its predecessor, an octagonal church built in 1699. Parishioners founded the church in 1677 in New Utrecht as the fourth Dutch Reformed Church in Kings County. After the American Revolution, in 1783, local residents erected a liberty pole in front of the church and flew an American flag from it to celebrate the evacuation of the British from Brooklyn. The pole has been replaced six times and still stands. In 1790 George Washington visited the church as part of a goodwill visit to Brooklyn.

■ Celebrations in Bensonhurst show off the creativity and religious devotion of its residents. Each spring on Good Friday, thousands of parishioners from the neighborhood's churches walk in procession to Our Lady of Guadelupe Church for High Mass. And in September, Bensonhurst sponsors the Festa of St. Rosalia, in honor of the patron saint of Sicily. This weeklong event, during which colored lights adorn the streets, rivals the Feast of San Gennaro in Manhattan's Little Italy.

■ Actor Elliott Gould, comedian Buddy Hackett, television host Larry King, baseball pitcher Sandy Koufax, opera singer Robert Merrill, actor Paul Sorvino, and investor Laurence Tisch all grew up in Bensonhurst.

■ Bensonhurst first became famous to outsiders as the home of Ralph Kramden (played by Jackie Gleason) in the 1950s television show *The Honeymooners*. The movie *Saturday Night Fever* (1978), set in both Bensonhurst and Bay Ridge, stars John Travolta as a hardware-store clerk who discos at night. (The disco was Bay Ridge's 2001 Odyssey.) Although outsiders may believe that cruising the neighborhood with car windows down and music blaring was created just for the movie, Bensonhurst residents know that it was a regular weekend occurrence on warm summer evenings along and beneath the elevated subway line at 86th Street.

■ New Utrecht High School has also starred on both the large and small screens: Frank Sinatra's character in the movie *It Happened in Brooklyn* (1947) is an alumnus of New Utrecht High School who revisits his old school. And the 1970s television show *Welcome Back Kotter* was set in the high school.

Fred Trump (father of Donald) built the Shore Haven Apartments at 21st Avenue near the Belt Parkway. In its day, the 5,000-apartment complex was the largest private housing development in Brooklyn. Originally part of Bensonhurst-by-the-Sea, it now falls within the boundaries of Bath Beach.

In the 1950s Bensonhurst was transformed by the arrival of thousands of immigrants from southern Italy. These new arrivals worked hard to establish prosperous businesses and bring over other family members, many of whom have continued to live in the same blocks of Bensonhurst for generations. By 1980 nearly 80 percent of the area's residents were of Italian descent, making the neighborhood one of the most

Small apartment buildings along Bay Ridge Parkway and 21st Avenue

homogeneous in New York City. Neighborhood houses, which are mostly one- and two-family semi-attached brick, stucco, and stone-faced buildings, sport vegetable gardens, grape arbors, and fig trees in their back yards and are decorated in the front by distinctive wrought-iron fences.

New Utrecht Reformed Church (1828) at 18th Avenue and 83rd Street

The Andrew G. Cropsey residence, ca. 1887, once stood in what is now historic New Utrecht (Long Island Historical Society Collection)

Bergen

Being less exciting than Coney Island can have its advantages. Bergen Beach, which was developed as a more modest-scale summer resort than Rockaway Beach and Coney Island, retains its expansive, relaxed feel. The neighborhood is composed primarily of large, custom-built, single-family homes, and those on East Mill Basin have private docks. Only one apartment building in Bergen Beach is as tall as seven stories. Indeed, the construction of three-story condominiums there in 1989 was so unusual that it was reported in the New York *Daily News.*

Long a refuge for the Canarsee tribe, the land that is today Bergen Beach was later within the original Dutch town of Flatlands, and the property on which houses are now situated was owned by the family of Hans Hansen Bergen, a seventeenth-century Dutch settler. The Bergen home was later occupied by British officers during the American Revolution. After several name changes, in the 1850s the island appeared on maps as Bergen Island. Around 1918 the island was connected to the mainland as part of a landfill project. Entrepreneurs Percy Williams and Thomas Adams, Jr. (of Chiclets fame), have the distinction of being the first to develop the area. Their resort, built in the 1890s on the old Bergen homestead, was created to attract seaside revelers. Even before Williams opened his amusement park in 1905, a 1900 *Brooklyn Eagle* guide noted that Bergen Beach had "many of

Beach

the midway attractions of the Chicago and Atlanta fairs, including the Ferris wheel." A casino, roller-skating rink, boardwalk, and vaudeville shows were among its entertainments.

But competition from the many at-tractions in Coney Island proved too stiff for the Bergen Beach resort. In 1925 Max Natanson and Mandelbaum & Levine, Manhattan real-estate devel-opers, purchased the land and its at-tractions for a reported $2 million. The partners planned a residential commu-nity with a bathing beach, pavilion, and a new amusement park.

The planned houses were never completed, although a few homes were eventually built and streets traversed the picnic groves. The land was sold, and the area remained unspoiled for many years. In 1932 there was still not a public bus to the area, and Bergen

Single family house at 72nd Street and Avenue W, typical of Bergen Beach development

Homes built in the 1960s at Avenue N and 68th Street in Georgetown

Beach comprised one of the largest parcels of undeveloped land in Brooklyn. Even after the Belt Parkway was constructed in 1939, and the consequent landfill added to the marshy, sandy soil around the beach, making it more buildable, the area remained nearly untouched until the 1960s. It did not become a popular residential area until the late 1980s and early 1990s.

During the 1960s **Georgetown,** a development with an unusual history, stimulated the construction of custom houses in Bergen Beach. It began when streets were paved and curbs and sidewalks put in place in anticipation of building "Georgetowne Greens" on a landfill area at Ralph Avenue and Avenue L. Four hundred two-story, semi-attached colonials were to sit on large, landscaped lots. But the plans lost luster when the mayor of New York City, John Lindsay, proposed to build Harborville, a middle-class project with 900 units on an adjacent 32-acre lot owned by the city, citing the 1955 Mitchell-Lama limited-profit housing companies law as his authority. Lindsay's proposal was eventually defeated, perhaps because of Lindsay's contentious relationship with middle-class voters and his reliance on deficit spending. In any case, the anticipated competition slowed development of Georgetowne Greens and fragmented the project. Completed homes were sold, and other developers stepped in to build three- and four-family attached and semi-attached houses. The neighborhood is now called Georgetown, and for the most part Italian and Jewish families have settled there.

Bergen Beach today is a primarily Italian neighborhood. The area is peaceful, and although some new families are moving in, many residents are older. For entertainment, residents can ride horses at the local stable, cruise or fish in Mill Basin, or shop on Veterans Avenue.

Boerum Hill

Painted advertisement for a Caribbean deli on 3rd Avenue

Boerum Hill is an oasis of gardens and beautiful nineteenth-century brownstones located at the hub of busy Downtown Brooklyn, Cobble Hill, and Gowanus. Its residents, many young and with non-native roots, add spirit and vitality to the neighborhood by organizing frequent sidewalk sales, street fairs, and art shows.

Most of Boerum Hill was developed between 1840 and 1870 on land owned by Charles Hoyt, Russell Nevins, and the Gerritsen and Martense families. The neighborhood was considered fashionable, though less grand than other, more affluent Brooklyn neighborhoods like Brooklyn Heights and Park Slope—a perception that persists to this day. Most houses had a kitchen and dining room on the basement floor, two parlors above, and one or two floors for bedrooms. Prominent visitors to Boerum Hill in this era included the writers Washington Irving and James Fenimore Cooper. Poet Sidney Lanier resided at 195 Dean Street.

During the 1920s many Irish lived in the area, and for some time the neighborhood was primarily home to craftsmen, accountants, surveyors, and carpenters, many of whom were just beginning to be able to afford single-family houses. The neighborhood's low profile at this time attracted many Prohibition speakeasies, such as the Boerum Hill Cafe (1851), at 148 Hoyt Street at Bergen Street, which is now the Brooklyn Inn. In the 1940s and 1950s, Puerto Rican families also discovered the convenience of living within walking distance of ten subway lines and the Long Island Rail Road Station at Atlantic Avenue. Today Boerum Hill is home to residents of many different cultures in a population considered middle to upper-middle class.

An 1838 map shows the streets between Court and 4th Avenue much as they are today. Indeed, Boerum Hill, then as now, is characterized by three- and four-story row houses, especially in the Boerum Hill historic district, six blocks near Dean Street that were landmarked in 1973. These houses are mostly Greek Revival and Italianate, and some blocks have exceptionally long stretches of identical row houses. Twenty-three row houses on State Street between Smith and Hoyt, built between 1847 and 1874, are also landmarked.

The small-scale, low buildings of Boerum Hill give it a more open, airy look than brownstone communities elsewhere in Brooklyn. Although this balanced development may seem an act of foresight given the authentic nineteenth-century homes that were preserved, it actually resulted from a period of economic decline in the area. By the early 1960s, many of Boerum Hill's brownstones had been turned into rooming houses. Sidewalks had become littered with garbage, broken furniture, and shattered glass. With little extra money for renovation, the owners of the brownstones left the original exteriors intact; none were updated with artificial stone facades.

Robert Diamond at the entrance to the nineteenth-century Long Island Rail Road tunnel (*Newsday* photo by Stan Honda)

Moreover, when in the late 1960s many of the buildings were slated for demolition, residents banded together in neighborhood block and community organizations to resurrect the area. Much of these organizations' work—including house tours of renovated homes, art shows, and creative campaigns to advertise Boerum Hill as revitalized—centered on building neighborhood pride. Around this time the neighborhood was renamed Boerum

Typical brownstone at Bond and Pacific Streets, built ca. 1880

the section between Smith Street and 3rd Avenue is a mecca for antiques buyers; during good weather, many stores display their wares on the sidewalk. Boerum Hill is also home to some of Brooklyn's finest mosques.

Institutions located in Boerum Hill include the YWCA on Dean Street; the Brooklyn House of Detention (ca. 1950), which replaced the City Prison (formerly the Raymond Street Jail) in Fort Greene; the Pacific Branch (1904) of the Brooklyn Public Library; and the Interborough Rapid Transit Atlantic Avenue subway kiosk (1908). The Baptist Temple was started in 1823 as the First Baptist Church. In 1893 it moved to Temple Square (also known as "Brimstone Square") and became the Baptist Temple, a Romanesque Revival fortress with a tower. The interior contains seats rather than pews, and it boasts a 1918 organ designed by J. W. Steere, known as the Stradivarius of the organ.

Hill, after Simon Boerum and his family, who had farmed the land during colonial times. The public-relations project worked. New homebuyers were attracted to Boerum Hill, and the enthusiasm of these new residents in turn reenergized the community organizations and contributed to an upturn in the local economy. Indeed, those prescient enough to invest about $20,000 in a Boerum Hill brownstone in the late 1960s and early 1970s have benefited from a nearly twentyfold increase in the value of their homes. In addition, two large housing developments, Gowanus Houses and Wyckoff Gardens, provide more than 1,600 apartments for Boerum Hill and Gowanus residents, and the former Ex-Lax factory at 423 Atlantic Avenue has been converted to cooperative apartments.

The piece of Atlantic Avenue that falls within Boerum Hill reveals the colorful ethnic diversity that continues to attract young, cosmopolitan residents. Between 3rd and 4th Avenues new stores and restaurants are opening to appeal to those interested in African and Islamic crafts and cuisine. And

Neighborhood grocery store, Pacific Street

Borough

With nearly 300 synagogues and 50 religious schools, known as yeshivas, Borough Park is as much an enclave of Orthodox Judaism as it is a community of Brooklyn. During the week, its sidewalks are filled with Orthodox families: men with long beards, dark suits, and dark hats; women wearing hats and *shatlech*, or wigs; little girls in long dresses; and boys sporting dark pants stroll past independently owned shops selling kosher meat, kosher pizza, and kosher wines. And during the Jewish holiday of Purim, which celebrates the rescue of the Jews of ancient Persia from their enemy Haman, the many children of Borough Park parade through the streets costumed as kings, queens, villains—even clowns—in one of several street parties that draw visitors from all over New York City.

Conservative religious beliefs have shaped Borough Park's recent history, but its colonial past is reminiscent of that of other Brooklyn neighborhoods. Borough Park was a part of New Utrecht, one of the six original Brooklyn towns, and until the early part of the nineteenth century its land was lush with commercial horticultural nurseries, dotted by the homes of the Dutch owners.

Midday on 50th Street and 14th Avenue

In 1887 Electus B. Litchfield bought land on which he built a number of cottages in a development that he named **Blythebourne**. Most of Blythebourne's residents were Protestant, but in 1902 a Catholic parish, St. Catherine of Alexandria, was founded. Nearly a hundred years later, the church still stands, on 41st Street. Borough Park was born soon thereafter, when State Senator William H. Reynolds (who later developed Dreamland

amusement park in Coney Island) purchased land north of Blythebourne and east of New Utrecht Avenue and subdivided it for homes.

The first synagogue in the area was built just after the turn of the century, in 1904, and in 1910 Russian Jews began resettling in Blythebourne from the Lower East Side of Manhattan. During this period the area still had a rural feel; local farms offered fresh eggs and produce to residents of both Blythebourne and Borough Park.

Park

After World War I, New Utrecht trains were elevated, providing more efficient transportation, and low-rise apartment buildings were built to accommodate a growing population. Borough Park attracted more Jewish residents, this time from the Lower East Side and Williamsburg. By the mid-1920s, Blythebourne had been integrated into the larger Borough Park, although the local post office is even today called the Blythebourne branch.

The Mapleton branch of the Brooklyn Public Library, located on 17th Avenue and 60th Street, reminds residents that another small community, **Mapleton,** was also encompassed by its larger sister neighborhood. Mapleton developed between 1913 and 1919, and is now considered a subneighborhood of Borough Park.

In 1930 about half the population of Borough Park was Jewish, while Italian and Irish immigrants were among those representing other cultures. During the Depression, everyone shared in the poverty and decline of the neighborhood, even as it continued to draw new residents. Hasidic Jews, primarily of the Bobover sect from Poland, began to arrive at this time. The neighborhood began to change quickly. Most Borough Park Italians relocated to Bensonhurst, and the majority of Hispanic residents moved to Sunset Park.

During the 1950s, two events brought even larger numbers of Hasidim to Borough Park: the 1956 uprising in Hungary and the construction of the Brooklyn-Queens Expressway in 1957, which displaced Hasidic Jews living in Crown Heights and Williamsburg. Although new housing had been built in Williamsburg, much of it was high-rise apartments, which the Hasidim consider undesir-

GREEN–WOOD CEMETERY

EIGHTH AVE
NINTH AVE
TENTH AVE
FT. HAMILTON PKWY
NEW UTRECHT AVE
TWELFTH AVE
BOBOVER PROMENADE (48 ST)
FOURTEENTH AVE
FIFTEENTH AVE
SIXTEENTH AVE
DAHILL RD

36 ST
37 ST
38 ST
39 ST
40 ST
41 ST
42 ST
43 ST
44 ST
45 ST
46 ST
47 ST
49 ST
50 ST
51 ST
52 ST
53 ST
54 ST
55 ST
56 ST
57 ST
58 ST
59 ST
60 ST
61 ST
62 ST
63 ST
64 ST
65 ST

BOROUGH PARK

TENTH AVE
ELEVENTH AVE
THIRTEENTH AVE
NEW UTRECHT AVE

SEVENTEENTH AVE
EIGHTEENTH AVE
OLD NEW UTRECHT RD
McDONALD AVE

WASHINGTON
CEMETERY

MAPLETON

NINETEENTH AVE
TWENTIETH AVE
TWENTYFIRST AVE
BAY PKWY
23RD AVE
24TH AVE
DAHILL RD

28 able because they cannot use elevators on the Sabbath.

Today almost all the residents of Borough Park are Hasidic Jews. The Bobover sect's headquarters is located at 15th Avenue and 48th Street, and 48th Street has officially been renamed Bobover Promenade. Other sects are also represented: the area is home to the Satmar, Munkatcz, Gur, and Belzer. In addition, a smaller group of modern Orthodox Jews has also flourished. The largest modern Orthodox synagogue in Borough Park, Young Israel Beth El, is situated on 15th Avenue, almost directly across the street from the main Bobover yeshiva.

When strolling down a Borough Park street, visitors are struck by the absence of chain supermarkets. Instead, a homey array of small shops entice everyone to partake in the Jewish culture. Almost all of Borough

NEIGHBORHOOD PROFILE

Boundaries: Borough Park: from 8th Avenue on the west to MacDonald Avenue on the east, from Green-Wood Cemetery and 36th Street on the north to 65th Street on the south. Mapleton: from 16th Avenue on the west to Dahill Road on the east, from 57th Street on the north to 65th Street on the south.
Subway: BMT West End Line B: 9th Ave., Fort Hamilton Pkwy., 50th St., 55th St., New Utrecht Ave., 62nd St. IND F: Ditmas Ave., 18th Ave., Avenue I, Bay Pkwy./22nd Ave., Avenue N, Avenue P. 4th Avenue N: 8th Ave., Fort Hamilton Pkwy., New Utrecht Ave., 18th Ave., 20th Ave.
Bus: B9: 60th St. B11: 49th St./50th St. B35: 39th St. B70: 8th Ave. B16: 13th Ave./14th Ave. B23: 16th Ave. B8: 18th Ave. B6: Bay Pkwy.
Libraries: Brooklyn Public Library Borough Park Branch (43rd St. near 13th Ave.) and Mapleton Branch (60th St. at 17th Ave.), Ryder Branch (23rd Ave. at 59th St.)
Community Board: No. 12
Police Precinct: 66th Precinct (5822 16th Ave.)
Fire Department: Engine 247 Thawing Apparatus 64 (1336 60th St.), Engine 282 Ladder 148 (4210 12th Ave.)
Hospitals and Clinics: Maimonides Medical Center (4802 10th Ave.), M. J. G. Nursing Home Co.–The Brenner Pavilion (4915 10th Ave.), Institute for Applied Gerontology (4914 Fort Hamilton Pkwy.)

Park's stores are "shomer shabbos," which means that they observe the Jewish sabbath and are closed from sundown Friday until at least sundown Saturday. In addition, many local buildings without yards have balconies for Sukkoth, the harvest holiday when Jews build temporary shelters to commemorate and reenact their ancestors' experience of wandering through the wilderness to the promised land.

The area is experiencing what some call an internal population boom. With traditional Orthodox families having five or more children, and

Homes along 36th Street

Bes Midrash and Synagogue Bes Yitzhak,
in the Shetl Revival style

Maimonides Medical Center

young adults reluctant to leave a place that so aptly reflects their traditional values, Borough Park has had to expand its housing. In recent years, many one- and two-family houses have been replaced by three- and four-family brick residences. Among the new occupants is a small community of Muslims who were attracted to Borough Park because of its residents' conservative religious beliefs.

NEIGHBORHOOD FACTS

■ Today's Maimonides Medical Center on 10th Avenue evolved from the New Utrecht Dispensary, a clinic established in 1911 by the women of Borough Park. That small medical center became Israel Hospital of Brooklyn, and in 1920 was reestablished as United Israel–Zion Hospital. The hospital was known for its polio rehabilitation service, its breakthrough surgical techniques, and its innovative procedures for caring for diabetic and coronary patients. In 1947 the facility merged with Beth Moses Hospital to become Maimonides Hospital, and in 1966 it took its current name.

■ Borough Park is home to a number of fine Jewish bakeries. Orthodox Jews who scoff at the boxed, supermarket matzohs buy their hand-baked matzohs fresh for Passover. Schick's, on 16th Avenue, produces Passover cakes and cookies for almost all of New York City's larger retail stores, which in turn ship the desserts all over the country.

Brighton

Detail of door at 711 Brightwater Court

Brighton Beach was designed with families in mind. Less rowdy than its sister Coney Island to the west, and not as exclusive as its sibling Manhattan Beach to the east, Brighton Beach is the perfect site for a relaxed summer day at the shore. A *Brooklyn Times* article dated June 16, 1890, paints a portrait of the era and the mood of a place where patrons were "chiefly good middle-class Brooklynites—people who brought books and babies and light luncheons with them and sat on the smooth sand, or occupied seats around the paths or walked around the magnificent lawns." Whereas subway service to Coney Island targeted Manhattan, rail lines to Brighton Beach were designed with stops accessible to middle-class Brooklynites. A casual atmosphere further enhanced the area's appeal to families.

Today, Brighton Beach is home to the liveliest and largest Russian community in Brooklyn, many of whom were attracted to "Little Odessa," as it came to be called, because it reminded them of the city on the shore of the Black Sea. The population of Russian immigrants in Brighton Beach is greater than 150,000 and represents approximately 80 percent of the area's residents. Russian is the language most commonly heard on Brighton's boardwalks, and a bustling section of Russian bookstores, fruit stands, nightclubs, and restaurants thrives under the elevated train tracks, on Brighton Beach Avenue from Ocean Parkway to West End Avenue. Mrs. Stahl's is a neighborhood favorite: her restaurant has been serving up tasty knishes—baked dough filled with spinach, cabbage, and potato—since 1935. And on Friday nights, while enjoying glitzy and raucous live Russian music at area restaurants, residents and visitors can feast on borscht, blinis, bureka, and boiled potatoes, and wash it all down with authentic Russian vodka.

Brighton Beach was not nearly as colorful in its earliest days. Originally part of the English town of Gravesend,

Beach

ATLANTIC OCEAN

NEIGHBORHOOD PROFILE

Boundaries: from Ocean Parkway on the west to West End Avenue on the east, from the Belt Parkway on the north to the ocean on the south.
Subway: <u>Brighton Line D</u>: Brighton Beach, Ocean Pkwy. <u>Brighton Line Q</u>: Brighton Beach
Bus: <u>B36</u>: Neptune Ave. <u>B68</u>: Brighton Beach Ave./Coney Island Ave. <u>Bx29</u>: Neptune Ave. <u>B49</u>: West End Ave. <u>B1</u>: Ocean Pkwy./Brighton Beach Ave.
Libraries: Brooklyn Public Library Brighton Beach Branch (Brighton First Pl. near Brighton Beach Ave.)
Community Board: No. 13
Police Precinct: 60th Precinct (2951 West 8th St./Coney Island), Mounted Troop E (28-01 Brighton 3 Street)
Fire Department: Engine 245 Ladder 161 (2929 West 8th St./Coney Island), Engine 318 Ladder 166 (2510 Neptune Ave./Sheepshead Bay)

the beach took its name from the British sea resort of Brighton. Until the mid-1800s, the area was used primarily for farming.

Development of restaurant pavilions and hotels at nearby Coney Island in the 1820s drew vacationers, as well as savvy developers who recognized the value of its real estate. Eventually as development increased, the original Coney Island became subdivided into four parts: Norton's Point, or "West End" (later Sea Gate); West Brighton, which was to encompass Luna Park, Steeplechase Park, and Dreamland; Brighton Beach; and Manhattan Beach. Of the two neighborhoods in the east, Brighton Beach and Manhattan Beach, Manhattan Beach was considered the more exclusive.

The first development at Brighton Beach was the brainchild of William A. Engeman, an entrepreneur who made a fortune during the Civil War selling supplies to both Union and Confederate troops. In his quest to acquire a huge tract of marshy and sandy land on which to build the neighborhood's first pier (1869), a hotel (the Ocean Hotel, 1873), and a bath house (1875) on the

beach, Engeman, with the aid of local resident William Stillwell, tracked down hundreds of heirs to 39 lots, some of whom lived as far away as Hawaii (then known as the Sandwich Islands). His hotel, the bathing facilities, and the completion of the Ocean Parkway (1876) drew crowds of Brooklyn family vacationers. So did Engeman's Brighton Beach Race Track (1879–1907), which offered an afternoon of betting on and cheering for a lucky horse. And to bring them even more quickly, entrepreneur Henry C. Murphy (who named Brighton Beach; he later became mayor of Brooklyn) built the New York and Brighton Beach Railroad (1878). That same year Murphy built the elegant Hotel Brighton (1878), later called Brighton Beach Hotel.

During the late 1800s, Brighton Beach indulged in some of the kinds of

32

■ In the late 1880s, when waves came too close to the Brighton Beach Hotel and threatened to pull it into the sea, a grand plan was devised to save it. Work began in the winter of 1887 to raise the hotel on logs, place 24 railroad tracks underneath, and use 112 cars to move it back from the ocean's edge. In 1888, over the course of three months, the 6,000-ton hotel was prepared for moving—and on April 4, 1888, the Brighton Beach Hotel was slowly pulled to drier land, as spectators and workers gave "shouts of joyous approval and triumph." It remained standing by the shore on Coney Island Avenue, 600 feet from its original lot, until 1924.

■ One of the restaurants renowned for its famous Friday and Saturday night feasts is the National, which was used as Robin Williams's refuge in the movie *Moscow on the Hudson* (1984). Waiters place vodka at every table instead of water. This restaurant had been the site of Brighton Beach's first "air conditioned" movie theater: the Lakeland featured a roof that opened on clear nights.

■ Famous residents of Brighton Beach include novelists Irwin Shaw and Wallace Markfield, comedians Phil Silvers and Mel Brooks, and singer Neil Sedaka.

Russian discount store on Brighton Beach Avenue

amusements that had made nearby neighborhoods famous. In addition to the racetrack, the Brighton Beach Music Hall (by 1892) and the more serious New Brighton Theater (1909)—which featured the first Yiddish vaudeville theater—captivated audiences with their lively entertainments. And Brighton Beach Park, the predecessor to the Brighton Beach Baths, featured a giant rollercoaster, midway, and fireworks, along with a carousel whose building still stands today.

From the beginning of the twentieth century, as nearby Coney Island became the amusement capital of Brooklyn, Brighton Beach began to seem attractive as a year-round residence to immigrants and to New Yorkers from more crowded neighborhoods like Brownsville, East New York, and

Manhattan's Lower East Side. To house the new arrivals, developers built more than 30 six-story apartment buildings, naming several after socialist leaders. These buildings still stand today, between Coney Island Avenue and Ocean Parkway, and some have been turned into cooperatives. Also during this period, the boardwalk was extended into Brighton (1926 and again in 1941). By the 1930s and 1940s, Brighton Beach was a crowded, year-round residential area. The neighborhood's summer bungalows, many of which had been built on the former Brighton Beach Race Track, were winterized to help accommodate the many new residents.

In the 1970s, just as Brighton Beach was beginning to seem a bit worn, with its elderly population in rent-controlled apartments and vacant

● **Brighton Beach Baths**

The Brighton Beach Baths, the 1907 inspiration of real-estate developer Joseph Day, was a 15-acre exclusive club that by the 1960s had 13,000 members. The baths, later named the Brighton Beach Bath and Racquet Club, offered members diverse pleasures: swimming in one of three pools, challenging others to a game of tennis or handball, sunbathing on the "public" beach (for 15 cents), or engaging in such diversions as miniature golf, mah-jongg, and cards. After all this competitive fun, members could relax in steam rooms or the solarium, or sip a drink while listening to a weekend concert by popular entertainers who over the years included such diverse figures as Milton Berle, Lionel Hampton, and Herman's Hermits.

But as Brighton Beach's population became less wealthy and elitist, the club found it difficult to attract members. In the mid-1980s the owner of the land saw its potential as prime residential real estate. After nearly ten years of protest from community residents, a court order in 1994 allowed building to commence, although neighborhood pressure led the developers to revise their plans: the luxury condominiums have been scaled back by 700 homes.

smaller houses (a plight depicted in the 1979 film *Boardwalk*), the Soviet Union eased its immigration policies and an infusion of immigrants, many young and eager to make their mark in their new home, began a new, vital chapter in the history of Brighton Beach. Although these former Soviets have been joined by newcomers from Puerto Rico, China, India, Pakistan, Vietnam, and other nations, the vibrant Russian culture is the most readily apparent.

Art Deco apartment building at Coney Island and Oceanview Avenues

Brooklyn

Brooklyn Heights, which in 1965 became the first New York City neighborhood to be designated both a New York City historic district and a national landmark, is a treasury of beautiful old houses that evoke the grandeur of nineteenth-century Brooklyn. Most historians agree that the beauty of the area's buildings is linked to the neighborhood's spectacular views of the Manhattan skyline, which enticed Brooklyn's first commuters to New York's bustling financial and commercial center. Indeed, after Robert Fulton launched the first steam-powered ferry service in 1814, the trip across the East River became safe and fast—it took less than 15 minutes for Brooklyn Heights residents to come home to "Manhattan's bedroom."

Before the steam-powered boats were put into service, few were adventurous or determined enough to make the trip by rowboat or sailboat. As of 1807, there were still only seven houses in Brooklyn Heights, then called Brookland Heights, with about 20 more near the river's edge. Earlier inhabitants include the Canarsee Indians, who called the area Ihpetonga, and Dutch farmers, who settled in the area during the mid-1600s.

Fulton's ferry sparked tremendous development. In 1816, when Brooklyn was incorporated as a village, streets in the neighborhood were planned and laid out. Advertising in the 1820s by a merchant, Hezekiah Pierpont, harbin-

The Esplanade (or Promenade) at 222 Columbia Heights Street

Heights

● **Plymouth Church of the Pilgrims**
The Plymouth Church of the Pilgrims at Orange and Hicks Streets, originally named Plymouth Church and completed in 1850, is a national historic landmark that is known best as the church once led by Henry Ward Beecher, a reformer and abolitionist. Beecher, whose sister was Harriet Beecher Stowe, author of *Uncle Tom's Cabin*, preached at Plymouth Church for 40 years. Once, as a powerful symbolic gesture, he brought a slave to the church and held an auction in which the highest bidder bought her freedom. The church was known as the "Grand Central Terminal of the Underground Railroad" because slaves seeking freedom in Canada were purportedly hidden in a tunnel under the building.

gered the promotion of the area to the well-to-do: he lauded Brooklyn Heights as "the nearest country retreat" for the Manhattan businessman. Recognizing a golden opportunity, enterprising landowners like John Hicks, Jacob Middagh Hicks, John Middagh, Henry Remsen, and Teunis Joralemon divided and sold their farms. The standard Brooklyn Heights lot, a space measuring 25 by 100 feet, was born.

Residential construction began in earnest in the 1820s and continued until the turn of the century. Beginning at the north side of Brooklyn Heights, builders created many frame and brick buildings in the Federal style, with pitched and gambrel roofs, examples of which still stand today on Middagh Street. The southern section of the Heights was developed soon thereafter, in the 1830s and 1840s, and different architectural styles were introduced, notably homes of brick and brownstone with details in the Greek Revival tradition. To keep up with the changing times and varied construction, owners of older houses added such details as cornices, bay windows, iron railings, or doorways, often in styles uncharacteristic of their homes' original architecture.

During this period a number of Brooklyn Heights' most beautiful churches were built, including New York City landmarks Grace Church (1847) on Hicks Street near Grace Court; Church of the Pilgrims (1846), now Our Lady of Lebanon Maronite Rite Roman Catholic Church, on Henry and Remsen Streets; and Holy Trinity Church (1847), now St. Ann and the Holy Trinity Episcopal Church, on Clinton Street at Montague

N E I G H B O R H O O D   P R O F I L E

Boundaries: from the Brooklyn-Queens Expressway and Esplanade on the west to Cadman Plaza and Clinton Street on the east, from the Brooklyn-Queens Expressway on the north to Atlantic Avenue on the south to Court Street.

Subway: <u>BMT 4th Avenue N and R</u>: Court St. <u>IRT 2 and 3</u>: Clark St. <u>IRT 4 and 5</u>: Borough Hall.

Bus: <u>B61</u>: Atlantic Ave. <u>B63</u>: Atlantic Ave. <u>B75</u>: Court St.

Libraries: Brooklyn Public Library Business Library (280 Cadman Plaza W. at Tillary St.), Brooklyn Public Library Brooklyn Heights Branch (280 Cadman Plaza W. at Tillary St.)

Museums: Brooklyn Historical Society (Pierrepont St.), Rotunda Gallery (Clinton St. between Pierrepont St. and Cadman Plaza W.)

Theaters: St. Ann's Center for Restoration and the Arts (Clinton St. near Livingston St.), The Heights Players (26 Willow Street)

Community Board: No. 2

Police Precinct: 84th Precinct (Downtown Brooklyn, 301 Gold St.)

Fire Department: Engine 205 Ladder 118 (74 Middagh St.), Engine 207 Ladder 110 (172 Tillary St.), Engine 224 (27 Hicks St.)

Hospitals and Clinics: Long Island College Hospital (Atlantic Ave.)

Street, which boasts the first stained-glass windows made in America. Not content with this honor, St. Ann's uses its 650-seat sanctuary for other "firsts": it sponsors an arts series and promotes avant-garde and new American performers. A block away from the church, at 129 Pierrepont Street, is St. Ann's Episcopal Church School, in the former home of the Crescent Athletic Club (1906–40).

Brooklyn Heights remained elegant throughout the nineteenth century, and it became Brooklyn's cultural and financial center. Two of the largest surviving Italianate mansions, the Alexander M. White and Abiel Abbot Low Houses (ca. 1857), stand at 2 and 3 Pierrepont Place. Attention was given to details throughout the area: houses that backed on the water sported second-floor porches, and warehouses along Furman Street planted trees and grass on their roofs as back gardens for residents on Columbia Street.

Developers who discovered a secondary market in catering to the wishes of middle-class Brooklynites continued to strive for elegance. In the 1880s apartment buildings were built and stand today as some of the finest early examples of the Queen Anne style: the Berkeley, Grosvenor, and Montague (1885), as well as the Arlington (1887), are all on Montague Street, between Henry and Hicks Streets. In addition to

Brooklyn Heights at the end of the nineteenth century (Brian Merlis Collection)

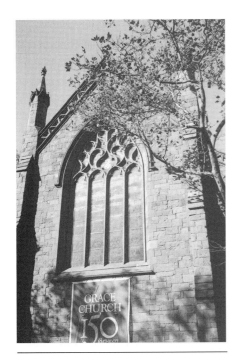

Grace Church at 254 Hicks Street, built by Richard Upjohn in 1847

■ The Brooklyn Historical Society, formerly the Long Island Historical Society, a research library and museum, houses artifacts, bound books, graphic images, and maps relating to the history of Brooklyn. Its current building, at 128 Pierrepont Street, underwent three years of rehabilitation to bring it into the modern age and make its holdings more accessible than ever. Constructed between 1878 and 1880, both the library and lobby interior and the building exterior are New York City and national historic landmarks.

■ After the American forces were defeated in the Revolutionary War's Battle of Brooklyn, General Israel Putnam withdrew his troops to Brooklyn Heights, where George Washington had his headquarters (in a house where today Montague Street meets the Esplanade). On August 29, 1776, two days after the Battle at Old Stone House, Washington and the American troops slipped across the East River to Manhattan, hidden by nighttime fog.

■ In 1909 a religious group now called the Jehovah's Witnesses established their headquarters in Brooklyn Heights. They used the former Squibb factory as a base and renamed their group the Watch Tower Bible and Tract Society. The Jehovah's Witnesses, known for their door-to-door proselytizing, continue to publish more than 25 million copies of their publications each year from this complex. Many members stay for a time in Brooklyn Heights to work at the Watch Tower.

■ In 1855, in the Rome Brothers' Printshop at what was the corner of Old Fulton and Cranberry Streets in Brooklyn Heights, Walt Whitman printed *Leaves of Grass*. The printshop was destroyed by urban renewal in 1964.

■ St. Francis College, at 180 Remsen Street, is the oldest Catholic school in Brooklyn. Founded by the Franciscans as a boys' school in 1859, it offered instruction in all levels, from elementary to college. In 1884 it was authorized to grant degrees, and in 1902 the lower divisions split off to form St. Francis Academy. In 1953 the college became coeducational, and in 1963 it moved to its present location, the former headquarters of Brooklyn Union Gas Company.

■ The 1960s television show *The Patty Duke Show* was set in Brooklyn Heights.

the Esplanade, these many beautiful homes and churches constructed before the turn of the century draw tourists to Brooklyn Heights. In warm weather, visitors wander the streets, guidebooks in hand, to marvel at the buildings.

After the Brooklyn Bridge opened in 1883 and the Interborough Rapid Transit Company came to Brooklyn in 1908, the area could no longer remain a retreat for wealthy commuters to Manhattan. As these upper-class residents found other, more exclusive havens, their mansions and row houses were divided into apartments and boarding houses. Several distinctive hotels were built, including the St. George (1885) on Clark Street, the Hotel Bossert (1909) on the corner of Hicks and Montague Streets, and the Hotel Margaret (1889) on Columbia Heights. The St. George, once the largest hotel in New York City, graced a full block of Brooklyn Heights and boasted the world's largest saltwater swimming pool. The Bossert housed one of Brooklyn's earliest radio stations. The Hotel Margaret burned down while being renovated into apartments.

Bedroom at 28 Pierrepont Street, ca. 1880 (Brooklyn Historical Society)

Association, which became a major galvanizing force in the neighborhood during this period, the community rallied to preserve the nineteenth-century character of Brooklyn Heights.

Additional construction since the 1950s includes the Cadman Plaza apartment buildings, built in the late 1960s on the site of the former Brooklyn Bridge trolley terminal. And many of the larger buildings in Brooklyn Heights have been converted into cooperatives.

Brooklyn Heights attracts young singles and couples with small children. Although quite a few homes are privately owned, the high cost of maintaining a single-family dwelling has again led to many brownstones being

Children still love the parks of Brooklyn Heights (Matthew Coleman)

In later years, writers and artists began to seek out the neighborhood. During the 1940s, composer Benjamin Britten, poet W. H. Auden, and novelist Carson McCullers lived together at what used to be a house at 7 Middagh Street. Writers Truman Capote, Henry Miller, Tennessee Williams, Arthur Miller, Norman Mailer, and the photographer Walker Evans all at some point called Brooklyn Heights home.

By the time of the Depression, the boarding houses in Brooklyn Heights had become low-income rooming houses—some people even described sections of the neighborhood as slums. The completion of the Brooklyn-Queens Expressway in 1957 changed Brooklyn Heights forever, as whole sections of brownstone row houses were demolished to make way for the large highway.

But the neighborhood was active in its own redevelopment. The Brooklyn Heights Association, founded in 1910 and one of the country's oldest civic associations, insisted on a compromise to total loss of the riverfront: construction of the Esplanade, a walkway and park along the East River, above the highway. A perfect place to take children, the Esplanade (called the Promenade by most Brooklynites) is a popular attraction into the evening, offering a clear view of downtown Manhattan and, in warm weather, refreshing breezes.

Grassroots organization and community interest also initiated the renovation of Brooklyn Heights brownstones during the 1950s. Aided by the Brooklyn Heights

St. George Hotel, Clark Street, ca. 1910 (Brooklyn Historical Society)

converted into apartments. And while some residents bemoan the loss of Brooklyn Heights' small boutiques, others have welcomed larger national stores, given that the landmarked buildings in which they are housed have not changed outwardly. Montague Street, always the heart of beautiful Brooklyn Heights, remains a lively, historic district full of restaurants and sites to explore.

Brownsville

Brownsville, on the eastern edge of Brooklyn, is surrounded by the neighborhoods of Bushwick, Bedford-Stuyvesant, East New York, East Flatbush, and Crown Heights. Like neighboring Bushwick and East New York, Brownsville is a community that is being rebuilt and reenergized. With every new home that is completed and occupied, the neighborhood's difficult years seem part of an ever more distant past.

Brownsville was named for Charles S. Brown, who bought the land and built 250 houses beginning in 1865. Brown's Village, as it was originally named, was a cozy cluster of small cottages and shops surrounded by meadows and a large dairy farm. The initial settlement stayed small because Brown's Village was inaccessible by sea and difficult to reach by land.

In 1887 the remote community of Brownsville, as it was now called, drew the interest of Aaron Kaplan, a New York City real-estate developer. Kaplan began to purchase tracts of land, construct tenement buildings, and encourage garment workers from Manhattan's Lower East Side to relocate there. The Fulton Street elevated railway, which opened in 1889, and the Williamsburg Bridge, which was completed in 1903, prompted more New Yorkers to move to

the area. As the neighborhood became crowded, two-family houses and tenements with streetside stores replaced single-family homes. By 1910 the large buildings were overflowing with immigrant families, and the area was a crowded slum of sweatshops and pushcarts, with few sewers or paved streets.

During these years, daily life in

World War I Memorial in Zion Park, Pitkin and East New York Avenues

Atlantic Plaza Towers, a Mitchell-Lama housing complex at Atlantic and Rockaway Avenues

Brownsville was guided by the customs and cere-
monies of the neighborhood's Jewish residents. At
the turn of the century, Brownsville was known as
the "Jerusalem of America," and by 1926, at least
75 percent of Brownsville's more than 400,000
residents were Jewish. The neighborhood was
filled with freethinkers, many of whom had fled
persecution in Russia and Poland. Indeed,
Brownsville elected socialists to the New
York State Assembly between 1915 and 1921
and later, in 1936, the neighborhood helped
an American Party candidate reach the
assembly. A statue of Emma Lazarus, author of "The New Colossus," the poem
inscribed on the Statue of Liberty,
stands in the neighborhood.

Also during the 1930s, the notorious "Murder, Inc.," an organization of criminals that included
Lucky Luciano, Meyer Lansky, Joe
Adonis, Frank Costello, Louis (Lepke)
Buchalter, and Albert Anastasia, was born
in Brownsville, although their activities covered the whole borough.

Meanwhile, new immigrants continued to arrive
in Brownsville. For some time a small, active community of North African Moors existed around Livonia Avenue and Rockaway Parkway.

After World War II, Brownsville underwent dramatic changes.
African Americans from other neighborhoods began moving to
Brownsville, but when they arrived, they faced discrimination, reduced social services, and lack of employment opportunities. Many longtime residents moved to eastern Brooklyn neighborhoods, Long Island, other
suburbs of New York City, or New Jersey. A majority of the largest, higher-qual-
ity stores on Pitkin Avenue closed, but some neighborhood institutions remained,
such as Slavin's Fish Market on Belmont Avenue, which has been serving Brownsville for 75 years.

For the next 20 years, Brownsville was plagued by the decay of old and abandoned
buildings, as well as by vandalism and arson. High-rise apartment buildings built in Brownsville during the 1950s and 1960s were intended to provide affordable, attractive housing. In-

NEIGHBORHOOD FACTS

■ In 1916 Margaret Sanger established the first birth-control clinic in America at 46 Amboy Street, but the clinic was shut down days later by local police. Although more than 150 clients had been in line on the clinic's opening day, Sanger was declared a public nuisance and sentenced to 30 days in jail.

■ The colorful daily life in Brownsville provided the impetus for some of the greatest accounts of Jewish immigrants in New York City. Henry Roth's *Call It Sleep* (1934), Irving Shulman's *The Amboy Dukes* (1947), Alfred Kazin's *A Walker in the City* (1951), and Norman Podhoretz's *Making It* (1967) were all inspired by the writers' experiences in and around Brownsville.

■ Brownsville was home to the Loew's Pitkin Theater, an opulent movie theater designed in 1930 by Thomas W. Lamb. The theater building still stands at the western side of the neighborhood, at the corner of East New York and Pitkin Avenues.

■ The Betsy Head Pool and Park was constructed by the Works Progress Administration in 1940, and for Brownsville's landlocked residents the Olympic-size pool became the local beach in the warm weather. Those living in the neighborhood still flock to Betsy Head in the summer.

■ Theater producers Joseph Papp and Sol Hurok, as well as comedians Zero Mostel, Danny Kaye, and Jerry Lewis, all lived in Brownsville at some point in their lives. The heavyweight boxers Mike Tyson and Riddick Bowe grew up in Brownsville, as did civil rights leader Mother Rosetta Gaston.

well received: it took time for the owners of the houses to adjust to the neighborhood and for the previous residents of Brownsville to become accustomed to the sight of owner-occupied, gated homes. But block parties and other activities sponsored by block and neighborhood associations have begun to bridge the residents' differences. Crime has decreased, and retail stores are healthy. More homes are planned for the neighborhood's vacant lots and should be completed by the year 2000.

At Brownsville's northwestern side is a small neighborhood sometimes referred to as **Ocean Hill**. The area is today within Bedford-Stuyvesant and Crown Heights, but historically, Ocean Hill was a part of Brownsville. Originally developed in the 1890s as an ex-

stead, they led Brownsville to become even more overcrowded and impoverished. Finally, in the early 1970s, a combination of efforts began to revitalize the community. Local residents and merchants banded together to ease racial tensions in the neighborhood, to fight for affordable and livable housing, and to create services for the neighborhood's young and old residents.

Between 1977 and 1985, more than a thousand housing units were built or renovated in Brownsville—housing that attracted, among others, immigrants from the Caribbean, who introduced the game of cricket to the neighborhood. Brownsville Heritage House was one such housing development; another was Marcus Garvey Village. Boasting low-rise row houses, front stoops, and trees, Marcus Garvey Village was completed in 1976 and heralded as an antidote to the problems created by early high-rises. In addition, the Council of East Brooklyn Churches, working with local neighborhood groups, built single-family row houses in the southeastern section of Brownsville. These homes were not initially

Margaret Sanger established the nation's first birth-control clinic in Brownsville (Library of Congress)

Belmont Avenue bazaar, 1910 (Brooklyn Historical Society)

clusive residential community, by the beginning of the twentieth century Ocean Hill had department stores, theaters, and some industry. In the 1930s, many Italians settled there.

During the 1960s Ocean Hill, along with Brownsville, was selected as one of three school districts to test community control over local schools. Conflicts ensued among school leaders, members of the community, and repre-

sentatives from the teachers' union. The disagreements led to one of the most intense teacher strikes in the history of education in New York City. (Indeed, although the neighborhood name Ocean Hill is now hardly ever used, we know roughly where it used to be because of the location of the schools that were involved in the strike.) More difficulties followed: in the 1970s the number of vacant lots dramatically increased as houses were abandoned and stores were destroyed or damaged by arson during the 1977 blackout. But the area is slowly being revitalized, and today most residents live in two-to four-family houses. In addition, the East Broadway Merchants' Association and the Ocean Hill Bushwick Bedford-Stuyvesant Development Corporation undertook the improvement of Broadway. The current population is mostly African American, with some Caribbean American residents.

NEIGHBORHOOD PROFILE

Boundaries: <u>Brownsville</u>: from Ralph Avenue, Eastern Parkway, and Rockaway Parkway on the west to Van Sinderen Avenue on the east, from Fulton Street on the north to the railroad tracks and Avenue D on the south. <u>Ocean Hill</u> (historic boundaries): from Ralph Avenue on the west and Fulton Street on the north to Eastern Parkway Extension on the east and south.
Subway: <u>IND A and C</u>: Ralph Ave., Rockaway Ave., Broadway/East New York Ave. <u>IRT 3</u>: Saratoga Ave., Rockaway Ave., Junius St. <u>BMT Canarsie</u>: Broadway/East New York Ave., Atlantic Ave., Sutter Ave., Livonia Ave., New Lots Ave.
Bus: <u>B35</u>: New Lots Ave. <u>B14</u>: Pitkin Ave./Sutter Ave. <u>B40</u>: Liberty Ave. <u>B15</u>: East 98th St. <u>B7</u>: Saratoga Ave. <u>B60</u>: Rockaway Ave. <u>B12</u>: East New York Ave. <u>B056</u>: East New York Ave.
Libraries: Brooklyn Public Library Brownsville Branch (Glenmore Ave. at Watkins St.), Stone Avenue Branch (Mother Gaston Blvd. at Dumont Ave.)
Community Board: No. 16
Police Precinct: 73rd Precinct/Service Station 3 (1470 East New York Avenue)
Fire Department: Engine 227 (423 Ralph Ave.), Engine 231 Ladder 120 (107 Watkins St.), Engine 233 Ladder 176 (25 Rockaway Ave.), Engine 283 (885 Howard Ave.)
Hospitals and Clinics: Brookdale University Hospital and Medical Center (One Brookdale Plaza), Brookdale Family Care Center (1380 Linden Blvd.), Linroc Nursing Home (650 Amboy St.)

44

Davis Medical Building, originally William Ulmer Residence, ca. 1885, at 670 Bushwick Avenue

Could it be true that Brooklynites, including children, once imbibed an average of two barrels of beer or ale a year? During the mid-1800s, in Bushwick—home of "Brewer's Row," 14 blocks containing 11 breweries—that was indeed the case. In this small city space, beer gardens, reminiscent of Bavarian beer halls, served up exuberant family entertainment, replete with oompah bands, dancing, sauerkraut with sausages, and, of course, steins of the local brew.

After this era of prosperity, the effervescence of Bushwick diminished somewhat, but in recent years the neighborhood has been renewed. Prohibition, the Depression, and a long strike by brewery workers closed down many of Brooklyn's nearly 45 breweries —most of them in Bushwick—and finally Rheingold and F. and M. Schaefer left in 1976. Further, during the blackout of 1977, a large proportion of Bushwick was destroyed by looting and arson. These setbacks challenged neighborhood residents to discover new ways of adding stability and vitality to a community once known as the "beer capital of New York."

When Peter Stuyvesant chartered Bushwick in 1661, one notable signer of its patent was Francisco de Niger, an African who had been enslaved in New Netherland but was free by 1660. Originally named Boswijck ("heavy woods," or as some interpret it, refuge or town in the woods), Bushwick was one of the original six towns of Brooklyn. (A subneighborhood called Ridgewood

Bushwick

QUEENS COUNTY

CYPRESS AVE

ST NICHOLAS AVE

SEIGEL ST
MOORE ST

FLUSHING AVE

BUSHWICK
HOUSES

NOLL ST
GEORGE ST
MELROSE ST
JEFFERSON ST
TROUTMAN ST
STARR ST
WILLOUGHBY AVE
SUYDAM AVE
HART AVE
DEKALB AVE
STOCKHOLM ST
STANHOPE ST
HIMROD ST
HARMAN ST
GREENE ST
BLEECKER ST
MENAHAN ST

MARIA
HERNANDEZ
PARK

IRVING AVE

WYCKOFF AVE

SUMNER PL
FAYETTE ST
ELLERY ST
PARK ST
LOCUST ST
BELVIDERE ST
ARION PL
MELROSE ST
JEFFERSON ST
DITMARS ST

SUYDAM AVE

MYRTLE AVE

GROVE ST
LINDEN ST
GATES ST
PALMETTO ST
WOODBINE ST

RIDGEWOOD

KNICKERBOCKER AVE

MADISON ST
PUTNAM AVE
CORNELIA ST
JEFFERSON AVE
HANCOCK ST
WEIRFIELD ST
HALSEY ST
ELDERT ST

WILSON AVE

CENTRAL AVE

EVERGREEN AVE

BROADWAY

HART ST
LAWTON ST
DODWORTH ST
KOSCIUSKO ST
KOSSGETH PL
LAFAYETTE AVE
VAN BUREN AVE
GREENE ST
GOODWIN PL

BUSHWICK AVE

BUSHWICK

COVERT ST
SCHAEFER ST
DECATUR ST
COOPER ST
MOFFAT ST

COOPER AVE

EVERGREEN ST
CHAUNCEY ST

CEMETERY
OF THE
EVERGREENS

PILLING ST
GRANITE ST
FURMAN AVE
ABERDEEN ST
DE SALES PL
VANDERVEER ST
STEWART ST
CONWAY ST

was origi-
nally part of the
Eastern District town
of Bushwick-Ridgewood.
This is now generally considered part of Queens and will be discussed in the forthcoming volume on the
neighborhoods of Queens.) The neighborhood
was primarily a farming community that produced
food and tobacco for local consumption and for export
to New York City. Heavy industries introduced during this
period included manufactured sugar, oil, chemicals, and glue. In
the 1840s, for example, Peter Cooper—inventor, manufacturer, philanthropist, onetime presidential hopeful, and founder of Cooper Union—built
his first factory, a glue manufacturing plant, in Bushwick.

By this time the original Dutch settlers had been joined by newcomers from
France, Scandinavia, and England. In addition, between 1840 and 1860, more
than a million German-speaking immigrants came to the United States, and many
settled in what was called the Eastern District of Brooklyn—the neighborhoods of
Greenpoint, Williamsburg, and Bushwick. Some continued their German migra-
tion by ferry, moving across the East River from crowded "Kleindeutschland" in
the Lower East Side of Manhattan.

In 1869, while breweries were being established in Bushwick, Adrian Marten-
ses Suydam began to subdivide his family farm, and by 1884, 125 residences had
been built on the site. Development of Bushwick gained momentum after 1888,
when the Broadway and Myrtle Avenue elevated railway reached the area and
made commut-
ing to Manhattan
easier. Bushwick Avenue,
especially between Myrtle Avenue and
Decatur Street, became home to the
large mansions of the brewers and
other professionals. Side streets in this
area were filled with rows of town-

NEIGHBORHOOD PROFILE

Boundaries: from Broadway on the west to the Queens County line on the east, from Flushing Avenue on the north to Conway Street and the L train line tracks on the south.

Subway: <u>BMT J</u>: Myrtle Ave. <u>BMT M</u>: Myrtle Ave, Central Ave., Knickerbocker Ave., Wyckoff Ave. <u>BMT Canarsie Line L</u>: Jefferson St., DeKalb Ave., Myrtle Ave., Halsey Ave., Bushwick Ave./Aberdeen St., Broadway-Eastern Pkwy.

Bus: <u>B40</u>: Broadway <u>B46</u>: Broadway <u>B20</u>: Broadway <u>B024</u>: Broadway <u>B7</u>: Broadway <u>B056</u>: Broadway <u>B60</u>: Wilson Ave./Cooper St. <u>B18</u>: Wyckoff Ave. <u>B26</u>: Wyckoff Ave./Halsey Ave. <u>B57</u>: Flushing Ave. <u>B38</u>: DeKalb Ave. <u>B52</u>: Gates Ave. <u>B20</u>: Schaeffer St.

Libraries: Brooklyn Public Library Bushwick Branch (Bushwick Ave. at Seigel St.), Washington Irving Branch (Irving Ave. at Woodbine St.), DeKalb Branch (Bushwick Ave. at DeKalb Ave.)

Community Board: No. 4

Police Precinct: 83rd Precinct (480 Knickerbocker Ave.)

Fire Department: Engine 218 (650 Hart St.), Engine 252 (617 Central Ave.), Engine 271 Ladder 124 (392 Himrod St.), Engine 277 Ladder 112 (582 Knickerbocker Ave.)

Hospitals and Clinics: Wyckoff Heights Medical Center (375 Stockholm St.), Bushwick Health Center (1420 Bushwick Ave.), Menorah Home and Hospital/Bushwick Avenue Division (871 Bushwick Ave.)

houses, some of which remain. In addition, two- to six-family homes were constructed throughout the neighborhood. Broadway began to develop into a vibrant, bustling shopping district that thrived until the late 1950s.

Many of the churches built in Bushwick during these years have survived. The Reformed Church of South Bushwick (1853) stands on Bushwick Avenue. Nicknamed the "White Church" because of its white steeple, it is a New York City landmark that was organized by members of the Old Bushwick Reformed Church, whose history dates back to 1654. St. Mark's Lutheran Church on Bushwick Avenue, originally St. Mark's Evangelical Lutheran German Church, was built in 1892. And a Jewish congregation formed Ahwis Achim in 1869.

In the meantime, the ethnic composition of Bushwick was changing from its Dutch origins. English, Irish, Russian, and Polish immigrants joined the largely German American population. After the Depression, the percentage of German Americans declined, and during the 1930s and 1940s, the neighborhood claimed a greater proportion of Italian Americans than any other community in Brooklyn. After World War II, many of these Italian Americans moved to Queens and the outer suburbs, and Bushwick gained new residents, including African Americans and immigrants from Puerto Rico. Small apartment buildings were constructed throughout the neighborhood to accommodate the newcomers.

But the economic hardships of the thirties and forties began to take their toll: after World War II, only seven local breweries remained in Bushwick. Housing began to deteriorate, and there was a rise in the number of fires in the area. Although revitalization was being discussed by the 1960s, further setbacks occurred. Businesses in the area declined, and city services were reduced. During the electrical blackout in 1977 that struck all of New York City and caused more than $300 million in damage overall, stores were looted and

entire blocks of the Broadway shopping district were burned to the ground. One-third of Bushwick's stores closed, and more than 40 percent of Bushwick's commercial and retail establishments went out of business within a year. Bushwick worsened, becoming a poor neighborhood lacking both housing and retail stores.

During the late 1970s and early 1980s, new low-rise apartment buildings were built in Bushwick to house the influx of new residents, one-third of whom were immigrants from the Dominican Republic. Others came to the neighborhood from Guyana, Ecuador, Jamaica, India, and Southeast Asia. But the new construction and renova-

NEIGHBORHOOD FACTS

■ Grove Street is named for Boulevard Grove, a park that used to be where Bushwick Avenue and Grove Street meet today. In the late 1800s, the park was a popular picnic spot.
■ St. Barbara's Roman Catholic Church, on Bleecker Street, was founded in 1893 and rebuilt in 1922; it was named not only after the saint but also after the daughter of local brewer Leonard Eppig. St. Leonard's Church, on Putnam Avenue, was named for Eppig's son.
■ Since the 1930s, Casa Borinquen, a Puerto Rican nightclub on Wyckoff Avenue, has been a favorite neighborhood hangout.
■ Three New York City landmarked buildings are still in use today. Public School 86, also known as the Irvington School, is on Irving Avenue and was built in 1893. It is a Romanesque Revival building with trios of arched windows and a large central gable with a massive semicircular arch. The 20th Precinct Police Station House and Stable, now Brooklyn North Task Force, at 179 Wilson Avenue, was built in 1895. It was designed as a mock-medieval fortress, complete with a round corner tower. Engine Company 252 (1897) on Central Avenue features beautifully scrolled and stepped gables.

New homes around St. Barbara's Roman Catholic Church on Menahan Street

Shops on Myrtle Avenue

tion of the 1980s did not keep pace with the demolition of unsafe dwellings. The neighborhood felt first overcrowded, as families moved in together when apartments were demolished; then vacant and desolate, as ever more lots became empty after buildings were taken down.

Over the past ten years, Bushwick has gained more than 500 new housing units, and more recently still, the neighborhood has undergone dramatic changes. New homeowners, such as residents of the new single-family houses on Jefferson Street, have

brought resources and stability to the neighborhood. And around these homes, walk-up brownstones and attached houses are being renovated, while others await rehabilitation. In recent years, a large Muslim community has settled along Bushwick Avenue and Myrtle Avenue. Older Italian Americans still live in Bushwick, and new immigrants from South Korea, Hong Kong, and Taiwan have arrived.

Many say that the upswing in the neighborhood's health is most evident on Broadway, where stores are coming back, in large part due to the efforts of

the East Broadway Merchants' Association and the Ocean Hill Bushwick Bedford-Stuyvesant Development Corporation. Some new shops have moved into renovated buildings undamaged by the fires of the 1970s, and the vacant lots along Broadway are being rebuilt. Some have been developed as rows of single-story retail stores; others have apartments above. Now neighborhood residents busy themselves with planting trees, painting fences, and cleaning up sidewalks and empty lots.

Canarsie

Canarsie is a warm and welcoming place to live. Overlooking Jamaica Bay, the onetime beach resort has become known as a stable, safe, middle-class neighborhood with a distinctively suburban spirit, epitomized by the two cars often visible in driveways of its brick houses. Today Little League batting practices enliven spring afternoons, golden age clubs enjoy walks on Canarsie Pier, and children bicycle and play kickball in the neighborhood's quiet streets. The clean, pleasant environment attracts wildlife as well. Migrating birds visit Fresh Creek Basin, and bronze plaques along renovated Canarsie Pier give passersby new appreciation for the area's indigenous species.

Attached homes at Paerdegat 12th Street

Perhaps Canarsie's relaxed pace is a result of its having remained rural longer than most Brooklyn neighborhoods: developers did not realize the community's potential until the 1950s. The area that is today Canarsie was originally part of the Dutch town of Flatlands. When the Dutch arrived, they named the area after the Native Americans living there, the Canarsees. But the etymology of the name Canarsie is still somewhat of a mystery. Some claim that it derived from *canard,* the French word for duck. Still others hypothesize that the Native Americans renamed the area after the fences erected by the Dutch farmers, using the word Canarsee. The entire area remained quiet until the late 1800s; fishermen fished in the waters of Jamaica Bay, clammers dug in the

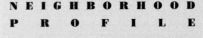

NEIGHBORHOOD PROFILE

Boundaries: <u>Canarsie</u>: from Ralph Avenue around the Glenwood Houses and along Paerdegat Avenue on the west to East 108th Street around the Breukelen Houses on the east, from the railroad tracks and Ditmas Avenue on the north to the Belt Parkway on the south. <u>Paerdegat</u>: from Paerdegat 1st Street on the west to Seaview Avenue on the east, from along Paerdegat Basin on the south to East 80th Street on the north.
Subway: <u>BMT Canarsie Line L</u>: East 105th St., Rockaway Pkwy.
Bus: <u>B17</u>: Remsen Ave./Avenue L <u>B42</u>: Rockaway Pkwy. <u>B60</u>: Rockaway Ave./Flatlands Ave. <u>B78</u>: Ralph Ave. <u>B6</u>: Flatlands Ave. <u>B82</u>: Flatlands Ave. <u>B6</u>: Glenwood Road <u>B8</u>: Foster Ave.
Community Board: No. 18
Police Precinct: 69th Precinct (9720 Foster Ave.)
Fire Department: Engine 257 Ladder 170 (1361 Rockaway Pkwy.)
Hospitals and Clinics: Long Term Home Health Care (1717 Ralph Ave.), Prospect Hospice (1717 Ralph Ave.)

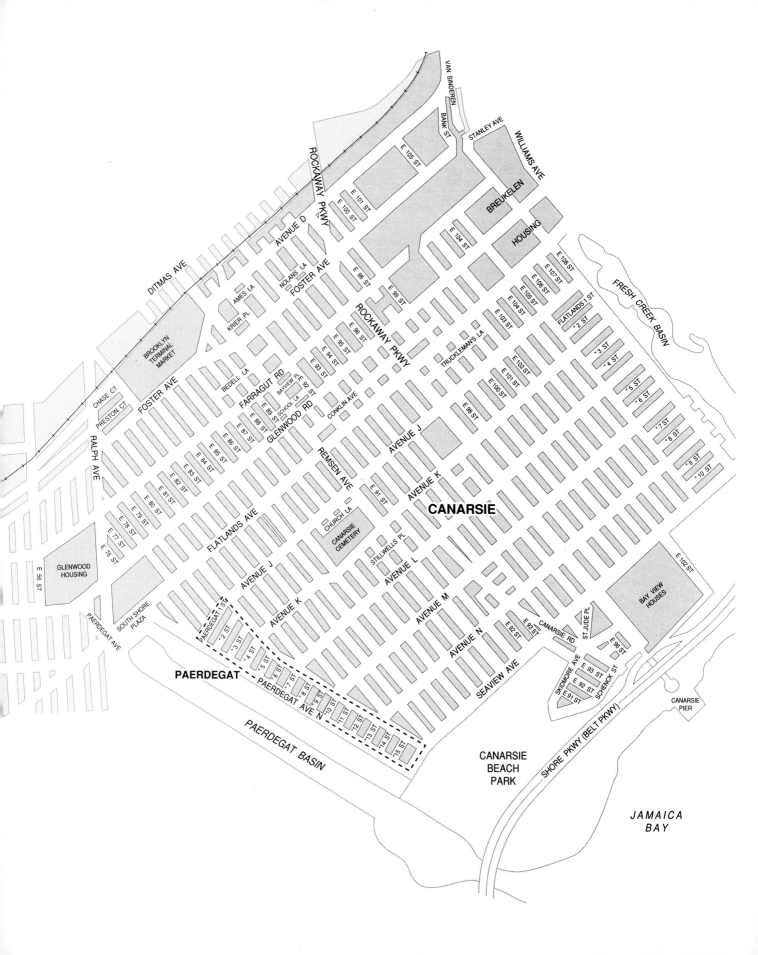

sands, and farmers harvested the land. The 200-year-old Vanderveer home, built ca. 1750 at today's East 107th Street and Flatlands Avenue, is a reminder of this bucolic period. It once had a grist mill that turned with the flowing waters of a creek that is now buried deep under East 107th Street.

In the 1860s the Brooklyn and Rockaway Beach Railroad was built, and a new, more dynamic period of growth began for Canarsie. Visitors were drawn to the shore, and soon the area became somewhat of a beach resort, as well as a halfway station to the Rockaway resorts on the other side of the Jamaica Bay ferry. Hotels were developed, and beer gardens and vaudeville houses soon followed. On warm

NEIGHBORHOOD FACTS

■ In 1942 the Brooklyn Terminal Market opened as a farmers' market. The market had an inn above its sale area, and farmers who could not return home the same day stayed upstairs. Today the Brooklyn Terminal Market is still a favorite shopping place for Brooklynites who seek fresh vegetables, fruits, plants, and flowers for their homes, restaurants, or other businesses.
■ So many World War II veterans returned home to Canarsie that the army built a compound of housing units modeled after the huts of the Quonset Indians. The one- and two-family units were referred to as the Jamaica Bay Housing Complex.
■ Although it now serves as an office, many Canarsie residents can remember a time in the 1940s and 1950s when the Log Cabin, a small log structure at 93rd Street and Flatlands Avenue, was a popular ice cream parlor.
■ Abbracciamento on the Pier, a restaurant that has been on Canarsie Pier for more than 13 years, sports a 900-foot dock so that diners can arrive by boat as well as car.

summer evenings, the well-to-do from northern Brooklyn arrived by carriage to gaze over Jamaica Bay. At least three churches in the neighborhood date to the nineteenth century, including Canarsie Reformed Church on Conklin Avenue (1877), Grace Protestant Church of Brooklyn New York (1840), and Canarsie Plymouth Congregational Church (1877) on East 96th Street, founded by a colony of blacks whose ancestors had been slaves in the area. They lived in "Colored Town" at Baisley's Lane (now Rockaway Parkway) and Avenue J.

The railroad also brought new resi-

The Log Cabin at 93rd Street and Flatlands Avenue was once an ice cream parlor

52 dents, especially German Americans, who came to Canarsie from neighboring East New York, and these newcomers were joined by Dutch, Scottish, and Irish immigrants. By the early 1900s, most of Canarsie's few thousand residents earned their living by fishing or oystering in Jamaica Bay.

In 1907 Golden City Amusement Park, the Coney Island of the southeastern shore of Brooklyn, opened at Seaview Avenue and Canarsie Road, where the Canarsie Pier is today. Many visitors from downtown Brooklyn and the northern central section of the borough were drawn to its rides, games, dance halls, and vaudeville. To get to the shore, beachgoers could hop on a trolley that ran down Rockaway Parkway. As riders approached the beach, they might be tempted to get off early to play the games being offered in the small shacks that lined the busy thoroughfare.

The early 1920s were a time of continued growth for Canarsie. Many Italian American and Jewish families who spent weekends in the area started to buy year-round houses in the neighborhood. Some of these homes, among the oldest in the neighborhood, are still standing on the streets in the east 90s.

The late 1920s and 1930s, however, were difficult years for Canarsie. Along with the Depression came pollution, which put a stop to the fishing and oystering in Jamaica Bay. Golden City Amusement Park burned down, and in 1939 the entire site was leveled to make room for the Belt Parkway.

But simultaneous with the construction of the Belt Parkway was the building of Canarsie Pier, a large publicly financed neighborhood waterfront project. Now a part of the Gateway National Recreation Area, an immense national urban park, Canarsie Pier, which adjoins Canarsie Beach Park, was designed as a gathering place for the community. Renovations in the late 1990s have ensured that it still is. More inclusive than the private yacht and canoe clubs of Canarsie, the Canarsie Pier is a meeting and recreational space for the whole neighborhood.

Although during the 1940s the trolley continued to run down Rockaway Parkway to the shore, and local truck farms were active into the 1950s, in general by the 1950s beautiful Canarsie was beginning to feel the effects of the development boom that was changing the landscape throughout Brooklyn. During this decade Canarsie's wetlands, which had long kept the neighborhood from being built up, were filled in. Two hundred acres of former marshlands became Seaview Village, 40 blocks of ranch-style and split-level houses and attached row houses at the northeastern side of the neighborhood. Additional row houses were constructed and soon covered much of the area. On the other side of the neighborhood, in the east 80s, a mix of housing endures, with homes that are almost a hundred years old standing next to houses built during this second period of Canarsie's development.

Canarsie's population grew rapidly in the 1950s as middle-class Italian Americans and Jews relocated from Crown Heights, East New York, Brownsville, Bedford-Stuyvesant, Bushwick, and Williamsburg. Two public housing projects were built during this period: the Breukelen Houses

Canarsie Pier, Gateway National Recreation Area

Canarsie Pier, early 1900s (Brian Merlis Collection)

(1951) on Williams Avenue, which straddle the Canarsie–East New York border, and the Bay View Houses (1955), between East 102nd Street and Rockaway Parkway. The Canarsie of 20 years earlier, with its swampy beaches, amusement park, and farms, had become a suburb, complete with neat, tree-lined blocks, cars parked in driveways, and shopping malls.

The **Paerdegat** subdivision, along the Paerdegat Basin, was one of the last areas of the neighborhood to be developed. The streets in this section are numbered 1 to 15 and have Paerdegat before the number; thus a house might stand on Paerdegat 1st Street, or Paerdegat 4th Street. Most who live in the brick two-, three-, and four-family houses that were built in the 1960s on these 15 blocks call their neighborhood Paerdegat, not Canarsie.

In the 1970s, ethnic furor surged in Canarsie as busing brought blacks and Puerto Ricans into the largely Italian American and Jewish community. The segregationist violence flared among the races as the inhabitants—themselves seeking solace from upheavals here and in Europe—felt that they had been abandoned by the liberal politicians and that they must fight for their way of life and very existence. As the integration continued during the 1980s, tensions calmed. Many African Americans and Caribbean Americans moved into Canarsie. The new residents—who came primarily from Jamaica, Guyana, Barbados, Trinidad and Tobago, and Grenada—live in the northeastern section of Canarsie. Many are homeowners. This area also counts Chinese immigrants, as well as immigrants from the former Soviet Union and Israel, among its residents. There are also smaller numbers of newcomers from Puerto Rico, Mexico, and the Dominican Republic. Many of these new Canarsie residents moved to the shore neighborhood from other Brooklyn communities, seeking a relaxed environment in which to raise their families.

The number of stores in Canarsie has not changed substantially in recent years, although more and more are Caribbean owned. Most shops are found along the neighborhood's largest streets, such as Rockaway Parkway, Flatlands Avenue, and Avenue L.

Canarsie has a large elderly population, residents who have lived in Canarsie all or most of their lives. Yet it now also welcomes young families, whose children travel the path of Canarsie's original trolleys, riding their bikes through the neighborhood out to the Canarsie Pier and to the 132 acres of Canarsie Beach Park.

Deep-set brownstone row houses and tall old trees

Naming a community is a symbolic task: it is a way for residents to reclaim and reshape their neighborhood's identity, to break with the past and yet at the same time forge new ties with their shared history. Residents of Carroll Gardens during the 1960s chose their name well. Brightly colored rose bushes spill over garden gates, and tendrils of ivy trail out of stoop window boxes. Tall old trees grow inside the unusually spacious front yards and along the sidewalk; deeply set brown-stone row houses grace quiet one-way streets. And Charles Carroll, an immigrant, Revolutionary War veteran (he sent troops from Maryland to aid the patriots in the Battle of Brooklyn), and the only Roman Catholic signer of the Declaration of Independence, is a fitting emblem of the neighborhood's proud heritage.

For at least a generation before its name change, the area that became Carroll Gardens existed as an independent but unnamed neighborhood. It was simply the section of South Brooklyn that was noticeably more Italian American than the areas surrounding it, and it was filled with bakeries, restaurants, and the sound of conversations in Italian.

In fact, what is today Carroll Gar-

NEIGHBORHOOD PROFILE

Boundaries: from the Brooklyn-Queens Expressway on the west to Hoyt Street between DeGraw and 5th Street and Smith Street between 5th Street and the Gowanus Expressway on the east, from DeGraw Street on the north to the Gowanus Expressway on the south.
Subway: <u>IND F</u>: Carroll St., Smith St./9th St. <u>IND Crosstown G</u>: Carroll St., Smith St./9th St.
Bus: <u>B71</u>: Sackett St./Union St./3rd St. <u>B75</u>: 9th St./Court St./Smith St. <u>B77</u>: 9th St.
Libraries: Brooklyn Public Library Carroll Gardens Branch (Clinton St. at Union St.)
Community Board: No. 6
Police Precinct: 76th Precinct (191 Union St.)
Fire Department: Engine 204 (299 DeGraw St.), Engine 216 Ladder 108 (187 Union St.)

Carroll

dens was settled in the early nineteenth century by Irish Americans. Until the middle of the century, the area was considered a part of South Brooklyn and was made up of the neighborhoods that are now known as Carroll Gardens, Boerum Hill, Cobble Hill, Gowanus, and Red Hook. Richard Butts planned and developed the oldest section of Carroll Gardens in 1846; he is responsible for creating the spacious front yards that add a sense of grandeur to the entire neighborhood. The more than 150 buildings on Carroll and President Streets, between Smith and Hoyt—and on Hoyt Street, between President and 1st—constitute the Carroll Gardens historic district designated in 1973, but blocks of buildings that follow this style extend from 1st to 4th Places between Henry and Smith Streets, and on 2nd Street between Smith and Hoyt Streets. All of the brownstone row houses with gardens were built between 1869 and 1884. Because the deep yards make for narrow streets, traffic is mostly one-way and the side streets stay quiet. Within the historic area is the landmarked John Rankin House, built in 1840. This handsome Greek Revival house was built on Clinton Street for the wealthy Mr. Rankin when the area was still rural. Now the building houses the F. G. Guido Funeral Home.

Five churches built during the nineteenth century stand in Carroll Gardens, three of which are still used as houses of worship. They include the landmarked South Congregational Church Parlor (1889), part of the South Congregational Church Complex on Court and President Streets; St. Paul's Episcopal Church of Brooklyn on Clinton and Carroll Streets (1884); and Sacred Hearts of Jesus and Mary and St. Stephen's Church, on Summit and Hicks Street (1860), originally St. Stephen's Church. The remaining two buildings, formerly Westminster Presbyterian Church and Calvary Baptist Church of Red Hook (originally South Congregational Chapel), are used for other purposes.

From the late nineteenth century to the 1950s, Italian immigrants sought out the quiet, beautiful streets of Carroll Gardens. At first many of these residents were dock workers in Red Hook, but in later years a great number worked in the shipyards of the Brooklyn Navy Yard. Between 1920 and 1950, most of the Irish American residents moved to other communities, leaving what is now Carroll Gardens inhabited predominantly by Italian Americans.

The completion of the Brooklyn-Queens Expressway in 1957 cut off the area from nearby Red Hook, as well as from a neighborhood on the eastern side of the roadway that now calls itself Columbia Street Waterfront District. The division of their formerly cohesive community drove many residents away. During the 1960s some young middle-class professionals were drawn to Carroll Gardens because of its safety, tranquility, and proximity to Manhattan. Some Carroll Gardens residents were upset by the lifestyles of

Gardens

these "hippie" newcomers, who had no ties to the area's churches and lived together in groups.

To those loyal to the neighborhood, restoration of this section of South Brooklyn seemed like a way to keep longtime residents from leaving. As one of the first steps in the renewal project, a new name for the community was sought. Carroll Gardens was chosen in honor of Charles Carroll, already the namesake of Carroll Street and Carroll Park.

Many of the yards of Carroll Gardens are decorated with religious shrines and statues throughout the year. But at certain holidays the area really shines. During Christmas and Easter, visitors from nearby neighborhoods flock to Carroll Gardens to view elaborate decorations and lights adorning the front yards and houses in the

NEIGHBORHOOD FACTS

■ During the 1930s and 1940s, Hamilton Avenue, which runs from the riverfront to the Gowanus Canal, served as the unofficial dividing line between Red Hook and what later became Carroll Gardens. Youth north of the avenue referred to themselves as Creekers, and those south of the avenue called themselves Hookers, after the hook-shaped peninsula of Red Hook.

■ Legends abound about the degree to which the Mafia has been present in Carroll Gardens. Many believe that because the neighborhood is located almost directly between the areas that have notoriously been controlled by the Gambino and Colombo families, it has been considered neutral turf and left alone by both sides. In 1918 Al Capone was married in the neighborhood, at St. Mary's Star of the Sea Church, on Court Street between Nelson and Luquer Streets.

■ Third Street in Carroll Gardens has had a complicated traffic history since the 1920s, when its front gardens were razed to widen the street to open it to two-way traffic. In the 75 years since, homeowners have lobbied to maintain the residential feel of the area by keeping the street one-way and less accessible to trucks.

■ The Cammareri Brothers Bakery on Henry Street, where bread is still baked in brick ovens, is where Cher and Nicholas Cage's characters meet in the movie *Moonstruck* (1987).

Court Street statue of St. Maria Addolorata, patron saint of Vola di Bari

neighborhood. Sometimes music is played. Neighbors often try to outdo one another, so two or three houses in a row may be especially embellished. In addition, a local procession marks Good Friday, and the neighborhood is known for its extravagant (albeit illegal) Fourth of July fireworks.

Several dialects of Italian are still spoken in Carroll Gardens, and many third- and fourth-generation Italian Americans are moving back to the

neighborhood to raise their families. Throughout the spring, summer, and early fall, you can usually find a pickup game of bocce in progress. The neighborhood is home to Italian markets, butchers, bakeries, and family-style restaurants. Smith Street has many stores, and Court Street from DeGraw to 4th Place is the heart of the shopping district.

Since the mid-1960s, Carroll Gardens residents have established a day-care center and helped to build low- and middle-class housing in both Carroll Gardens and Red Hook. In addition, during the past few years local

Spacious front yards characterize the
brownstones of Carroll Gardens

St. Paul's Episcopal Church of Brooklyn,
at Clinton and Carroll Streets

grassroots organizations have maintained the community's voice in dis-
cussions of the reconstruction of the
Gowanus Expressway, and are actively
fighting for clean-up of the Gowanus
Canal.

Clinton Hill

One of the greatest luxuries of living in a historically wealthy neighborhood may be that such communities can afford to create and preserve architecturally significant homes. Strolling along the streets of Clinton Hill, for example, visitors can step back in time to discover residences built in styles that exemplify different periods of the neighborhood's development. Elegant Romanesque mansions, classic Victorian row houses, Italianate frame villas, and pre–Civil War frame houses each contribute to a beautifully distinctive streetscape.

Today's mostly middle-class residents of "the Hill" share an appreciation of their unique neighborhood. Students from Pratt Institute and St. Joseph's College mingle with longtime Italian American homeowners, African American professionals, Caribbean immigrants, and middle-class families of many ethnic backgrounds. A large number of architects, artists, photographers, and craftspeople also live in the area, many of them Pratt alumni and affiliates who cannot bear to leave.

The neighborhood that is today Clinton Hill occupies the highest ground in the area and was part of a parcel of land acquired by the Dutch in the 1600s. Dutch residents continued to own most of the land in the area until the mid-1800s. In 1832 Clinton Avenue was laid out as a tree-lined boulevard along the crest of a hill, named for De Witt Clinton (1769–1828), onetime mayor of the City of New York, governor and senator of New York State, and presidential hopeful. Soon thereafter, by the 1840s, grand homes

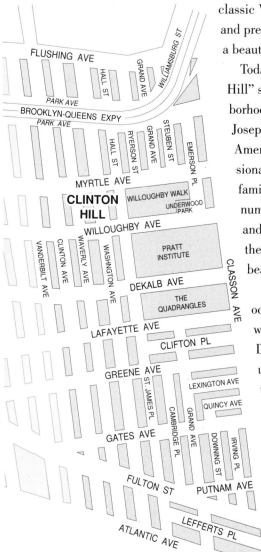

Decorative details on a home in Clinton Hill's historic district

with lawns, stables, and carriage houses had been built. The area was considered a rural retreat until the 1860s, when developers began building the row houses that by 1880 lined many streets and attracted affluent professionals.

In 1875 oil executive and philanthropist Charles Pratt, owner of the Astral Oil Works (see Greenpoint), chose Clinton Avenue as the site for his mansion. Indeed, Pratt liked the area so much that he built houses in Clinton Hill for four of his sons as each married. (The house that Pratt built for his son Charles Millard, at 241 Clinton Avenue, is now the residence of the Roman Catholic bishop of Brooklyn.) Pratt's enthusiasm for the area prompted many of Brooklyn's other wealthy industrialists to build mansions on Clinton and Washington Avenues between 1880 and 1915. Many of these mansions, along with late nineteenth-century row houses, were designed by such prominent Manhat-

tan and Brooklyn architects as William Tubby and Montrose Morris. Notable residents included the Pfizers, of the drug manufacturing company, the Bristols, of Bristol-Myers pharmaceuticals, the Underwoods, of Underwood Typewriters, and the Liebmanns, of Rheingold Breweries.

In the 1900s the area's first apartment buildings were constructed, and during the 1920s and 1930s, they replaced some of the neighborhood mansions. In the 1940s housing was built for the families of navy personnel working at the Brooklyn Navy Yard in nearby Fort Greene. In 1954 Robert Moses, head of the mayor's committee on slum clearance, cleared a five-block area south of Pratt Institute for urban

282–290 DeKalb Avenue at the corner of Waverly Avenue, built in 1889

● **Pratt Institute**

In 1887 Charles Pratt founded the Pratt Institute, an art and industrial school that from its outset accepted both women and men of all races. The institute buildings originally faced out onto city streets, and the campus did not appear as it does today until Pratt expanded in the 1950s and 1960s. At that time, many of the streets and buildings were razed: now the main campus comprises five square blocks. Pratt is well known for programs in art and design, architecture, and computer and library sciences. (Its engineering program has been transferred to Brooklyn Polytechnical Institute.) In addition, the faculty has been very active in assisting Brooklyn during its struggle to redevelop its neighborhoods. The institute is perhaps the single most important institution in the decades-long campaign to bring housing and commercial redevelopment to the borough.

The Pratt Institute Free Library (1896) was Brooklyn's first free library, although in 1940 it was restricted to students, and it shares the distinction of being a New York City landmark with the main building complex, constructed between 1885 and 1927, and the Pratt row houses on Willoughby Avenue, Steuben Street, and Emerson Place. These three sections of row houses, 27 homes in all, remain from a group of 38 built by the Pratt family. According to the New York City Landmarks Commission, they were intended for "people of taste and refinement, but of moderate means."

Notable alumni of Pratt Institute include Ellsworth Kelly, who had a recent retrospective at the Guggenheim Museum; cartoonist Ed Koren; journalist Pete Hamill; actor and playwright Harvey Fierstein; and Morrison Cousins, the designer of Tupperware.

renewal, and during the 1950s and 1960s, many one-family homes became rooming houses. In the 1970s many of the neglected brownstones and carriage houses in the neighborhood were restored.

In 1981 a portion of Clinton Hill was designated a New York City historic district. The neighborhood also has a number of individual landmarked buildings, including the Church of St. Luke and St. Matthew (1889) at 520 Clinton Avenue, which is often described as one of the grandest nineteenth-century churches in Brooklyn; Emmanuel Baptist Church (1887) at 279 Lafayette Avenue, which was

financed by Charles Pratt; St. Mary's Episcopal Church (1859) at 230 Classon Avenue, a Gothic Revival church; and the Royal Castle Apartments (1911–12), one of Clinton Hill's earliest apartment buildings. The Lincoln Club (1889), which is today the Mechanics Temple, is also landmarked. The club, at 65 Putnam Avenue, was organized in 1878 by a group of affluent gentlemen from the area as a social gathering place where they could also promote the activities of the Republican Party. The political agenda was dropped soon after the club was developed, but the club stayed active until 1931. And even after it was taken

Pratt Institute Building, ca. 1929 (Library of Congress)

NEIGHBORHOOD PROFILE

Boundaries: from Vanderbilt Avenue on the west to Classon Avenue on the east, from Park Avenue or Flushing Avenue on the north to either Fulton Street or Atlantic Avenue on the south.
Subway: <u>IND Crosstown G</u>: Clinton Ave./Washington Ave., Classon Ave.
Bus: <u>B57</u>: Flushing Ave. <u>B61</u>: Park Ave. <u>B54</u>: Myrtle Ave. <u>B38</u>: DeKalb Ave./Lafayette Ave. <u>B52</u>: Greene Ave. <u>B25</u>: Fulton St. <u>B26</u>: Fulton St. <u>B45</u>: Atlantic Ave. <u>B69</u>: Vanderbilt Ave. <u>B48</u>: Classon Ave.
Libraries: Brooklyn Public Library Clinton Hill Branch (Washington Ave. near Lafayette Ave.); Pratt Institute Free Library
Community Board: No. 2
Police Precinct: 88th Precinct (298 Classon Ave.)
Fire Department: Engine 210 (Fort Greene, 160 Carlton Ave.)

Mid-nineteenth-century row houses were rural retreats for affluent professionals

over in the 1940s by the Mechanics, it continued to be a social club.

Today, although DeKalb Avenue is a main thoroughfare through Clinton Hill, Clinton and Washington Avenues represent the heart of the neighborhood. These broad streets retain a tree-shaded elegance, and their large mansions give the area a sense of unusual space and graciousness. It has been said that in Clinton Hill's heyday these lawns drew people away from the luxurious homes of Brooklyn Heights.

Cobble Hill

Three tenets of great communities—continual renewal, an openness to diversity, and an appreciation of the past—have guided the development of lovely Cobble Hill. If you stand on Court Street and look down such streets as Baltic, Kane, and DeGraw into the heart of the neighborhood, your eye is drawn to sidewalks shaded by large trees and stoops framed by wrought-iron railings. On Court Street itself, generations-old businesses and stores offer a tie to the past, while new restaurants, cafes, and shops tempt passersby with trendier fare. This rich, ongoing history is why much of Cobble Hill has been named a historic district by New York City's Landmark Commission.

Cobble Hill was first settled in the mid-seventeenth century when Dutch governor Peter Stuyvesant began to allow farming north of Red Hook. The neighborhood was originally named Ponkiesbergh (in English, "Cobles Hill") by Dutch farmers because of the cobblestones in the area. The corner of Atlantic Avenue and Court Street offered a commanding view, so it became the site of Cobble Hill Fort, a strategically important military location during the Revolutionary War's Battle of Brooklyn. The name Cobble Hill died out by the 1800s and the neighborhood was basically considered a part of Brooklyn Heights until the 1950s, when an enterprising realtor saw the name on a 1766 map and the neighborhood was reborn.

The neighborhood remained rural until 1836, when the South Ferry began crossing the East River, ushering passengers between Atlantic Avenue and Manhattan's Whitehall Street. This new connection with the financial and business center of New York City prompted development in the neighborhood, which was then considered part of South Brooklyn. The largely agrarian community became home to a primarily middle-class population, and some of Brooklyn's finest nineteenth-century houses were built. Row houses, constructed between 1840 and

---

Arab-American shops along Atlantic Avenue and Clinton Street

the late 1870s, the philanthropist Alfred T. White—a cousin of Seth Low, Republican reformer and mayor of Brooklyn and New York—built experimental housing projects in the area that are still standing. His Tower and Home buildings, on Hicks Street at Baltic Street, were apartments designed to offer working-class tenants unusual amenities for the time: sunlight, good ventilation, and common plumbing. Warren Place (between Warren and Baltic, just east of Hicks),

Sahadi Importing, one of many Middle Eastern shops along the Atlantic Avenue border of Cobble Hill

1880 in the Greek Revival and Romanesque styles, also stand as testament of this early development boom. Also at this time Long Island College Hospital (1848) was established; a teaching hospital (without a medical school), it occupies several buildings on Henry Street and Amity Street.

One of the earliest surviving examples of the period's grand architecture is the DeGraw Mansion (1845), at the corner of Clinton and Amity Streets. In 1891 the building was made even grander; the renovations included a tower, which gave a view of Brooklyn harbor from the first residential elevator in Brooklyn.

Cobble Hill was one of the first Brooklyn neighborhoods to have residences that were not private homes. In

NEIGHBORHOOD FACTS

■ Winston Churchill's mother, Jennie Jerome, later Lady Randolph Churchill, was born in 1854 in Cobble Hill, at 197 Amity Street near Court. Don't be confused by a plaque at 426 Henry Street, which identifies that building as her birthplace: that marker actually identifies Jennie Jerome's uncle's house, where her family stayed before she was born.

■ Louis Comfort Tiffany designed the original windows, high altar, altar railings, pulpit, and lectern of the Episcopalian Christ Church and Holy Family at 320 Clinton Street, built in 1842.

■ Richard Upjohn, architect of Trinity Church in lower Manhattan, designed and lived in a house at 296 Clinton Street, constructed in 1843.

■ During the 1930s, writer Thomas Wolfe lived in a house on Verandah Place, between Henry and Clinton Streets.

■ The still-active Congregation Baith Israel Ashei Emes is descended from Brooklyn's oldest Jewish congregation. Members gather for services at the Kane Street Synagogue, on Kane Street at Tompkins Place. The synagogue was constructed as the Middle Dutch Reformed Church (1856) on Kane Street.

64 which White also built, is a cluster of tiny one-family "Workingmen's Cottages," built around a private courtyard. Each of these cottages is only 11.5 feet wide. Warren Place residences were built for supervisory workers and originally rented for a pricey $18 a month.

During the early twentieth century, an influx of immigrants from Ireland, Italy, and the Middle East settled in Cobble Hill. Atlantic Avenue between Court and Hicks Streets features one of the largest concentrations of Middle Eastern businesses in New York City and is home to Middle Eastern stores that are 25 to 50 years old. There Yemenis, Lebanese, and other Arabs sell delicious food, exotic spices, and indigenous clothing to the discriminating and the adventurous.

In the 1950s brownstone enthusiasts moved into the neighborhood and began to renovate and restore the area block by block. The Cobble Hill historic district (first designated in 1969, and extended to include more homes in 1988) is also noted for its outstanding preservation of churches that predate the Civil War. These include St. Frances Cabrini Chapel, originally Strong Place Baptist Church (1852), located on DeGraw and Strong Streets, and St. Peter's Our Lady of Pilar Roman Catholic Church (1859–60), located on Warren and Hicks Streets.

NEIGHBORHOOD PROFILE

Boundaries: from the Brooklyn-Queens Expressway and Hicks Street on the west to Court Street on the east, from Atlantic Avenue on the north to DeGraw Street on the south.
Bus: B61: Atlantic Ave. B63: Atlantic Ave. B75: Court St.
Community Board: No. 6
Police Precinct: 76th Precinct (191 Union St.)
Fire Department: Engine 216 Ladder 108 (Carroll Gardens, 187 Union Ave.)
Hospitals and Clinics: Long Island College Hospital (340 Henry St.), Cobble Hill Nursing Home (380 Henry St.)

A view of Kane Street in Cobble Hill, a New York City landmarked district

Alfred White's rendering of a "cottage" on Warren Place, 1880 (Brooklyn Historical Society)

The mix of old and new residents keeps Cobble Hill ever changing. Families who have owned brownstones for generations live next door to young professionals who rent apartments. Many of the newer occupants who have purchased row houses are renovating, reclaiming as single-family homes houses that had been divided into apartments during the 1970s and 1980s. The results are beautiful, as evidenced by the increased marketability of these homes. In 1997, a row house on Congress Street sold for a record amount, just over $1 million.

Cobble Hill residents take pride in the architecture and atmosphere of the neighborhood. Newcomers to Cobble Hill, most of whom are white-collar professionals, have been drawn by its distinctive architecture and historic flavor. But nearly everyone in Cobble Hill agrees that they also value the neighborhood because it is diverse, family oriented, and cosmopolitan.

Cobble Hill Park, one of the first vest-pocket parks in New York City, was originally developed when community residents blocked construction of a supermarket at an abandoned site. The park, which is paved with bluestone and shaded by more than 300 trees, won a Municipal Art Society award for a renovation completed in the spring of 1990. The park features old-fashioned benches and tables for relaxing, a lively children's play area, and marble columns for all to enjoy. New young families in the neighborhood have especially appreciated the play area, and their influence has resulted in renovations at playgrounds at Pacific and Henry Streets.

Columbia

NEIGHBORHOOD PROFILE

Boundaries: from the East River on the west to the Brooklyn-Queens Expressway and Hicks Street on the east, from Atlantic Avenue on the north to Hamilton Avenue and the Brooklyn Battery Tunnel entrance on the south.
Bus: B61: Columbia St. B71: Sackett St. Bx27: Hamilton Ave./Manhattan Bx28: Hamilton Ave./Manhattan Bx29: Hamilton Ave./Manhattan
Community Board: No. 6
Police Precinct: 76th Precinct (191 Union St.)
Fire Department: Engine 204 (Carroll Gardens, 299 DeGraw St.), Engine 216 Ladder 108 (Carroll Gardens, 187 Union Ave.)

The Columbia Street Waterfront District is undergoing a rebirth. The area is home to musicians, artists, blue-collar, white-collar, and telecommuting workers and families—as well as many longtime residents who never lost faith in their community. In recent years, nurses and other staff members of Long Island College Hospital in nearby Cobble Hill have also sought out the

Typical stores on Warren and Court Streets

Waterfront

Street

District

Columbia Street Waterfront District. The resilient community is destined to grow even stronger and more desirable as Long Island College Hospital expands and local parks are refurbished.

Those who have been in the neighborhood since the 1950s may marvel at how the community has rebounded from the trials of that period. The Brooklyn-Queens Expressway (1957) cleaved working-class Columbia Street, with its mixed brick and sided row houses, from its more prosperous neighbors Cobble Hill and Carroll Gardens. And when a plan to build a commercial containerization port in the neighborhood was unveiled in 1953, many residents left to seek homes in new communities.

But the history of Columbia Street Waterfront District as a neighborhood begins much earlier than this difficult time. Like Red Hook and Carroll Gar-dens, from the early 1800s to the 1880s nearly all of Columbia Street's residents were Irish, and the men who lived in the area worked at nearby piers. By the 1920s these recent arrivals had been joined by immigrants from Puerto Rico. Through the world wars, the area remained unchanged. The lives of its working-class residents, who occupied row houses that were not as well maintained as those on the east side of Hicks Street, were dictated by the demands of the shipping industry.

Meanwhile, Columbia Street's stores had a remarkable turn-of-the-century flavor, which they retained until the 1970s. Originally home to Italian bakeries and grocery stores, Columbia Street in the 1940s and 1950s was lined with pushcarts selling fruits and vegetables. Newspaper photographs taken as late as the 1970s show that shoppers were still sidestepping live chickens on the sidewalks.

During the 1950s, however, the neighborhood began to change in other ways. Homes were demolished to make way for the Brooklyn-Queens Expressway. Most of the shipping industry moved to Port Elizabeth, New Jersey, which had more land and accessible roads than the Brooklyn port. The result was massive layoffs and unemployment in the Columbia Street district. Many of those who moved at the threat of the containerization facility had even sold their homes to the city at less than market value rather than risk owning an undesirable property next to such a port.

The container port did not materialize, to the relief of the stalwart residents who had remained. But recovery of the Columbia Street Waterfront District was gradual. Puerto Rican residents began building small wooden clubhouses called *casitas* in the prevalent empty lots. And during the 1970s, a large infrastructure project was undertaken in the neighborhood. For more than a year, residents of this small, struggling neighborhood endured incredible disruption as Columbia Street was completely dug up and new sewers laid. Trucks could not pass through the area, and stores closed. Moreover, building foundations were undermined: some buildings fell, and many others were in danger of collapsing. The neighborhood became isolated and unpopular.

But in the early 1980s, the city named the area a renewal district and began to tear down unusable buildings. The housing and preservation department designed a multiphase development plan for the neighborhood and mandated that new buildings in the area could not be built higher than three stories.

Signs of Columbia Street's renaissance can be seen in many places. Although waterfront renovation plans are still in flux because of environmental issues, the five-acre Van Voorhes Park is due to undergo a $5 million renovation. Mothers wheel baby carriages along Columbia Street, five thriving community gardens grow flowers and vegetables, and on side streets neighbors chat on stoops. Although Columbia Street residents walk to Court Street and Atlantic Avenue in nearby Cobble Hill for shopping, new restaurants in the neighborhood welcome longtime residents, newcomers, and visitors to a reinvigorated Columbia Street Waterfront District.

Candy store at 153 Union Street

Coney Island

To visit Coney Island is to remember a time when Brooklynites first experienced mixed-sex bathing in the Atlantic, tasted the funny-shaped innovation called the frankfurter, and marveled at Luna Park, a fantasyland lit by more than a million lightbulbs. But the enchantment of Coney Island stems from a longer and broader history than summertime amusements. Most likely taking its name from *konjin*, the Dutch word for rabbits (which were once the most lively occupants of the area), Coney Island has evolved from the mid-1600s into a neighborhood with a unique character.

Coney Island became part of the town of Gravesend when it was founded in 1643 by an Englishwoman, Lady Deborah Moody. Until the late 1700s and early 1800s, the area was used primarily for grazing animals. A somewhat exclusive resort, Coney Island House, was built by the Terhune brothers in 1824 near what is today Shell Road to entertain wealthy vacationers from Brooklyn and surrounding locales. (Although open to all, the resort could be reached only by a toll road, which restricted its visitors to the well-heeled.)

Between 1840 and 1870 Coney Island became a popular summer attraction, although year-round residents were few. After the Civil War, five railroads were built, connecting the area

Even on a winter day Coney Island attracts visitors

with the rest of the city. A development boom resulted, with new neighborhoods springing up to accommodate those who wished to stay year-round (including homeless Civil War veterans and criminals on the lam). Norton's Point, later renamed West End and then Sea Gate, is one such neighborhood. So are Manhattan Beach and Brighton Beach, both located on the eastern side of the peninsula. West Brighton, a name still used by some

Homes built in the 1980s along West 22nd Street

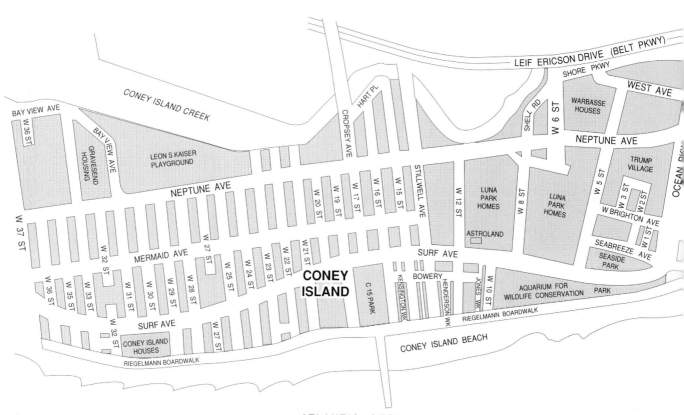

residents who live between Ocean Parkway and West 8th Street, is today the area most visitors refer to as Coney Island.

The first Coney Island amusements were developed with the blessing of political boss John Y. McKane, whose policies during the late 1800s (before his 1894 imprisonment in Sing Sing for election fraud) encouraged the building of concessions, race tracks, casinos, hotels, bath houses, saloons, and restaurants. In an area next to Ocean Parkway known as the Gut, brothels, dance halls, and gambling dens proliferated. In 1899 Jim Jeffries and Tom Sharkey faced off in a famous boxing match at the Coney Island Athletic Club in West Brighton. But working-class families who traveled by train for a day at the shore inspired entrepreneurs to offer more seemly entertainment as well. In the 1870s German immigrant Charles Feltman opened Feltman's, a restaurant in West Brighton that specialized in German food, while from a boardwalk stand he showed off his new invention: hot dogs. And by the 1890s visitors of all ages could climb up inside Colossus, a 122.5-foot-tall pachyderm made of wood and tin, or try Captain Paul Boyton's Shoot the Chutes water ride at his Sea Lion Park.

At the turn of the century, while owners of fashionable resorts on Manhattan

Parachute Jump at Steeplechase Park, ca. 1960 (Brian Merlis Collection)

Beach and Brighton Beach were cultivating their highbrow status and distancing themselves from local entertainments, three new amusement parks opened along Surf Avenue to appeal to the summertime crowds. The 15-acre Steeplechase Park, at West 17th Street, was launched in 1897 by George C. Tilyou and continued operation even after a devastating fire in 1907 resulted in many of the rides being moved indoors. In the Steep-

NEIGHBORHOOD FACTS

■ In 1920 five cents in the Nickel Empire (Coney Island) could buy a subway ride or a hot dog at Nathan's Famous, which has been serving hot dogs for more than 80 years and hosts an annual Fourth of July hot dog eating contest.

■ Year round, school groups and families visit the Aquarium for Wildlife Conservation to see giant sea turtles, sharks, sea otters, dolphins, sea lions, and Casey, the oldest beluga whale born in captivity in the United States.

■ Mardi Gras Parade was launched in 1905 by Louis Stauch to raise money to rebuild the Home for Wayward Girls, which had burned. Its first year the celebration lasted a full two weeks and was held at the end of the season, around Labor Day. Finally reduced to a one-day parade with floats, parades, and celebrities, it wound down in the late 1950s. Dick Zigun started the Mermaid Parade in 1983; held at the beginning of the season, it welcomes in the summer solstice and allows King Neptune to officially open the sea. Coney Island residents also gathered each year to watch fireworks on the Fourth of July and to marvel at the Blue Angels, an Air Force precision flying exhibition.

■ On an average weekend in 1907, visitors mailed approximately 250,000 postcards from Coney Island to relatives and friends.

■ In a time-honored tradition, members of the Polar Bear Club meet on New Year's Day, strip to bathing suits, and swim in water that can be as cold as 30 degrees Fahrenheit.

■ Just north of the Belt Parkway, thousands of subway cars are lined up at the Metropolitan Transportation Authority's rail yards, the largest rail car facility in the world.

■ Coney Island's Half Moon Hotel was once a favorite hideout for prosecution witnesses because all the windows in its "rat suite" faced the ocean, for safety. There in 1940, famous gangster-turned-witness Abe (Kid Twist) Reles helped New York police fill 75 notebooks with details about 85 mob-related killings in Brooklyn. Reles, though closely guarded by police, died November 12, 1941, after jumping—or being pushed—from a window in the hotel. The suitcase and sheets with which Reles planned to make his "getaway" are in the Municipal Archives (32 Chambers Street, Manhattan), which stores material evidence used in court cases. In a 1960 film, *Murder, Inc.*, Reles is played by a young Peter Falk with scenes filmed in the Half Moon Hotel. The hotel, later converted into a geriatric home, was demolished in 1997.

lechase Race (rebuilt after the fire), the park's most famous attraction, customers astride mechanical horses attached to iron rails as high as 35 feet rode from the Pavilion of Fun outside toward the ocean, then circled round to reenter the other side of the building. At the finish line, racers were paddled by clowns. Indeed, a touch of physical risk and surprise were thematic to the Steeplechase Park. On the Human Roulette Wheel, people tried to sit on an enormous disk as it spun around. In the Blowhole Theater, jets of air blew women's skirts above their waists as they walked unsuspectingly (or not) over strategically placed iron grates. And the landmarked Parachute Jump, built for the World's Fair in 1939 and moved from the New York City World's Fair to the site, offered riders the delicious thrill of waiting several seconds for the parachute to open as they plunged to the ground. The jump remained in use until the park closed in 1964.

Luna Park was the brainchild of Frederic Thompson and Elmer Dundy, who opened the 50-acre amusement center in 1903 at West 10th Street. Designed to resemble the fabled city of Baghdad, the outlines of its buildings were illuminated each evening. In 1904 the average daily attendance at Luna Park was 90,000—four times that of a well-attended major-league baseball game. Minute-long rides and brief (less than 20 minutes) theatrical performances allowed visitors to sample every attraction. One such per-

Luna Park may have been the most popular park, but it was not the brightest spot on Coney Island. Dreamland, which opened in 1904, had even more lights—so many that immigrants sailing into Ellis Island could reportedly see Dreamland's tower long before they were able to make out the Statue of Liberty. William H. Reynolds envisioned his $3.5 million Dreamland as a retreat from urban over-population. Advertisements for the park trumpeted plenty of open space ("No crowding"), inclined walks ("No stairs"), and quiet environs, while murals depicting Switzerland, the canals of Venice, and the fall of Pompeii lent a leisured, cosmopolitan air. Perhaps Dreamland was too sleepy for the tastes of summer revelers. Its few thrilling attractions—such as the Leap-Frog Railway, in which two full-size electric railroad cars threatened to collide on a single track, and the Fighting the Flames show, where customers could watch women and children being saved from blazing buildings—could not sustain it.

Annual Polar Bear Club swim, January 1998

formance was the Trip to the Moon, moved from the Buffalo World's Fair, which dramatized an imaginary journey into outer space. The park was a popular destination for sightseers until the 1940s, when it burned down.

The Cyclone, built in 1927 on site of the world's first roller coaster (1884), is now a city landmark

Luna Park, which opened in 1903 along Surf Avenue, in 1929 (Brian Merlis Collection)

After Dreamland was destroyed by fire in May 1911, it was not rebuilt. The Aquarium for Wildlife Conservation now occupies its site.

During the first decade of the twentieth century, a true year-round community began to develop in Coney Island as predominantly Irish and then Italian residents settled on West 15th, 16th, and 17th Streets between Surf and Neptune Avenues. Our Lady of Solace Roman Catholic Church was founded in 1900, and its current building, on West 17th Street, was completed in 1926. Jewish immigrants also found the area appealing. Two-story stucco houses and apartment buildings were created to accommodate residents of all ethnicities.

Meanwhile, the Coney Island Creek had been filled in in about 1920, transforming the area from an island to a peninsula, and the New York City subway had been extended to the area on former steam-line tracks. By 1920 the number of summer visitors each day reached 1 million. The area could scarcely contain that many vacationers, but few options remained for relieving the congestion: the amusement parks were unable to grow because of the many railroad tracks and cottages that had been built around them. In 1923 the city answered the need for more room by building the current seaside walkway. The 2.6-mile-long Riegelmann Boardwalk (named for Edward J. Riegelmann, Brooklyn borough president at the time) stretches from

Apartment buildings from the 1960s near the bridge to the Aquarium for Wildlife Conservation

Robert Moses disliked the noisy commercialism of places like Nathan's at Coney Island. He created Jones Beach in Long Island as an alternative. (Brian Merlis Collection)

Sea Gate to Brighton Beach. It was later straightened by Robert Moses, commissioner of the city parks department between 1934 and 1960, who also widened the beach.

During Moses's tenure at the parks

Mural on Mullins Lumber Store on Neptune Avenue

department, other dramatic changes occurred. Moses was strongly opposed to purely commercial, lascivious amusements and sought to create a more natural environment. Under his stewardship, Jones Beach was created in Long Island as an alternative to the dirtier and more crowded beaches in the city.

After World War II, severe housing shortages led residents to attempt to winterize beach bungalows. But the lightweight structures were not strong enough to withstand everyday living, and by the 1960s almost 50 acres in Coney Island had been cleared for new

housing, mostly large apartment buildings on the streets around Neptune, Mermaid, and Surf Avenues. More recent developments include large apartment buildings, such as the Luna Park Homes and Warbasse Houses, as well as the Astella Houses, close to 900 single-family homes built in the 1990s between West 15th and West 37th Streets and Surf and Mermaid Avenues. Recent immigrants to the area include Chinese and West Indians from Jamaica, Barbados, and Trinidad and Tobago. All add to the rich diversity of a historic landscape that includes the original Nathan's Famous hot dog restaurant; the B & B Carousell and 150-foot-high Wonder Wheel; and Philip's, a confectionery that offers freshly twirled cotton candy and saltwater taffy.

The tradition of having fun at Coney Island will continue. Astroland, the last remaining full-sized amusement park in Coney Island—opened in 1954 on the site of Feltman's restaurant—features rides like the Astrotower and the landmarked wooden Cyclone roller coaster. The neighborhood also boasts popular handball courts in Seaside–Asser Levy Park and skating at Abe Stark Ice Skating Rink. Keyspan Park, home of the Brooklyn Cyclones, has been one of Coney Island's biggest draws with all season tickets sold out every year since it opened in 2001.

"Master of the slide," Jackie Robinson, coming home (Associated Press; National Baseball Hall of Fame Library, Cooperstown, N.Y.)

THE BROOKLYN

"Wait till next year" was the melancholy motto of the Brooklyn Dodgers, the baseball club that between 1916 and 1953 played in seven World Series—and lost all seven. "Dem Bums," as they were affectionately dubbed, began as a minor league team in 1883. The franchise, variously called the Bridegrooms, the Superbas, and the Robins over the years, took its enduring name—short for Trolley Dodgers—from the practical response of Brooklyn pedestrians to the spread of rapid transit. Although the Dodgers put some strong teams on the field in their first half-century in the National League, which they joined in 1890, some of the best-loved squads were the most inept, like the "Daffiness Boys" of the late 1920s and the 1930s—a gang whose outfielders sometimes let fly balls bounce off their skulls and whose baserunners once congregated three deep at a single base.

The Dodgers began to improve on the field after Larry MacPhail became their general manager in 1938, but when Branch Rickey succeeded MacPhail a few years later, the Dodgers changed the game itself. Organized baseball had been an all-white fraternity since the 1880s, but Rickey flouted the "gentleman's agreement" that barred blacks, signing Jackie Robinson in 1945 and several other Negro Leagues stars in the following years. Robinson joined the major league club in 1947, and the Dodgers won the pennant, as they would in five of the following nine seasons, as black players like Robinson, Roy Campanella, Don Newcombe, and Joe Black meshed seamlessly with white teammates like Duke Snider, Carl Erskine, and Pee Wee Reese. But every time the Dodgers finished atop the National League during this span, the invincible New York Yankees were waiting for them in the World Series. "Next year" finally came in 1955. The Dodgers prevailed in seven games against their rivals from the Bronx, and the borough wept with indescribable joy. Two years later, the tears came from indescribable pain and a sense of betrayal, as owner Walter O'Malley announced that the team would move to the West Coast. Some longtime residents still refuse to recognize the existence of the Los Angeles Dodgers.

A bird's-eye view of Ebbets Field in 1947 (Brian Merlis Collection)

Fans outside Ebbets Field in the early 1950s (Brooklyn Public Library; National Baseball Hall of Fame Library, Cooperstown, N.Y.)

DODGERS

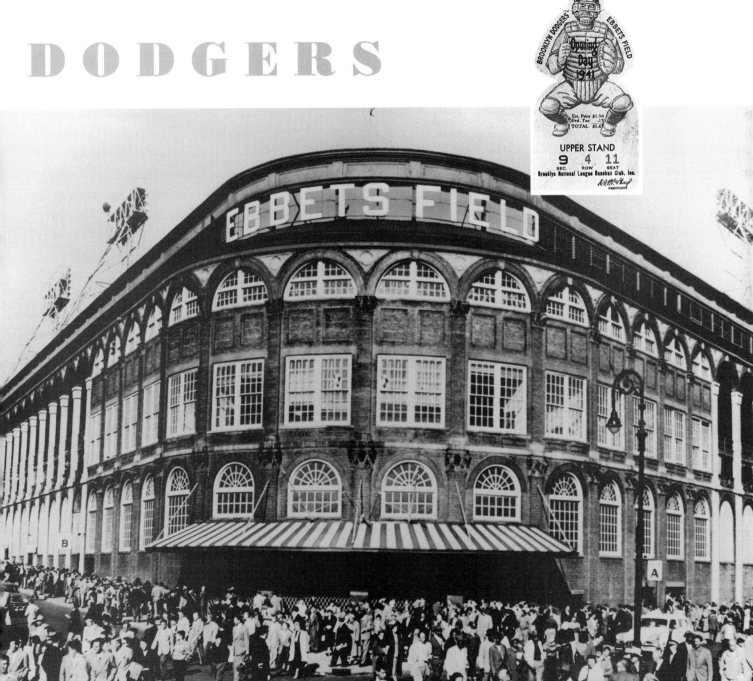

Crown

■ According to Brooklyn lore, the area that is today Crown Heights was at one time known as Crow Hill, after its tallest hill, whose trees were always filled with crows. In 1873 the *Brooklyn Eagle* suggested that the name was a reference to the original African and African American settlement in the area, which was established as early as 1830. The whites of the area, the paper reported, called the Africans and African Americans "crows." Others say that the "crows" were the inmates in the Kings County Penitentiary, which was located within the county buildings in Crow Hill from 1846 until its demolition in 1907.

■ In 1868 Eastern Parkway was completed. Designed by Frederick Law Olmsted and Calvert Vaux of Central and Prospect Parks fame, it was the first six-lane parkway in the world, built eight years before their Ocean Parkway. Its magnificent median strips brought promenades and equestrian paths to the neighborhood and offered side service roads for carriages. The part of the parkway between Grand Army Plaza and Ralph Avenue has been designated a New York City scenic landmark.

■ Crown Heights is home to the Brooklyn Children's Museum (1899; 145 Brooklyn Avenue at St. Marks Avenue), the first and oldest children's museum in the United States. The museum was the first to use interactive, hands-on exhibits to help teach children about their physical and cultural environment. Most of the museum is underground.

■ Costumes are so important a part of the West Indian Carnival that from January to September the elaborate, brightly colored garments are prepared in what are called *mas camps*. These local stores or apartments are rented for the sole purpose of creating the costumes for this single event and are filled with volunteers day and night. A storefront museum of carnival costumes is located on Flatbush Avenue.

Every Labor Day is a celebration of diversity in Crown Heights. With jubilant music provided by 2,000–3,000-member bands, elaborate feathered and sequined costumes like those seen in Trinidadian carnivals, and West Indian dancing, Crown Heights is electric with community and cultural pride as more than 2 million revelers join in the colorful West Indian Carnival and parade. True to the inclusive nature of the neighborhood, Crown Heights's carnival, a tradition since 1969, features aspects of all the West Indian cultures represented in Brooklyn.

As parade participants—many with ties to Haiti, Jamaica, Trinidad and Tobago, Barbados, and Grenada—wend their way through Brooklyn, their celebration passes by the worldwide headquarters of the Lubavitch movement of Hasidic Jews at 770 Eastern Parkway. And fittingly so, for the West Indian community both encompasses and is influenced by the Lubavitchers, who represent another important and distinct culture in Crown Heights. Although they are a minority in the neighborhood, the Lubavitch Hasidim play a vital and visible role in the community.

Heights

Where exactly does Crown Heights begin and end? The best answers to this question consider social as well as geographic boundaries. With residents of different cultures drawn to friends and family in nearby communities, it is not surprising that the geographic limits of Crown Heights are somewhat ill defined. Some claim the area between Eastern Parkway and Atlantic Avenue as part of Crown Heights, for example, whereas others consider this section a piece of Bedford-Stuyvesant. Most residents agree on Park Place as the boundary between the two neighborhoods. This puts developments like the Albany Houses and the former African American neighborhoods of Weeksville and Carrville in Bedford-Stuyvesant, and they are discussed in that entry. And Eastern Parkway is lined with low brick apartment buildings, whereas inner Crown Heights has many single-family homes.

Crown Heights was first settled in the 1600s and was farmed by African American slaves—the first African Americans in the area—for their Dutch owners. After emancipation, some of these African Americans purchased property in the earliest free black communities of Weeksville and Carrville.

During the second half of the nine-

Friends of Crown Heights day-care center

teenth century, the northern section developed: mansions were built where farms once stood, and limestone row houses were constructed. After Eastern Parkway was completed, the splendor of the grand boulevard made the northern part of Crown Heights a desirable residential area, and more large houses sprang up. One of these sections is

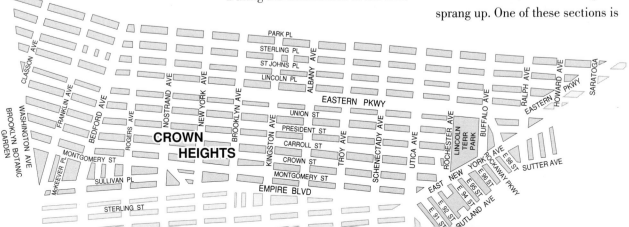

Shopping along Kingston Avenue

called "Doctor's Row" because medical professionals—originally white Protestant, then Jewish, and most recently, West Indian—have inhabited the houses since their construction. Other elegant homes in the neighborhood include the nineteenth-century houses on President Street, between New York and Brooklyn Avenues.

At the turn of the century, the population in Crown Heights grew. Brick and brownstone row houses, which fill many side streets today, were built. In addition, the southern section of Crown Heights was developed: mansions, one- and two-family row houses, and semi-detached houses were constructed.

It was in the early twentieth century, about the time the neighborhood took on the name Crown Heights, that immigrants from the Caribbean began to settle there, although during the 1920s the population was largely composed of Protestants, Catholics, and Jews with ties to Germany, Scandinavia, Ireland, and Italy. By the mid-1940s, Crown Heights had attracted a number of Lubavitch Hasidim who had emigrated from the Soviet Union; a large proportion of the neighborhood's Jews belonged to this group. Walk-up apartment buildings were constructed to accommodate the Hasidim, who are not allowed to use elevators during

West Indian Carnival on Eastern Parkway, 1975 (Tony Sanchez, Brooklyn Historical Society)

NEIGHBORHOOD PROFILE

Boundaries: from Washington Avenue on the west to Rutland and Sutter Avenues on the east, from approximately Park Place on the north to Empire Boulevard on the south.

Subway: <u>Franklin Avenue Shuttle S</u>: Dean St., Park Pl., Botanic Garden <u>IRT 2</u>: Eastern Parkway/Brooklyn Museum, President St., Sterling. <u>IRT 3</u>: Franklin Ave., Nostrand Ave., Kingston Ave., Utica Ave. <u>IRT 4</u>: Franklin Ave., Utica Ave. <u>IRT 5</u>: President St., Sterling.

Bus: <u>B65</u>: Dean St./Bergen St. <u>B45</u>: St. John's Pl./Washington Ave. <u>B71</u>: Eastern Pkwy. <u>B17</u>: Eastern Pkwy. <u>B14</u>: Eastern Pkwy. <u>B15</u>: Bergen St. <u>B48</u>: Classon Ave. <u>B49</u>: Bedford Ave./Rogers Ave. <u>B44</u>: Nostrand Ave./New York Ave. <u>B43</u>: Brooklyn Ave./Kingston Ave. <u>B46</u>: Utica Ave. <u>B40</u>: Ralph Ave. <u>B7</u>: Saratoga Ave./Thomas S. Boyland Ave. <u>B12</u>: East New York Ave.

Libraries: Brooklyn Public Library Crown Heights Branch (New York Ave. at Maple St.), Brower Park Branch (St. Mark's Ave. near Nostrand Ave.), Eastern Parkway Branch (Eastern Parkway at Schenectady Ave.)

Community Board: No. 8

Police Precinct: 77th Precinct (127 Utica Ave.), 71st Precinct (421 Empire Blvd.)

Fire Department: Engine 234 Ladder 123 (1352 St. John's Pl.), Rescue Co. 2 (1472 Bergen St.), Engine 240 Ladder 113 (Rogers and Maple)

Hospitals and Clinics: Catholic Medical Center–St. Mary's Hospital (170 Buffalo Ave.), Interfaith Medical Center (555 Prospect Pl.), Interfaith Medical Center (1545 Atlantic Ave.), Brookdale Family Care Center (1873 Eastern Pkwy.), Lola Cuffee Family Health Center (485 Throop Ave.), Eastern Parkway Family Health Clinic (391 Eastern Pkwy.), CNR Healthcare Network–Center for Nursing and Rehabilitation (520 Prospect Pl.), Lowenstein Adult Day Care Center (520 Prospect Pl.)

residents began to establish what has become the largest West Indian neighborhood in the city. Parts of Crown Heights are sometimes called La Saline, after a section of Haiti's Port-au-Prince. Utica and Nostrand Avenues are filled with stores carrying West Indian delicacies; many of these were founded during the area's renaissance in the 1970s and 1980s.

The nation's attention was drawn to Crown Heights during the summer of 1991 when a Guyanese child was killed by a car driven by a Lubavitch Hasid. Riots followed, and a Hasidic student was killed. These tragic events created a negative image of the area that did not always fit residents' perceptions, but neighborhood organiza-

Two Hasidim stop to chat on the corner of President Street and Kingston Avenue

the Sabbath, and apartments of all kinds were built to house other growing populations in Crown Heights.

After World War II, however, something of an exodus began. Many veterans moved to outlying suburbs with the assistance of the G.I. Bill. The neighborhood declined through the 1960s, as apartment buildings were abandoned

and the community grew poorer. But by the late 1960s and early 1970s, new immigrants from the Caribbean had settled in Crown Heights, and a new university opened, Medgar Evers College of City University of New York (1969), which has since moved to Fort Greene. By joining families and friends already in the community, these new

Ebbets Field Houses, at Bedford Avenue and Sullivan Place, where Ebbets Field once stood

tions and grassroots groups viewed the incident as deplorable yet as providing an opportunity to respond to the long-standing tensions with positive, community-building ventures. Many antibias projects were initiated, like Project CURE, which brought together young men of different ethnicities, to foster racial understanding. Unity Day, created jointly by Caribbean and

Hasidic residents through the 71st Precinct Community Council, gathers together more than 10,000 persons each June and offers a happy example of how a community can be strengthened through diversity.

Black heroes grace a mural on Nostrand Avenue

Cypress

Homes along Grant Avenue in City Line

Sometimes considered a part of East New York, Cypress Hills is a multiracial community with a colorful past and a bright future. Echoes of the rowdy din of roadhouses and the roar of crowds at one of the earliest thorough-bred racetracks in the country have faded; in their place are the sounds of families enjoying a fully developed suburban area filled predominantly with single- and multifamily townhouses.

Cypress Hills was settled in the early 1700s as a part of New Lots of the town of Flatbush. African American slaves farmed the area for Dutch, French, Huguenot, and English landowners, and the community remained rural until the early 1800s. One of the first signs of development was the construction of Jamaica Plank Road (1807), a wooden structure along what is now Jamaica Avenue: two of the road's toll gates were within today's Cypress Hills. A Dutch farmhouse, the Wilhelmus Stoothoff House (1841), still stands on this thoroughfare, facing Highland Park. Fulton Street was also laid out during the early 1800s.

When Union Course racetrack was constructed in 1821, just over the county line in Queens, settlement spread to Brooklyn. A community

Hills

called **Union Place,** with roadhouses, blacksmiths, retail shops, and hotels, sprang up to meet the demands of gamblers, sightseers, and new residents. The settlement was later called Unionville and then Union Course, after the track, where races were held until after the Civil War.

By 1835 the first building lots were sold, on Eldert Lane and extending south from Jamaica Plank Road. Meanwhile, on the western side of Cypress Hills, John Pitkin, a wealthy merchant from Connecticut, was developing farms in an attempt to build a manufacturing city that he named East New York. While Pitkin developed his shoe factory in East New York, he may have lived within Cypress Hills, on Atlantic Avenue between New Jersey and Pennsylvania/ Granville Payne Avenues. Pitkin later gained prominence in Cypress Hills by donating land for the East New York Dutch Reformed Church, which was built at Fulton Street and New Jersey Avenue in 1839.

The Long Island Railroad had also begun to serve the area with a line called the Great Eastern Railroad, on tracks that, although nearly inaccessible today, still exist under Atlantic Avenue. These tracks were once elevated west of

Fulton Street, ca. 1944 (Brian Merlis Collection)

Warwick Street. As reaching Cypress Hills via public transportation became easy, residents were attracted to the area. Detached houses were constructed during this period to accommodate the flood of newcomers. Increased pedestrian traffic from the Long Island Railroad service also led to the commercial development of Atlantic Avenue, which by the mid-nineteenth century featured stores to meet the needs of the newest residents. By the end of the century, the avenue was also home to industries like dairies, numbering-machine factories, cabinet and embroidery factories, and greenhouses.

In 1852 the town of New Lots, which encompassed Cypress Hills, was incorporated. The New Lots Town Hall, built in 1873, still stands at 111 Bradford Street, although it has since become an apartment building. By this time, although the center of Cypress Hills had yet to be developed, streets had been laid out in both the eastern and western sections of the neighborhood.

In the mid-1800s, cemeteries north of the neighborhood, including the federal Cypress Hills Cemetery (1848), were planned and developed. It is not certain whether the neighborhood takes its name from this cemetery; possibly both were named for the trees that grew on the local hills. Eighteen cemeteries were eventually developed around and within Cypress Hills.

In 1886 the City of Brooklyn annexed the town of New Lots, including what is now Cypress Hills. Soon there-

● Cypress Hills Cemetery

In 1862 Cypress Hills Cemetery was made a part of the National Cemetery System, which was established by an act of Congress and authorized by President Abraham Lincoln. Cypress Hills is the only national cemetery in New York City. Some of the earliest dead to be interred there were Union and Confederate casualties of Civil War battles. Later the cemetery became the final resting place for writers Emma Lazarus and Sholem Aleichem, actors Mae West and Edward G. Robinson, baseball players Jackie Robinson and Lou Gehrig, and magician Harry Houdini. Six notorious Mafia figures—Joseph Profaci, Charles (Lucky) Luciano, Vito (Don George) Genovese, Joseph Colombo, Carlo Gambino, and Carmine Eyalente—are also buried in Cypress Hills. And in the 1930s remains in Brooklyn Navy Yard graves, which may include early African Americans, were moved to the cemetery.

Legend has it that the headless ghost of Fiji Island chief Veindovi haunts the cemetery. Chief Veindovi was captured by the U.S. Navy and charged with cannibalism because in the 1830s he allegedly ate eight American sailors from the whaling ship *Charles Doggett*. Chief Veindovi never had a trial; he died of tuberculosis after reaching Brooklyn. His head, removed from his body, now resides in the Smithsonian Institution in Washington, D.C., and his body, once buried in the Brooklyn Navy Yard Hospital Cemetery, was moved in the 1920s to Cypress Hills.

The gatehouse of the cemetery has been restored and is now used as the offices of a local nonprofit group.

after, the neighborhood developed rapidly into a thriving suburban area. Paved streets and sewers were laid. Trolleys began to rattle along Jamaica Plank Road, and two-family detached residences were built. By the end of the century the area was attracting a number of immigrants, mainly German.

Meanwhile, Ridgewood Reservoir and the 141-acre **Highland Park** were developed. Highland Park's formal opening was in 1903, and thereafter large houses overlooking the park were

Front yard Catholic shrine, Sheridan Avenue in City Line

NEIGHBORHOOD FACTS

■ Half of a roadhouse from the days of Union Course racetrack still stands in Cypress Hills. William I. Shaw's Hotel, built in the 1840s, was the site of the first New Lots town election in 1852 and once stood at Jamaica Avenue and Eldert Lane. In 1902 the hotel was split and both halves were moved to Danforth Street, where they were placed on opposite ends of the block. The half still standing, on Danforth and Hemlock, was apparently placed backward; its porch is at the back of the house instead of the front.

■ Two schools in Cypress Hills are New York City landmarked buildings. Public School 65K, on Richmond Street, was built in 1870 and enlarged in 1889. Public School 108, on Linwood Street, was built in 1895.

■ The Arlington Branch of the Brooklyn Public Library, one of the first Carnegie libraries to be built in Brooklyn, was completed in 1906.

■ The Eastern Park Ballground was once home of the Bridegrooms, later known as the Brooklyn Dodgers.

built. Residents of these homes consider their community both part of and distinct from the neighborhood of Cypress Hills.

Soon after the turn of the century, row houses were constructed throughout Cypress Hills, many to join previously built detached houses. Two women, Mrs. A. P. Price and Catherine Kampfe, became leaders in the development of row houses in Cypress Hills. Believing that they knew better than men what women wanted in a new house, they braved a traditionally male-dominated field to build structures that are still standing today.

By the early 1920s, almost every block of the neighborhood was filled with houses, and by the mid-1920s apartments were even being constructed above Fulton Street stores.

During the 1930s, the population of the area doubled, and construction continued apace. Today Cypress Hills looks much as it did during the bustling 1930s; it has stayed a stable working-class neighborhood, and much of the original housing stock has remained intact. During the 1990s, some new housing was added to the western side of the neighborhood.

The population has changed and grown with the neighborhood. At the beginning of the twentieth century, Cypress Hills was inhabited primarily by Americans of German, Irish, Italian, and Polish descent. This ethnic mix remained primarily the same until the middle of the twentieth century, when African Americans, Central Americans, and South Americans moved into Cypress Hills. Today Haitian, Jamai-

Veterans Day ceremony at Highland Park National Cemetery

Hindu shrine in front of two-family detached house

and the community center has always been St. Sylvester's Roman Catholic Church. In 1943 the neighborhood raised money to build a war memorial at Liberty Avenue and Eldert Lane. Every year City Line's Memorial Day parade of scouts and elected officials ends at this landmark.

In the 1970s most of the Italian and Irish American residents moved out of City Line and new, Hispanic residents

can, Indian, Pakistani, Korean, and Chinese residents also call Cypress Hills home, and a Lithuanian population, which still has a cultural center in the neighborhood, has roots there.

City Line is a small neighborhood within Cypress Hills that is separated from the rest of the larger community by the tracks of the Long Island Rail Road and the busy North Conduit Avenue. The area was called City Line even before Brooklyn was incorporated into the city of New York, and residents of the area—who have a different racial and ethnic makeup from that of Cypress Hills and East New York (which also sometimes claims City Line), as well as their own shopping area—are proud to consider themselves a separate neighborhood.

The residents of the area used to be primarily of Italian and Irish descent,

NEIGHBORHOOD PROFILE

Boundaries: <u>Cypress Hills</u>: from the intersection of Fulton Street, Jamaica Avenue, and Broadway on the west to Eldert Lane and the Queen's County border on the east, from Jackie Robinson Parkway on the north to Atlantic and North Conduit Avenues on the south. <u>Highland Park</u>: from Marginal Street West on the west to Ridgewood Reservoir on the east, from Jackie Robinson Parkway on the north to Jamaica Avenue on the south. <u>City Line</u>: from Conduit Avenue on the west and south to the Queen's County border on the east to Atlantic Avenue on the north.

Subway: <u>BMT Jamaica Line J</u>: Alabama Ave., Van Siclen Ave., Cleveland St., Norwood Ave., Crescent St., Cypress Hills, 75th St./Eldert Lane

Bus: <u>B024</u>: Atlantic Ave. <u>B056</u>: Jamaica Ave. <u>B20</u>: Broadway <u>BQ24</u>: Broadway <u>B13</u>: Crescent St. <u>B18</u>: Crescent St./Hemlock St.

Libraries: Brooklyn Public Library Cypress Hills Branch (1197 Sutter Ave.), Arlington Branch (203 Arlington Ave.)

Community Board: No. 5

Police Precinct: 75th Precinct (1000 Sutter Ave.)

Fire Department: Engine 332 Ladder 175 (165 Bradford St.)

Hospitals and Clinics: Wartburg Lutheran Home for the Aging–Wartburg Nursing Home (50 Sheffield Ave.)

Mural depicting Brooklyn history at corner of Autumn and Jamaica Avenues

arrived, most of whom were Puerto Rican. The neighborhood's racial diversity served it well during the unsettled 1970s. Although nearby neighborhoods were battling rioting, arson, and abandonment during this period, City Line remained intact, perhaps because these neighbors had had experience living and working together. And the neighborhood continues to change. Slowly, Dominicans and Ecua- dorians have also moved in. And in recent years Guyanese and Bangladeshi immigrants have become a part of the community as well.

City Line has one- and two-family homes, but small apartment buildings and row houses accentuate side streets. Liberty Avenue, where the City Line Theater once stood, has always been the commercial center of the neighborhood. Today the avenue, from Crescent Street to Eldert Lane, is a vibrant, bustling shopping area where one can hear lively conversations in many languages.

Downtown

Downtown Brooklyn is a vital, lively hub of the borough, where commercial, government, and financial interests converge. When they aren't being tempted by the stores at Fulton Street Mall, Brooklynites in downtown conduct business at MetroTech Center, take care of legal business in Brooklyn courtrooms, fill out paperwork at Brooklyn Borough Hall, and join others studying for degrees at Brooklyn Law School, Long Island University, and New York City Technical College.

Building after building in Downtown Brooklyn tells a story of Brooklyn's colorful history, but most who live and work there are so busy hurrying through the neighborhood's streets that they barely have time to notice the architectural treasures that surround them. One of the newest additions to this architectural legacy is also an important symbol of the renewal of Brooklyn in general, and Downtown Brooklyn in particular. Once the first hotel in 50 years opened its doors in November 1998, the New York Marriott Brooklyn at Renaissance Plaza on Jay and Adams Streets, visitors were able to find everything they needed for an extended stay in Brooklyn right downtown.

The first European settlers attracted to the site of Downtown Brooklyn were Dutch farmers and tradespeople, who acquired the land from its original in-

Brooklyn

Corner of Sands and Washington Streets,
ca. 1920 (Brian Merlis Collection)

habitants, the Munsee-speaking
Lenape, or Delaware, Indians. The first
superintendent of Brooklyn was appointed in 1625. In 1646 the settlers,
who lived close to the East River in
wooden houses, were granted a charter
by the Dutch West India Company and
named their town Breuckelen. A road
linked Breuckelen to another settlement, Bedford Corners (see Bedford-
Stuyvesant entry), which stood at
what is now Fulton Street and
Bedford Avenue.

As early as 1642,
rowboats and sail-
boats for hire
shuttled adventurous
travelers between
today's Fulton Ferry
and Manhattan, but
it was not until 1814,
when Robert Fulton
introduced steam-
powered ferries to the
area, that safe, regularly
scheduled boat service
across the East River became
available. The ferries were im-
mensely popular. By the middle
of the nineteenth century, thousands of Brooklynites boarded
ferries each day to shop, work,
and even attend church in
Manhattan.

The steady flow of ferry-

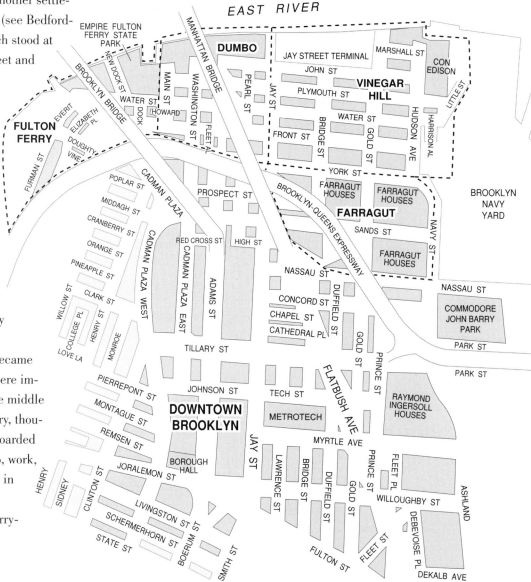

bound commuters down what was called Old Ferry Road and Old Fulton Street—parts of which are today Cadman Plaza West—inspired restaurateurs and store owners to develop new businesses. Their timing was perfect. The population grew enormously during this period: in 1790 Breuckelen had approximately 1,600 residents; by 1820 this number had reached about 7,000. By 1834 banks and financial offices had also been built near the ferries.

In 1834 the City of Brooklyn was chartered over opposition from New York City, and in 1835 a parcel of land one mile from the waterfront was designated

Junior's, the Brooklyn mecca for cheese-cake fans, on DeKalb and Flatbush Avenues

---

NEIGHBORHOOD PROFILE

Boundaries: <u>Downtown Brooklyn</u>: from the East River, Cadman Plaza West, and Clinton Street on the west to the eastern border formed by the Brooklyn Navy Yard, Navy Street, Prince Street, and Ashland Street, from the East River on the north to State Street and Fulton Street between Smith and Ashland Streets on the south. <u>Fulton Ferry</u>: from the East River on the west and north to Main Street on the east to the Brooklyn-Queens Expressway on the south. <u>Vinegar Hill</u>: from Jay Street on the west to the Brooklyn Navy Yard on the east, from the East River on the north to York Street on the south. <u>Farragut</u>: from the Manhattan Bridge overpass on the west to Navy Street on the east, from York Street on the north to Nassau Street on the south. <u>DUMBO</u>: from Main Street on the west to Jay Street on the east, from the East River on the north to the Brooklyn-Queens Expressway on the south.

Subway: <u>IND F</u>: York St., Jay St./Borough Hall <u>IND A and C</u>: High Street/Brooklyn Bridge, Jay St./Borough Hall <u>Brighton Line D and Q</u>: DeKalb Ave. <u>BMT Jamaica Line M</u>: Court St., Lawrence St./MetroTech <u>BMT 4th Avenue N and R</u>: Court St., DeKalb Ave. <u>IRT 2 and 3</u>: Clark St., Borough Hall, Hoyt St./Fulton Mall <u>IRT 4 and 5</u>: Borough Hall, Nevins St.

Bus: <u>B61</u>: Atlantic Ave. <u>B63</u>: Atlantic Ave. <u>B37</u>: Livingston St. <u>B45</u>: Livingston St. <u>B51</u>: Livingston St. <u>B75</u>: Livingston St./Court St. <u>B65</u>: Boerum Pl. <u>B25</u>: Cadman Plaza West <u>B41</u>: Cadman Plaza West <u>B51</u>: Cadman Plaza West <u>B25</u>: Cadman Plaza West/Tillary St./Adams St. <u>B41</u>: Cadman Plaza West/Adams St. <u>B52</u>: Cadman Plaza West/Tillary St./Adams St. <u>B38</u>: Cadman Plaza West/Adams St. <u>B26</u>: Cadman Plaza West/Jay St. <u>B61</u>: Jay St. <u>B54</u>: Jay St./Flatbush Ave./Duffield St.

Libraries: Brooklyn Public Library Business Library (280 Cadman Plaza West), Brooklyn Heights Branch Library (280 Cadman Plaza West)

Theater: BACA Downtown Theater (195 Cadman Plaza)

Community Board: No. 2

Police Precinct: 84th Precinct (301 Gold St.)

---

the site for a city hall, the first building in Brooklyn to be a true civic center. The city hall on Joralemon Street, the building that Brooklynites have known since 1898 as Brooklyn Borough Hall, was not completed until 1849 (with its cupola taking even longer to finish). It was landmarked in 1966 and restored in 1989. Another distinct building from the period is the Friends Meeting House at 110 Schermerhorn Street, which was constructed in 1857 in the beautifully proportioned, plain style of the Quakers. In 1867 the Quakers started a coeducational elementary and secondary school in the basement of the meeting house, one of the earliest schools to feature an ethnically and

● **The Manhattan Bridge**

The Manhattan Bridge, which opened in 1909, was actually designed by Leon Moisseiff, although Gustav Lindenthal often gets the credit. (In 1903 Lindenthal submitted a plan for the bridge, but it was rejected because it included too many structural innovations.) The Canal Street entrance features a grand arch and colonnades designed by Carrère and Hastings, famous for their work on, among other structures, the New York Public Library. The bridge is 6,855 feet long and has a main span of 1,470 feet.

Intersection of Fulton Street and Flatbush Avenue, ca. 1940 (Cezar Del Valle)

racially mixed student body. (In 1972 the school, now the Brooklyn Friends School, moved to 375 Pearl Street in Brooklyn Heights.) The Quakers also formed antislavery groups like the New York Colored Mission (1871), as well as the Society for the Prevention of Cruelty to Children (1875). The City of Brooklyn began annexing its surrounding neighbors, and by 1860 Greenpoint, Williamsburg, and Bushwick were added to Brooklyn, making it, by area, the third largest city in the country.

If the ferries had encouraged a steady stream of new residents, the Brooklyn Bridge, completed in 1883, inspired a flood of newcomers—as well as the demise of Brooklyn-Manhattan ferry service in 1924. Following the construction of the bridge, many hotels, theaters, businesses, and newspaper offices began to open around Brooklyn's City Hall. The area still had foundries, refineries, and vinegar works. But by 1898, when Brooklyn was incorporated into New York City, Fulton Street in Downtown Brooklyn was an animated commercial district that had grown naturally, with little planning. A construction boom occurred during the late 1800s to mid-1900s. In 1892 the landmarked Brooklyn Fire Headquarters was built on Jay Street. The U.S. Post Office's Brooklyn Central Office, also a landmarked

Gage & Tollner (established 1879) at 372 Fulton Street (Brooklyn Historical Society)

● The *Brooklyn Eagle*

Brooklyn boasted a prominent national newspaper in the *Brooklyn Eagle*, founded in 1841 as the *Brooklyn Eagle and King's County Democrat* and located on Johnson Street (now Cadman Plaza East). One of its most illustrious editors was Walt Whitman, chief editor from 1846–47, who resigned because of his support for the Free Soil Party. But the *Eagle*, though partisan, nonetheless embraced Whitman's dream of speaking to all the people of Brooklyn —and beyond; by the early 1860s the paper was the most widely read afternoon newspaper in the United States. By 1931, when it absorbed the *Brooklyn Times-Union*, its chief competitor, it was the largest daily and Sunday newspaper in Brooklyn. Boasting such writers as St. Clair McKelway, Hans von Kaltenborn, Edward Bok, Nunnally Johnson, and Winston Burdett, the newspaper four times won the Pulitzer Prize. In 1955, plagued by declining circulation, a long-running dispute with the New York Newspaper Guild, and a lengthy strike, it ceased publication, although it revived for a few months in 1960 as a weekly and for a year in 1962–63 as a daily.

building, rose in 1891 on Cadman Plaza. And on Fulton Street, the Dime Savings Bank was erected in 1907 and expanded in 1932. Both the interior and exterior of this building are New York City landmarks.

The building that formerly housed the New York City Board of Education (1926–2002) was constructed in 1926, as was the Brooklyn Municipal Building on Joralemon Street. The New York City Board of Transportation Building at Jay Street, now the Transit Authority headquarters, was completed in 1950.

Privately endowed schools established for Brooklynites were also constructed in Downtown Brooklyn. The first, Brooklyn Female Academy, opened in 1844; when it closed in 1853 because of a fire, Packer Collegiate Institute opened. The Brooklyn Collegiate and Polytechnic Institute offered their first classes in 1854. Graduates of these programs (and others) who wish to continue their studies in Downtown Brooklyn can choose from Brooklyn Law School (1901), Long Island University (1926), and New York City Technical College (1946).

Economic and social upheaval in the late 1950s and 1960s caused a retailing slump in Downtown Brooklyn and other urban areas. Manhattan's larger variety of stores, easily accessible by subway, exacerbated the problem of luring shoppers to the downtown area. Consequently, several large stores and businesses closed. One de-

NEIGHBORHOOD FACTS

■ For 84 years, the Bridge Street African Wesleyan Methodist Episcopal Church, the oldest black congregation in the borough, was located on Bridge Street in Downtown Brooklyn. It moved in 1938 to Bedford-Stuyvesant.

■ In 1776 General George Washington evacuated his soldiers from the Battle of Brooklyn at what is now the Fulton Ferry dock.

■ In 1799 Kings County's first newspaper, *The Courier, and Long Island Advertiser*, began publishing weekly near Fulton Ferry.

■ There are only two streets named United States in the whole country. One is in Pittsburgh, and the other, now a private road located within the Consolidated Edison facility, is located in Vinegar Hill.

■ Parts of the original Interborough Rapid Transit System (IRT) have been landmarked by New York City. One of the landmarked "underground stations," as they were called at the time they were built, is the Lexington IRT stop at Borough Hall, which was redesigned and restored in 1987.

■ The first Roman Catholic church on Long Island, organized in 1822, was St. James Procathedral, on Jay and Chapel Streets. Before this building was constructed, Brooklyn's Roman Catholics had to take ferries to Manhattan to worship.

■ Bargemusic, a stationary barge that has been docked at the foot of Cadman Plaza West since 1977, is a favorite spot for Brooklyn music enthusiasts. Formerly Erie-Lakawanna Coffee Barge 375, it is an intimate setting where listeners can hear renowned musicians performing in twice-weekly chamber music concerts.

including what was then Abraham & Straus, the centerpiece store. Also within the mall is Gage & Tollner, a favorite Brooklyn restaurant since 1879. The site it inhabits now was built in 1892, and its interior is landmarked. Junior's, at nearby Flatbush and DeKalb, has been serving the most famous cheesecake in Brooklyn since 1929, when it was known as Enduro's Sandwich Shop.

The shopping center attracted other new construction that continues today. During the 1980s office buildings were built, and by the 1990s businesses seeking lower rents than they could find in Manhattan began to move to Downtown Brooklyn. The old downtown remains much the same since the construction of the Fulton Street Mall, whereas the new downtown,

A majority of Vinegar Hill, DUMBO, and Fulton Ferry residents are artists or employees of art-related businesses

partment store, however, Abraham & Straus, held on through Downtown Brooklyn's troubled retail years. Founded in 1865 as Wechsler & Abraham, the retailer moved to 420 Fulton Street in 1883, and by 1899 it was known as the largest dry goods store in New York State. In 1949 Abraham & Straus was taken over by Federated Stores; it became part of the Macy's chain in 1995.

In 1977, in an attempt to win back some of the borough's shoppers, construction began on the Fulton Street Mall, New York City's first pedestrian shopping mall and the site of more than a hundred retail outlets,

Empire Stores warehouses in
Fulton Ferry in the 1930s
(Brooklyn Historical Society)

double in size. Because of
the new business develop-
ment in the western part of
the neighborhood, perhaps
20 years from now two
smaller neighborhoods
could spring out of what is
today Downtown Brooklyn
—Downtown East and
Downtown West.

Downtown Brooklyn al-
ready encompasses four
smaller neighborhoods that
sit at its northern shore:
Fulton Ferry, Vinegar Hill,

between the mall and the Flatbush
Avenue Extension, is expanding
rapidly.

MetroTech Center, a 16-acre complex of new and renovated buildings
with landscaped grounds, has helped
to bring more than 6,000 jobs to Downtown Brooklyn. The center was inspired by work at the present Polytechnic University, an outgrowth of the
Polytechnic Institute, and it represents
a movement begun in Brooklyn to forge
new ties between technical institutes
and employers. The Chase building,
at 4 MetroTech Center, is the second-
tallest building in Brooklyn, at 450
feet. The new hotel, New York Marriott
at the Brooklyn Bridge, with confer-
ence rooms, underground garage, and
day-care center, adds more employment opportunities and plans to

Farragut, and DUMBO. Each of the smaller neighborhoods differs markedly from
the others, although all have a variety of housing: row houses, warehouses converted to studio space, lofts, and apartments. In fact, the four neighborhoods have
virtually indistinguishable boundaries. An estimated two-thirds of the residents
that call these neighborhoods home identify themselves as artists or employees of
arts-related businesses.

Fulton Ferry, located where ferries once carried Brooklynites to Manhattan,
is a tiny, quiet enclave, the only commercial district in Brooklyn that has been
designated a landmark. The Greek Revival Long Island Insurance Company
building at 5–7 Front Street was built in 1834; it may be New York City's earliest
surviving office building. Also in this area is the landmarked Brooklyn City Railroad Company building on Old Fulton Street (1861), off Cadman Plaza West. Established in 1853, the railroad operated horsecar lines that brought people to and
from the Fulton Ferry Terminal.

The exteriors of the buildings in this area have barely changed since the eighteenth century. The Eagle Warehouse and Storage Company of Brooklyn, for example, on Old Fulton Street, is a large brick structure completed in 1893. Once
the main storage facility in the area for household furnishings and silverware,
the building, like other local warehouses, has been renovated into cooperative
apartments.

Also in Fulton Ferry are the old Empire Stores (1869) on Water Street; these are nineteenth-century warehouses that held the animal hides, sugar, and other raw materials to be loaded from Brooklyn trains onto barges docked at Fulton Ferry piers. The warehouses have also been used to store coffee.

Fulton Ferry offers a mixture of restaurants and offices—as well as hidden, redeveloped residences—within its history-filled commercial buildings. In addition, Empire Fulton Ferry State Park offers unmatched panoramic views of Manhattan and the Brooklyn Bridge. The scenic spot has been used for many locally produced music videos as well as for movies like *Scent of a Woman* (1992) and *King of New York* (1990). Empire Fulton Ferry State Park will merge into the proposed Brooklyn Bridge Park within the next decade.

In 1800 John Jackson bought a large tract of land on the northeasternmost section of Downtown Brooklyn and named part of it **Vinegar Hill,** after the location of the final battle in the Irish Revolution of 1798. The earliest residents were Irish Americans (which accounts for the neighborhood's other early name, Irish Town), Lithuanian Americans, Italian Americans, Latin Americans, and African Americans.

Gold Street was named for the gold coins that were discovered when the area was developed. Local lore has it that Captain Kidd's treasure is buried in the area under cobblestones brought from Ireland as ship ballast.

By the mid-1800s, Sands Street, then the main street of the area, was home to a row of bars, gambling houses, and brothels that attracted thieves and, later, drug peddlers. These blocks were later nicknamed Hell's Half Acre. In the 1920s, the commandant of the Brooklyn Navy Yard ordered the Sands Street entrance to the Navy Yard closed so that his sailors would not be enticed by these unsavory activities.

The building of the Farragut Houses, a high-rise public housing project, and the necessary razing of all of Sands Street's neighboring houses, was heralded in the early 1950s as a sure way to clean up the neighborhood. Today these blocks and the Farragut Houses make up their own neighborhood, **Farragut** (not to be confused with the Farragut that used to be one of the smaller neighborhoods within East Flatbush). Farragut has about 3,000 residents, Vinegar Hill about 150.

During World War II Farragut pros-

Light and shadow Down Under the Manhattan Bridge

Between the Bridges Pub in DUMBO

pered because its residents, who were mainly Irish American, worked in such nearby industries as the Brillo steel wool factory and the shipyards of the Brooklyn Navy Yard. When a section of Vinegar Hill's nineteenth-century row houses was landmarked recently, these homes were acknowledged as residential survivors of a larger neighborhood that stretched from the Brooklyn Bridge to the Navy Yard. Today many of these house artists.

Near Vinegar Hill is the small neighborhood of **DUMBO**, the acronym for Down Under the Manhattan Bridge Overpass. As the area grows in size, character, and desirability, its boundaries are changing, and it is now sometimes called Between the Bridges, referring to the area between the Brooklyn and Manhattan Bridge overpasses. DUMBO is an up-and-coming neighborhood of artists and young people living in warehouses converted to apartments and studios. The neighborhood became a true community in the 1970s when artists and loft lovers seeking space outside Manhattan moved into commercial lofts illegally. Now quite a few of the commercial buildings have been officially converted to living lofts. The neighborhood has a scattering of streetside galleries.

THE BROOKLYN

Although the idea of a bridge between Brooklyn and New York City had been around since 1788, it wasn't until early in 1867 that serious plans were mooted. At that time John Augustus Roebling, the inventor of an improved wire cable and an accomplished bridge builder, proposed the Brooklyn Bridge to William C. Kinsley, the publisher of the *Brooklyn Eagle*. He imagined a bridge with two massive stone towers, a network of steel cables suspended from the towers, and vertical wires connecting the roadbed to the cables, reinforced by diagonal stays from the towers and iron trusses underpinning the suspended floor to stiffen the roadbed. Nature gave Roebling's plan an unexpected boost: the winter

The Brooklyn Bridge is a cultural icon, inspiring such masterpieces as Hart Crane's *The Bridge* (1930) (UPI/Corbis-Bettmann)

BROOKLYN BR

DEPT OF TRAFFIC

BRIDGE

of 1866–67 was a cold one, and the elements disrupted ferry service. Residents demanded a solution—and in April 1867 a bill to incorporate the New York Bridge Company was introduced in the legislature. In 1869, however, just after the necessary approvals were in place, Roebling was killed as a result of a ferry accident. His son Washington Roebling took over the project, but in 1872 he contracted the bends; he remained an invalid for the rest of his life. With the help of his wife, Emily Warren Roebling, however, he was able to oversee the rest of the bridge's construction from a room in his home on Columbia Heights. The project faced further difficulties, but when the Brooklyn Bridge, now a New York City landmark, finally opened in 1883, it deserved its local appellation of "the eighth wonder of the world." The bridge has a span of 1,595.5 feet. Today, commuters still crowd foot and bicycle paths on the bridge during rush hour, taking in the spectacular views and fresh breezes on their way to and from work.

Pedestrian and bike traffic on the bridge

Recent repair work on the bridge (Matthew Coleman)

Dyker

Christmas decorations on 84th Street between 11th and 12th Avenues

The evening is crisp, the snow luminous. Christmas Eve is only a week away, and many residents of 84th Street in Dyker Heights are immersed in preparations. Thousands of lightbulbs are strung, 40-foot Nutcrackers are hoisted into position, and crèches with as many as 50 characters are decorated and polished for their seasonal performance. Many Brooklynites enjoy trimming their homes for Christmas, but few are more enthusiastic than Dyker Heights residents, some of whom spend thousands of dollars and devote weeks of preparation—often with professional assistance—to the joyful task.

With its low, cozy buildings, most of which are single-family homes surrounded by yards, Dyker Heights is a place where people can put down roots. Indeed, it is said that once families have settled in this charming neighborhood, they don't leave for generations. Sometimes considered a part of Bay Ridge, the almost exclusively residential neighborhood is dotted with a few apartment buildings and some two-

Heights

family brick homes among the single-family houses; almost no buildings (other than churches) are taller than three stories. But the high ground offers all residents attractive views. The highest, most desirable section of Dyker Heights is 11th Avenue around 80th and 81st Streets. Mansions built along that avenue provide spectacular views of the Narrows.

Dyker Heights also boasts Dyker Beach Park, a 242-acre green space on Gravesend Bay. Children and adults flock to the park to play soccer, tennis, and bocce. Golf lovers are drawn to Dyker Heights, too, attracted by Dyker Beach Golf Course, which is also in the park. What other Brooklyn neighborhood allows a golfer to live just blocks away from the first tee (near the corner of 7th Avenue and 86th Street)?

On May 27, 1643, 200 acres of today's Dyker Heights were acquired by Anthony Jansen van Salee. Originally part of the Dutch town of New Utrecht, the area was used for farmland; even after the English took over the colony in 1664, Dutch farmers and their slaves remained. But the English established a firm hold in New Utrecht: the area now called Dyker Heights,

along with the rest of Brooklyn, remained occupied by British troops until the end of the American Revolution.

The naming of Dyker Heights remains a bit of a mystery. It may have been named for the two Van Dykes who divided and developed the area in 1719, or the name could refer to the dikes that were used to drain the marshland that once covered the neighborhood.

In the nineteenth century, fishermen of Scandinavian heritage from Bay Ridge settled in Dyker Heights, which was filled with farms until well after the turn of the century. When the subway reached the neighborhoods that surround Dyker Heights—Bay Ridge, Fort Hamilton, and Bensonhurst—Irish American residents joined those who had already made Dyker Heights home. During the

GRAVESEND BAY

102

■ Poly Prep Country Day School, formerly Brooklyn Polytechnic Preparatory School (1924), is located on the border of Dyker Heights and Fort Hamilton, at 92nd Street and 7th Avenue. The school has also opened a branch for the elementary grades in Park Slope on Prospect Park West.
■ The families of Dyker Heights gather several times each year for festivals in spacious, 8.5-acre McKinley Park. Fresh pumpkins attract children to the fall festival, and during both the spring and fall festivals a pie-eating contest, dance contest, and flea market enliven the celebrations.

Homes overlooking the Narrows

1960s, Italian American residents who had the means to move into Dyker Heights's large houses came as well. Developers began to construct one- and two-family homes to replace mansions that could no longer be maintained, planning Dyker Heights as a suburban neighborhood with spacious residences and lush front lawns. Although the community remains primarily Italian American, some of the neighborhood's newest residents include Russian and Chinese immigrants. A small community of Arab Americans has also been developing in recent years.

Although Dyker Heights has a store for convenience items, residents seem content to visit nearby neighborhoods to make larger purchases. A quiet and lovely haven, Dyker Heights remains primarily a place to relax and enjoy family and community.

The whole neighborhood dresses up for Christmas in Dyker Heights

East

Sounds, sights, and flavors of the Caribbean tantalize visitors to East Flatbush. Tin awnings shade first- and second-floor porches of red-brick homes; lush flowers adorn tiny front yards; and the intoxicating aroma of jerk chicken, oxtail soup, plantains, pastries, fresh rotis, and codfish drifts out of restaurants, roti shops, and bakeries. Street vendors tempt passersby with freshly cut sugarcane, coconuts, mangoes, ginger beer, and sorrel drinks. Local Haitian ska bands, warming up for performances in the neighborhood nightclubs, add their rhythms to the mix. And for dessert, Taste of the Tropics shops (one of the oldest businesses in East Flatbush) offer homemade Caribbean fruit-flavored ice cream.

East Flatbush is a dynamic neighborhood that has experienced tremendous growth since the early 1980s. Until recently the area was considered an

This Ecuadorean barber shop has been doing business in the neighborhood for some thirty years

amalgam of smaller neighborhoods—Remsen Village, Rugby, Wingate, Farragut, and Erasmus, as well as the large apartment complex of Vanderveer Estates—but it is now a unified and primarily Caribbean American community that embraces these earlier boundaries. Although the names of the

Flatbush

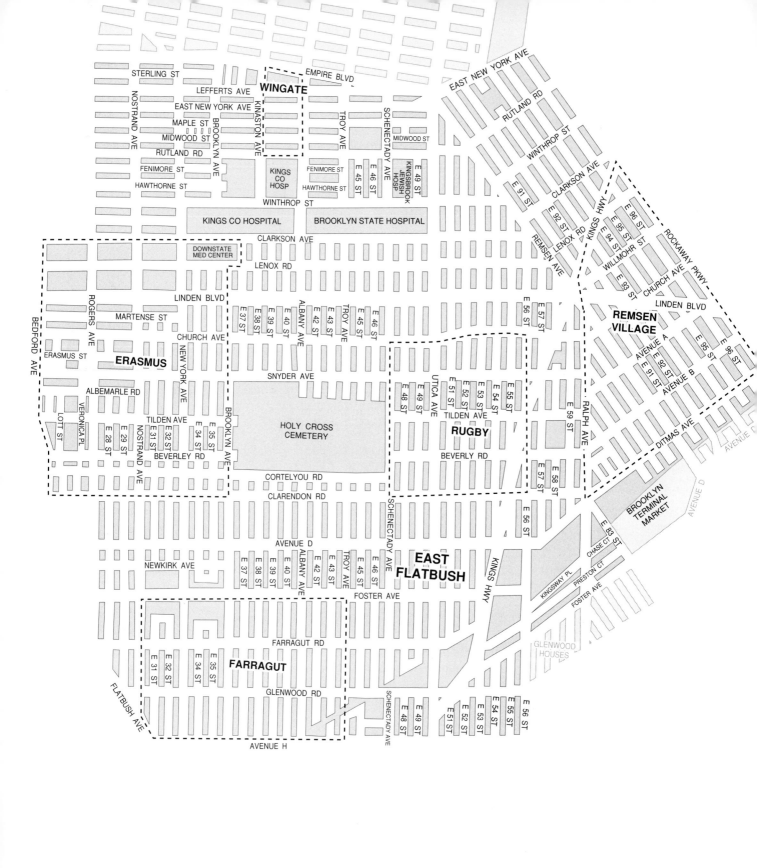

smaller neighborhoods still appear on local schools, libraries, and post office branches, only Erasmus—located just south of Prospect-Lefferts Gardens, near Flatbush's famed Erasmus Hall High School—remains a recognizable entity within East Flatbush, perhaps because it is organized by the 20-year-old Erasmus Neighborhood Federation.

One of the most obvious changes in East Flatbush during this recent period of development has been the appearance of additional churches. Every block seems to hold at least one church: stores, homes—even movie theaters and meeting halls—have been transformed into houses of worship. During the summer months, many of these churches hold tent revivals in local parks, parking lots, and private homes. The music of these celebrations can be heard for blocks.

The western section of today's East Flatbush was a part of the original

NEIGHBORHOOD FACTS

■ Pieter Claesen Wyckoff House, on Clarendon Road and Ralph Avenue, was originally built in 1652, with additions made around 1740 and 1820. Wyckoff descendants lived in the house until 1901, and in 1965 the building was the first to be landmarked in New York City. In 1969 the house was donated to the Historic House Trust, a private arm of the New York City Parks Department; it was restored in the 1980s as a museum depicting farm life in Brooklyn during the seventeenth and eighteenth centuries. In 2003, the Wyckoff Association acquired a barn (1800; used 1850–2000) from a branch of the Wyckoff family. A Brooklyn barn raising is expected in 2005.
■ From 1948 to 1949, baseball legend Jackie Robinson, who pioneered the integration of the sport, lived at 5224 Tilden Avenue. The house is now a national historic landmark.

Dutch town of Flatbush; parts of the eastern side were within the original Dutch town of Flatlands. Before the late 1890s, much of the land was used for farming. Development of East Flatbush into residential neighborhoods began at around the turn of the twentieth century after Henry Meyer's Germania Land Company purchased 65 acres of farmland (including some of the Vanderveer homestead) in 1892 in anticipation of a promised subway extension and consolidation with other Brooklyn neighborhoods.

An early area within East Flatbush to be developed was **Rugby,** a name bestowed on the area by the developers in the 1890s, when it was covered by potato farms. In 1900 the real-estate firm Wood, Harmon and Company purchased many acres of farmland and made a deal with Brooklyn Rapid Transit that the firm would build 50 houses within a year if the transit company would extend the trolley service.

Rugby grew even larger after 1912, when the Interborough Rapid Transit started to extend the subway along

An old movie theater turned tropical deli, Nostrand Avenue at Clarkson Avenue

NEIGHBORHOOD PROFILE

Boundaries: <u>East Flatbush</u>: from Rogers Avenue to Clarkson Avenue to Bedford Avenue to Clarendon Road back to Rogers Avenue to Flatbush Avenue on the west to Rockaway Parkway through Brooklyn Terminal Market to East 83rd Street to Foster Avenue and East 56th Street on the east, from Empire Boulevard and East New York Avenue on the north to Avenue H on the south. <u>Rugby</u>: from Schenectady Avenue on the west to East 56th Street on the east, from Church Avenue on the north to Clarendon Road on the south. <u>Remsen Village</u>: from Ralph Avenue on the west to Rockaway Parkway on the east, from Kings Highway on the north to Ditmas Avenue on the south. <u>Wingate</u>: from Kingston Avenue on the west to Albany Avenue on the east, from Empire Boulevard on the north to Rutland Road on the south. <u>Farragut</u>: from Nostrand Avenue on the west to Troy Avenue on the east, from Foster Avenue on the north to Avenue H on the south. <u>Erasmus</u>: from Bedford Avenue on the west to Brooklyn Avenue on the east, from Clarkson Avenue on the north to Clarendon Road on the south.
Subway: <u>IRT 2</u>: Sterling St., Winthrop St., Church Ave., Beverley Rd., Newkirk Ave., Flatbush Ave./Brooklyn College <u>IRT 5</u>: Sterling St., Winthrop St., Church Ave., Beverley Rd., Newkirk Ave., Flatbush Ave./Brooklyn College
Bus: <u>B43</u>: Empire Blvd. <u>B12</u>: Clarkson Ave./East New York Ave. <u>B35</u>: Church Ave. <u>B8</u>: Avenue D <u>B6</u>: Glenwood Rd./Avenue H <u>B49</u>: Rogers Ave. <u>B44</u>: Nostrand Ave./New York Ave. <u>B46</u>: Utica Ave. <u>B7</u>: Kings Highway/Lenox Rd. <u>B78</u>: Ralph Ave./Clarkson Ave.
Libraries: Brooklyn Public Library Clarendon Branch (2035 Nostrand Ave.), East Flatbush Branch (9612 Church Ave.), Rugby Branch (1000 Utica Ave.)
Museums: Pieter Claesen Wyckoff House Museum (Clarendon Rd. and Ralph Ave.)
Community Board: No. 17
Police Precinct: 67th Precinct (2820 Snyder Ave.), 71st Precinct (421 Empire Blvd.)
Fire Department: Engine 248 (2900 Snyder Ave.), Engine 310 Ladder 174 (5105 and 5101 Snyder Ave.)
Hospitals and Clinics: University Hospital of Brooklyn–SUNY Health Science Center at Brooklyn (445 Lenox Rd.), Kings County Hospital Center (451 Clarkson Ave.), Kingsbrook Jewish Medical Center (9585 Schenectady Ave.), The Samuel and Bertha Schulman Institute for Nursing and Rehabilitation–The Brookdale University Hospital and Medical Center (555 Rockaway Pkwy.), Rutland Nursing Home at the Kingsbrook Jewish Medical Center–David Minkin Rehabilitation Institute (585 Schenectady Ave.)

Nostrand Avenue. Most of the one- and two-family detached and semidetached houses that still stand in East Flatbush within the old boundaries of Rugby were built during the 1920s and 1930s. A few apartment buildings were constructed after World War II. From the 1920s to the 1960s, most residents were Italian Americans and American-born Jews. Utica and Church Avenues have remained major commercial centers.

In the late 1930s the developer Fred Trump, father of Donald Trump, built bungalows on Remsen Avenue near East New York and Clarkson Avenues, on the site that was once the winter home of the Barnum and Bailey Circus. **Remsen Village** took its name from this avenue, which bisects the area and has always been the neighborhood's main attraction for shoppers. Small businesses and shopping areas also line Ditmas Avenue and Linden Boulevard. Remsen Village's modest attached and semi-attached brick homes were built in the early twentieth century to house its growing Jewish population, who remained in the area until they started to move into the outer suburbs in the 1970s, a trend that continues today. More recent immigrants are mainly from Haiti, Jamaica, and Guyana.

Wingate had originally been called Pig Town, after the many small animal farms in the area, but it was renamed in 1954, when General George Wingate High School, named for the founder and president of the National Rifle Association, was built on Kinaston Avenue. From the 1920s to the 1950s, detached and semidetached wooden frame houses, row houses, and walk-up apartment buildings sprang up in Wingate. Two-story townhouses with interior gardens and courtyards were built in the 1920s on Miami, Tampa, and Palm Courts, north of Kings County Hospital. Although Wingate's population for the most part mirrors that of the rest of East Flatbush, an ever shrinking enclave of Orthodox Jews still lives in its northern section.

Wingate is known for its expansive parks, including the Wingate Playground, Alexander Metz Playground, and All Boys' Athletic Field. Bright and tasteful stores along Nostrand Avenue and Empire Boulevard attract residents and visitors alike.

Farragut is named for Admiral David G. Farragut, who distinguished himself in the Mexican and Civil Wars.

School groups crossing Linden Boulevard at Nostrand Avenue in Erasmus

From 1925 to 1950 most residents of Farragut were Jews and Italian Americans who lived in one- and two-family detached and semidetached houses built between 1920 and 1930. By the 1990s most residents were African American and Latin American. The area has fewer Caribbean residents than do other parts of East Flatbush.

Farragut changed radically after World War II, when many apartment buildings sprang up. Until 1950, a six-acre plot of land called Farragut Woods had remained home to otters, raccoons, muskrats, and the Flatbush Water Works. The need for housing led to the construction of Vanderveer Estates. This middle-income apartment complex of 59 buildings is home to more than 12,000 residents, most of whom are African American or Latin American. Not surprisingly for land that supported aquatic animals, Vanderveer Estates sits atop many underground streams and wells; even today, when it rains heavily, water seeps up and floods the subway between the Flatbush Avenue and Beverley Road stops.

The area around Erasmus Hall High School informally defined the neighborhood of

● **Kings County Hospital**
In 1831 Kings County Hospital was founded as a one-room infirmary. By the 1870s it had become the core of the county buildings, and by 1939 it was the third largest hospital in the United States, a distinction it retained until the mid-1990s, when it served nearly a million people each year. In 1956 the hospital became affiliated with the State University of New York–Downstate Medical Center, now called University Hospital.

Today many of the neighborhood's Haitian, Caribbean, and Jamaican residents work as health care providers at Kings County Hospital and University Hospital as well as at other East Flatbush hospitals like Kingsbrook Jewish Medical Center and Kingsboro Psychiatric Center. Indeed, although a mixed-income area, East Flatbush has one of the highest concentrations in New York City of Caribbean, Caribbean American, and West Indian doctors and nurses (as well as teachers and lawyers).

Erasmus from the time the school was founded in 1786, but it became known as a part of East Flatbush in the late 1970s as residents banded together to improve their community.

From the 1960s to the 1980s, a shift in population from Italian American and Jewish to Caribbean and Caribbean American led to the development of a great many new neighborhood associations. The groups worked to foil real-estate agents' blockbusting and to encourage cooperation between new and old residents. The slogan of one

Pieter Claesen Wyckoff House (1652) on
Clarendon Road and Ralph Avenue
(Brooklyn Historical Society)

local alliance was "United we can see
it through; united there is nothing we
can't do."

By the 1980s East Flatbush was
well on its way to becoming almost entirely composed of residents with ties
to the Caribbean, Jamaica, Guyana,
and Trinidad and Tobago. In the late
1980s and early 1990s the Haitian
population doubled, and many of these
new residents have settled in the area
from Flatbush Avenue in Bedford-
Stuyvesant to Nostrand Avenue and
from Linden Boulevard to Church Avenue. Ten of the 12 Catholic churches in
East Flatbush have congregations that
are almost completely Haitian.

Plans are under way to revitalize the
"Junction," where Flatbush Avenue
and Nostrand Avenue intersect and
where the Number 2 and Number 5
trains make their last Brooklyn stop,
near Brooklyn College. Many hope that
this area will become a major retail
attraction that will lure central Brooklyn's shoppers away from the south
shore's Kings Plaza and rejuvenate
East Flatbush's commercial economy.

East

Can grassroots community efforts renew a neighborhood that has faced persistent challenges? Residents of East New York not only know the answer; they live it. During the past decade, the neighborhood, for many years a partially abandoned, run-down haven for drug dealers and drug users, has regained its warmth and vitality: community gardens offer a shady gathering place, and residents once again sit outside to catch up on local news and gossip. Perhaps the poorest residents of the neighborhood have made the most impressive turnaround. They have been empowered to reclaim their neighborhood; and to accelerate these improvements, they have extended a hand to the community's new, enthusiastic homeowners.

A reduction in crime and the construction of affordable housing have contributed greatly to East New York's revitalization. Brooklynites' fading memory of the old East New York has been replaced by a positive new image of residents working together for the betterment of the neighborhood—and themselves.

Some residents feel that East New York includes the smaller neighborhoods of Cypress Hills, Highland Park, City Line, Starrett at Spring Creek, and the enclave called New Lots. In this book, Highland Park and City Line are identified as smaller neighborhoods in Cypress Hills, while New Lots and Starrett at Spring Creek are discussed here.

East New York's neighborhood organizations focus on supporting and nurturing with recreational and educational programs the more than 60,000 children and young adults who live in the area. They have also singled out the lack of adult literacy as a key obstacle to overcome: almost half of the neighborhood's adults have not gradu-

NEIGHBORHOOD FACTS

■ Since around 1970, East New York residents have gathered each September at the annual East New York Street Fair and Music Festival, held on New Lots Avenue. For the past quarter-century or so, the Latin Souls Little League has also celebrated their opening day in May with a parade in East New York.

■ Science fiction writer Issac Asimov and composer George Gershwin once lived in East New York. Actor Jimmy Smits, known for his role in the 1990s television show *NYPD Blue,* grew up in the neighborhood during the 1960s.

■ In January 1998 carousel building—a Brooklyn specialty—returned to the borough through the efforts of Fabricon Carousel Company, located in East New York. Among its projects, the only manufacturer of carousels in New York City is creating a carousel designed by artist Red Grooms for export to Nashville, Tennessee.

New York

Community garden at Livonia Avenue and Schenck Avenue on the edge of the old neighborhood of New Lots

ated from high school. Economic revitalization continues to be a priority as well. East New York's residents are working to develop retail establishments in the neighborhood. One recent success is the 1998 opening of a 14-screen movie theater on Linden Boulevard. Residents hope that the multiplex theater (one of whose screening rooms is named for photographer Gordon Parks), built by National Amusement, will attract more businesses.

The area that is today East New York was once called Ostwout (east woods). In the 1670s farmers from Flatbush moved east seeking new land and renamed the area **New Lots,** to contrast with a part of Flatbush near the village center, which was then called Old Lots. Village streets were laid out in 1677. Just before the American

Revolution's Battle of Brooklyn began, colonial forces were posted throughout the eastern farmlands. Unfamiliar with the rural landscape of the East Woods, the soldiers accidentally allowed British forces to pass through at the northwestern edge of East New York, close to the junction of Atlantic and Alabama Avenues today. As a result, the British were able to attack the Americans from the rear, winning the battle.

After the Battle of Brooklyn, the area continued to be farmed by the Dutch. The New Lots Reformed Dutch Church, which is also called the New Lots Community Church, was built in 1824, and this landmarked building still stands on New Lots Avenue. Headstones in the church's graveyard are engraved with the names of some of the most prominent families of the

area. The section of East New York around this church is even today referred to by some as the New Lots area of East New York.

New Lots remained mostly rural until 1835, when John Pitkin, a wealthy Connecticut merchant, bought land north of New Lots Avenue and named the area East New York because it was at the eastern end of metropolitan New York City. Pitkin built a shoe factory at Pitkin Avenue and Williams Avenue. His company seemed poised to grow and attract other industries and residents, but the Panic of 1837 kept it from large expansion. Residents of the area at the time were mostly Pitkin's employees.

In 1852 New Lots was incorporated as a town, and its land included what is today East New York, Cypress Hills, and parts of Brownsville. In the late 1800s a large German population settled in East New York and worked at the Union Course Race Track in Woodhaven, Queens. These German residents founded the Deutsche Evangelische Lutherische St. Johannes Kirche, which was built circa 1885 on New Jersey Avenue and is today Grace Baptist Church. In 1886 New Lots was annexed by the City of Brooklyn.

After the Williamsburg Bridge opened in 1903 and the Interborough Rapid Transit subway reached New Lots in 1922, East New York expanded. Over the next 20 years German, Italian, Russian, Polish, and Lithuanian immigrants moved into the neighborhood, and by the 1940s a large part of

112 East New York was densely populated. The buildings were mostly walk-up apartments and row houses, but side streets were dotted with freestanding houses designed for two, three, and four families (many of these homes still stand today). There are also a number of large housing complexes in East New York, including the Louis H. Pink Houses, Cypress Hills Housing, Linden Houses, Linden Plaza Houses, and Boulevard Housing.

As nearby Brownsville was changed by urban renewal in the 1950s and 1960s, many African Americans moved to East New York. Subsequently, many longtime residents left the neighborhood. The area experienced a period of decline, exacerbated in part by corruption in the U.S. Department of Housing and Urban Development, which led to foreclosures on housing by the federal government. The vacant buildings encouraged arson and so did the rioting that broke out sporadically because of high unemployment and other difficulties. By 1966 more than 80 percent of East New York's residents had been in the area only a short time.

The community began working to rebuild and redevelop East New York in the late 1970s, but initially progress was slow. The East Brooklyn Industrial Park was created in 1980 in a 70-acre site in the middle of Powell Street in Brownsville and Atlantic, Sheffield, and Sutter Avenues. By the mid-1980s, federally subsidized housing for the neighborhood's elderly residents had been built; more than 100 buildings

NEIGHBORHOOD PROFILE

Boundaries: <u>East New York</u>: from Van Sinderen Avenue on the west to Conduit Avenue and the Queens County line on the east, from Atlantic Avenue on the north to the Belt Parkway on the south. <u>New Lots</u>: from Pennsylvania/Granville Payne Avenue on the west to Fountain Street on the east, from New Lots Avenue on the north to Linden Boulevard on the south. <u>Starrett at Spring Creek</u>: from Louisiana Avenue on the west to Van Siclen Avenue on the east, from Flatlands Avenue on the north to the Belt Parkway on the south.
Subway: <u>IND A and C</u>: Liberty Ave., Van Siclen Ave., Shepherd Ave., Euclid Ave. <u>Canarsie Line L</u>: Atlantic Ave., Sutter Ave., Livonia Ave., New Lots Ave.
Bus: <u>BQ24</u>: Atlantic Ave. <u>B12</u>: Liberty Ave. <u>B14</u>: Sutter Ave. <u>B20</u>: Linden Blvd. <u>BQ8</u>: Pitkin Ave. <u>BQ7</u>: Pitkin Ave. <u>B13</u>: Crescent St./Fountain St. <u>B15</u>: New Lots Ave. <u>B20</u>: Pennsylvania Ave. <u>B6</u>: Cozine Ave./Ashford St. <u>B83</u>: Van Siclen St./Vandalia Ave. <u>B60</u>: Williams Ave. <u>B40</u>: Liberty Ave.
Libraries: Brooklyn Public Library New Lots Branch (New Lots Ave. at Barbey St.), Spring Creek Branch (Flatlands Ave. near New Jersey Ave.)
Community Board: No. 5
Police Precinct: 75th Precinct (1000 Sutter Ave.)
Fire Department: Engine 225 Ladder 107 (799 Lincoln Ave.), Engine 236 (998 Liberty Ave.), Engine 290 Ladder 103 (480 Sheffield Ave.)
Hospitals and Clinics: Brookdale Family Care Centers (1110 Pennsylvania Ave., 2554 Linden Blvd., 465 New Lots Ave.), Nephrology Foundation of Brooklyn, East Unit (63 Pennsylvania Ave.)

had been renovated; and 50 owner-occupied homes had been constructed.

During the early and mid-1980s, a consortium of local organizations, church congregations, and homeowner associations working with the Council of East Brooklyn Churches began to develop private houses in East New York. Many of these Nehemiah Houses (named after the biblical reformer)—two-story one-family row houses created by Reverend Johnny Ray Youngblood through his St. Paul Community

Baptist Church and the Council of East Brooklyn Churches—were built on Blake and Dumont Avenues between Cleveland and Warwick Streets. More than a thousand of these new homes have been built in East New York, and more than 600 additional houses are planned by the year 2000. All of the completed houses are occupied, and on blocks where the first houses were built, the young trees now supply welcome shade.

In the mid-1980s, immigrants from

New Lots Reformed Dutch Church (1824)
at 630 New Lots Avenue

the Dominican Republic, Jamaica,
Guyana, Haiti, Honduras, Ecuador,
Panama, and Trinidad and Tobago began to settle in East New York. As of
the mid-1990s, the neighborhood still
had many African American and Latin
American residents, as well as a small
number of inhabitants of Asian descent. Soaring crime rates during this
period have since been overcome by a
combination of community policing

Starrett at Spring Creek, 46 apartment
buildings on 153 acres between Flatlands
Avenue and the Belt Parkway

and the increased involvement of community groups. The main commercial areas of East New York are Pitkin Avenue, New Lots Avenue, and Pennsylvania Avenue.

The area south of Linden Boulevard remained rural, sporting farms even as the rest of the neighborhood began to change. This area was sometimes

Mural on Blake Avenue and Linwood Street relating the history of East New York

Looking west along Atlantic Avenue from Georgia Avenue, 1923 (Brian Merlis Collection)

called Nanny Goat Boulevard because of the local goat farms; residents recall buying local eggs south of Linden Boulevard as late as the mid-1960s. In 1972 construction began on the 153-acre Starrett City (now **Spring Creek Towers**)—46 apartment buildings, each with as many as 20 stories. This land had originally been developed by the National Kinney Corporation and was designed by Herman J. Jessor as

Twin Pines Village. When the Starrett Corporation took over the project, they named it Starrett City, and in 1989 the name changed to Starrett at Spring Creek, though it is now known as Spring Creek Towers.

Spring Creek Towers is the largest federally assisted housing project in the United States, and it has its own power plant, private security force, and cable television station. In 1975, when

the apartments were first rented, 65 percent were reserved for Caucasian residents and 35 percent for non-Caucasian residents. It seemed that not-for-profit developers feared that if no quota existed, Starrett would soon become 100 percent black. Was it more important to provide low-income housing, or integrated housing? In 1979 the quota system was abolished. In recent years, many of Starrett's residents have been Russian and Eastern European immigrants, demonstrating how the ethnic circumstances of today are dramatically different from those that existed in the 1970s. In 1994 Spring Creek Towers had 20,000 residents.

Today East New York residents consider the development where these buildings stand interspersed with ball fields, parks, and shopping areas a part of their community and shop at many of Starrett's stores.

Flatbush

Flatbush is a mosaic of architectural styles and ethnic and racial backgrounds. Large Victorian mansions with yards and porches, owned by well-to-do young families, merge gracefully with apartment buildings that attract many of Brooklyn's newest immigrants. Sprinkled into the mix are small attached brick homes, Art Deco apartment buildings, neighborhood shops, and, along its major thoroughfares, a string of brightly decorated discount stores.

As members of a large neighborhood located in the heart of Brooklyn, residents of Flatbush have perhaps always searched for ways to harmonize eclectic perspectives. After the Dutch acquired the land from the Canarsee Indians (ca. 1652), the Eskemoppas Sachem of the Rockaway Indians proclaimed that Flatbush belonged to them. To avoid conflict, the Dutch settlers paid for the land a second time. And for some time boundary disputes with the town of Brooklyn kept residents wonder-

NEIGHBORHOOD PROFILE

Boundaries: <u>Flatbush</u>: from Coney Island Avenue, Beverley Road, East 19th Street, and Church Avenue on the west to Bedford Avenue, Clarendon Road, and Rogers Avenue on the east, from Parkside Avenue on the north to Avenue H on the south. <u>Ditmas Park</u>: from East 16th Street on the west to Ocean Avenue on the east, from Dorchester Road on the north to Newkirk Avenue on the south. <u>Ditmas Park West</u>: from Coney Island Avenue on the west to East 16th Street on the east, from Dorchester Road on the north to Newkirk Avenue on the south. <u>Albemarle-Kenmore Terraces</u>: from East 21st Street on the west to Flatbush Avenue on the east, from Church Avenue on the north to Albemarle Road on the south. <u>Beverley Square East</u>: from East 17th Street on the west to East 19th Street on the east, from Beverley Road on the north to Cortelyou Road on the south. <u>Beverley Square West</u>: from Argyle Road on the west to East 17th Street on the east, from Beverley Road on the north to Cortelyou Road on the south. <u>Fiske Terrace</u>: from the Brighton Line subway tracks on the west to Ocean Avenue on the east, from Glenwood Road on the north to Avenue H on the south. <u>South Midwood</u>: from Ocean Avenue on the west to Bedford Avenue on the east, from Foster Avenue on the north to Glenwood Road on the south. <u>West Midwood</u>: from Coney Island Avenue on the west to the Brighton Line subway tracks on the east, from Foster Avenue on the north to Avenue H on the south. <u>Midwood Park</u>: from the Brighton Line subway tracks on the west to Ocean Avenue on the east, from Foster Avenue on the north to Glenwood Road on the south. <u>Caton Park</u>: from Rugby Road on the west to East 16th Street on the east, from Caton Avenue on the north to Church Avenue on the south.
Subway: <u>Brighton Line D</u>: Parkside Ave., Church Ave., Beverley Rd., Cortelyou Rd., Newkirk Ave., Avenue H <u>Brighton Line Q</u>: Church Ave., Newkirk Ave.
Bus: <u>B16</u>: Caton Ave. <u>B35</u>: Church Ave. <u>B23</u>: Cortelyou Rd. <u>B8</u>: Foster Ave. <u>B68</u>: Coney Island Ave. <u>Bx29</u>: Coney Island Ave. <u>B41</u>: Flatbush Ave. <u>B49</u>: Bedford Ave./Rogers Ave.
Libraries: Brooklyn Public Library Cortelyou Branch (Cortelyou Rd. at Argyle Rd.), Flatbush Branch (Linden Blvd. near Flatbush Ave.)
Community Board: No. 14
Police Precinct: 70th Precinct (154 Lawrence Ave.)
Fire Department: Engine 255 Ladder 157 (1367 Rogers Ave.), Engine 281 Ladder 147 (1210 Cortelyou Rd.)
Hospitals and Clinics: The Brooklyn Hospital Center, Caledonian Campus (100 Parkside Ave.), New York Congregational Home for the Aged (123 Linden Blvd.), Brookdale Family Care Center (1095 Flatbush Ave.)

ing whether Flatbush's northern boundary was at the crest of the hills or nearer the bottom of the declivity.

Named from the Dutch word *vlackebos* (wooded plain), Flatbush was in the center of Brooklyn's Midwout, or middle woods. What are today the neighborhoods of New Lots (see East New York), East New York, and Cypress Hills were all within Flatbush but were considered the Ostwout (east woods), to distinguish them from Midwout. Other remnants of Dutch names can be found as well. Today's corner of Empire Boulevard and Flatbush Avenue was once called Steenraap (stone gathering place) for its stony soil. A bit east was Steenbakkery, after Steenbakkery Pond—a pool of water that can still be seen on an 1842 map of the area.

As late as the 1860s and 1870s, gently turning windmills dotted the landscape; perhaps the only indication then of Flatbush's importance as one of the first six towns of Brooklyn was its courthouse, established as early as 1686. But change was imminent. The arrival of the Brooklyn, Flatbush and Coney Island Railroad in 1878 made the land attractive to developers.

The 1894 incorporation of Flatbush into the City of Brooklyn encouraged even more development. The area was converted from farmland into fashion-

Four- and six-story apartment buildings at Albemarle Road and Ocean Avenue

118 able suburban enclaves, which were originally named Vanderveer Park, Manhattan Terrace, Matthews Park, Slocum Park, and Yale Park. Only parts of these initial developments remain, but this entire section of Flatbush is now popularly referred to as Victorian Flatbush. Even today, many residents of the mostly intact developments consider the name of their development to be their "neighborhood" name.

In the 1920s large apartment buildings were built along Ocean Avenue as far south as Kings Highway.

The suburban developments and older row houses on side streets were left untouched, but between 1920 and 1940 almost all of the other land in Flatbush was filled with four- and six-story apartment houses, both walk-ups and elevator buildings.

The new availability of apartments attracted new residents to Flatbush. Many of the apartment dwellers were Jewish immigrants who had moved from the Lower East Side or from more crowded Brooklyn neighborhoods like Williamsburg and Brownsville. As the neighborhood's population soared, Flatbush Avenue became a busy shopping area. During the 1920s and 1930s, Flatbush also had a wonderful array of movie theaters: the Albemarle, the Astor, the College, the Cortelyou, the Parkside, the RKO Kenmore, and the Loew's Kings (the largest) drew crowds every weekend.

Ebbets Field, where the Brooklyn Dodgers played from 1913 to 1957, was technically located in Crown Heights, but Flatbush developed a romantic and lasting association with both the team and the ballpark. The attention they brought to Flatbush helped earn it a reputation as the quintessential Brooklyn neighborhood.

After World War II, many of the children of the original apartment dwellers moved out of the neighborhood, but others moved into the large, romantic Victorian houses. Other population shifts occurred as well.

Much of the Jewish population of Flatbush was replaced by newer immigrants, many from the Caribbean, Pakistan, Afghanistan, Cambodia, Korea, Central America, and the Soviet Union. By the 1980s most immigrants were arriving from the Caribbean, and one-third of all immigrants were Haitian. (During this period, the Haitian immigrants living in Flatbush made up almost a quarter of all of the Haitian immigrants arriving in New York City.) Other immigrants arrived from Jamaica, Guyana, Trinidad and Tobago, Grenada, Panama, Barbados, St. Vincent and the Grenadines, Asia, and the Dominican Republic. From 1970 to 1980 the neighborhood was transformed from 85 percent Caucasian to 80 percent non-Caucasian. Nearly all of these new arrivals lived in the apartment buildings of Flatbush.

It took some time for all of these groups to learn to live together in a single neighborhood. But a peaceful coexistence was achieved, in part because landlords and homeowners remained throughout the changes and because the immigrants helped create a new community that included longtime residents. The result of this community building is a vibrant and beautiful neighborhood.

Albemarle Road at Ocean Avenue

Albemarle Terrace as seen in a *Brooklyn Eagle* postcard (Brooklyn Historical Society)

120   Flatbush Avenue, for example, is recovering from the effects of "white flight" to become closer to the way it was during its heyday in the late 1960s and early 1970s, when from Prospect Park to Foster Avenue—a short mile and a half—it was overflowing with more than 500 stores. Merchants have banded together to spur development, and a recently built municipal parking lot is likely to encourage shoppers to sample the diverse array of cultures represented by the new small shops. Among the more famous Flatbush businesses are New York City's first Sears (1925), at Bedford Avenue and Clarendon Road; Ebinger's Bakery (1898–1972), on Bedford Avenue; and Loehmann's (1921), on Duryea Place off Flatbush Avenue.

In 1990 tensions flared between some Flatbush natives, mostly Caribbean blacks, who perceived Korean grocers in the neighborhood as taking away their livelihood; in return, the

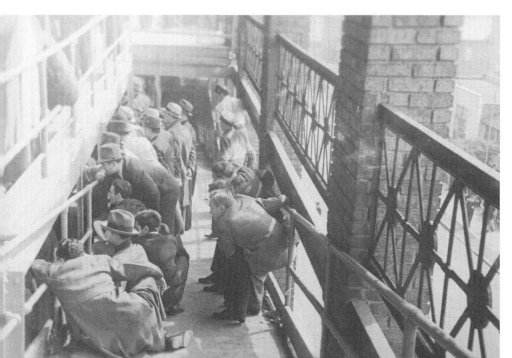

Koreans accused the blacks of stealing. When a black woman was accused of shoplifting, a boycott of the grocery stores followed. Political action and community building finally ended the hostilities. But even isolated events of discord cannot undermine the fundamental respect for one another that various ethnic groups share. Every fall residents of Flatbush celebrate their

Watching a game from the ramps at Ebbets Field (Brian Merlis Collection)

● Erasmus Hall

Erasmus Hall Academy (now Erasmus Hall High School and Academy of the Arts), founded in 1786 with the help of a group that included Alexander Hamilton, John Jay, and Aaron Burr, was the first secondary school chartered by New York State. In 1896 the institution became a public school—the second-oldest in the United States. Today the original wooden clapboard building, a New York City landmark, stands in the courtyard of the neo-Gothic high school, which was erected early in the twentieth century at 911 Flatbush Avenue. Entertainers Neil Diamond, Barry Manilow, and Barbra Streisand—as well as chess champion Bobby Fischer—are among the school's famous graduates.

unity at the Flatbush Frolic along Cortelyou Road.

Several planned developments built at the turn of the century retain an autonomous perspective because of block associations; their descriptions follow. Some of the more distinct of these have their own entries in this book (Prospect Park South, Prospect-Lefferts Gardens, and Midwood). Three of the original developed neighborhoods within Victorian Flatbush—Ditmas Park, Albemarle Terrace, and Kenmore Terrace— are now landmarked enclaves. But the other small neighborhoods, Beverley Square East and West, Ditmas Park West, Fiske Terrace, South Midwood, West Midwood, Midwood Park, and Caton Park, also retain much of their original character. Although apartment houses were built between some of the

large houses in the 1920s and 1930s, residents of Victorian Flatbush neighborhoods have continually banded together to maintain these tiny neighborhoods and the feeling of small-town living they provide.

Ditmas Park, now a New York City historic district, was created in 1902 and is its own neighborhood within Flatbush. Developed by builder Lewis H. Pounds and architect Arlington Isham, Ditmas Park was unusual in that all of its sewers, sidewalks, paved streets, and landscaping were designed before a single home was constructed. The development team even had the area graded so that the planned community would have level, smooth land. Ditmas Park is filled with freestanding, single-family homes with wide front lawns. Most of the towering shade trees that line the streets were planted when the neighborhood was built. Some of the most spectacular of the neighborhood's 175 homes are on Ocean Avenue, and East 16th Street has the longest row of bungalow-type houses in Brooklyn, all built in 1908 and 1909. After completing Ditmas Park, Pounds built **Ditmas Park West**, a mirror neighborhood, on the opposite side of the Brighton railroad tracks (now the subway line).

The two dead-end streets of Albemarle and Kenmore Terraces are just off busy Flatbush Avenue. These two cul-de-sacs have been designated a New York City historic district. To enter these blocks is to step back to the early 1900s. **Albemarle Terrace**'s red-brick row houses have a colonial look and are two to three stories high.

Erasmus Hall High School

By 1918, when construction began on **Kenmore Terrace,** automobiles were prevalent in Brooklyn. The houses on Kenmore Terrace reflect this influence: they are among the first urban row houses to have built-in garages. The style of the houses on the southern side are derived from the English Garden City style, an architectural form that paralleled the rise in popularity of the car.

In 1898 T. B. Ackerson began buying land in Flatbush and building houses with his own construction company. **Beverley Square East** was his first development; he went on to build **Beverley Square West** after 1901. No two Beverley Square East houses are the same because they were built to order. Ackerson was well aware of the value of public transportation: he had two subway stations established only a block apart (on Beverley and Cortelyou Roads), making them the two closest stations on the Brighton Line subway. Ackerson's own home was on Marlborough Road in Beverley Square West. The developer also purchased a huge tract of land from George and Elizabeth Fiske for $285,000—less than the cost of a large house in Victorian Flatbush today— and constructed **Fiske Terrace.**

Henry Meyer, who built **South Midwood,** designed **West Midwood** as well. In 1904 Meyer sold land to Ackerson, who built two houses for his family within West Midwood, on East 12th Street and Glenwood Road. The population of Flatbush was growing so

Single-family homes on East 18th Street in Midwood Park

quickly at that time that only 18 months after construction began, all the homes had been sold.

Midwood Park, completed before 1908 by John R. Corbin Company, is notable because it is the only community within Victorian Flatbush that has repeated architecture. Corbin's houses were the first mass-produced houses of the day, and he boasted that he could build a thousand houses a year in this manner using basic models on which variations could be made. On East 18th Street is the Knickerbocker Field Club, a tennis establishment that at one time offered members a huge Victorian clubhouse to relax in. The club still stands, but the clubhouse was destroyed by fire.

Caton Park, with approximately 50 freestanding homes, sits just south of the Prospect Park Parade Grounds and just north of Prospect Park South. It was developed by a number of people between 1902 and 1909: John Sawkins, one of the Ditmas Park West builders, built the houses on East 16th Street and the houses on the northern end (up to No. 25) on Marlborough Road; Edward Strong oversaw construction on houses on both sides of Rugby Road; and William A. A. Brown built the houses on the south end of Marlborough Road.

In the early 1900s and 1920s, when these houses were new, a small African American community coalesced to the east of the large homes. Servants of the homeowners, these residents wished to live close enough to walk to the "big houses," so they settled on Lott Street and Veronica Place. The community founded Salem Missionary Baptist Church on Veronica Place in 1910. The church is now located on East 21st Street.

Flatlands

If the subway and bridges to Manhattan have accelerated the pace of living in much of Brooklyn, it is perhaps not surprising that Flatlands is serene. Long ago, however, the neighborhood was a center of activity. The sparsely populated marshland settlement was in turmoil the night of August 26, 1776, when Lord Cornwallis and his British troops marched down Kings Highway on their way to outflank the Americans at the Battle of Brooklyn. And the Ascot Heath, a flat racetrack built in 1781, was all the rage for eighteenth-century New Yorkers. Now, away from the hubbub of shopping districts and

Flatlands Dutch Reformed Church in 1907 (Brooklyn Historical Society)

subway stops, Flatlands is a small, quiet, residential oasis near the middle of the borough.

One of the original six towns of Brooklyn, Flatlands was at one time so expansive that it encompassed what are today Marine Park, Mill Basin, Bergen Beach, Georgetown (see Bergen Beach), Canarsie, East Flatbush, and Starrett at Spring Creek (see East New York). Today blocks of one- and two-family homes with driveways hint at the importance of the automobile to this community's development.

The rich soil of Flatlands was a lure

NEIGHBORHOOD PROFILE

Boundaries: Flatlands: from Nostrand Avenue on the west to Ralph Avenue on the east (except for the Glenwood Houses, which are considered a part of Canarsie), from Avenue H on the north to the southern border formed by Flatlands Avenue, between Nostrand Avenue and Flatbush Avenue, and Avenue T, between Flatbush Avenue and Ralph Avenue. Futurama: From Utica Avenue on the west to Ralph Avenue on the east, from Avenue J on the north to Avenue L on the south.
Subway: None
Bus: B7: Kings Highway B6: Avenue H B82: Flatlands Ave. B41: Avenue N B100: Fillmore Ave./Avenue T B035: Flatbush Ave. B41: Flatbush Ave. B78: Ralph Ave.
Libraries: Brooklyn Public Library Flatlands Branch (Flatbush Ave. at Avenue P), Paerdegat Branch (850 East 59th St.)
Community Board: No. 18
Police Precinct: 63rd Precinct (1844 Brooklyn Ave.)
Fire Department: Engine 309 Ladder 159 (1851 East 48th St.), Engine 323 (6405 Avenue N)
Hospitals and Clinics: Beth Israel Medical Center Kings Highway Division (3201 Kings Highway)

to the Canarsee Indians, the original inhabitants of the area, who called their village Keschaechqueren. Dutch settlers followed: in 1636 Jacob van Corlear, Andries Hudde, Wolfert Gerritsen van Kouwenhoven (sometimes identified as simply Wolfert Gerritsen), and Wouter Van Twiller, the governor of New Netherland, acquired land. Settlements developed near what are today Kings Highway and Flatlands Avenue. By 1647 these villages together had formed New Amersfoort, named after a Dutch city in the province of Utrecht.

In 1640 van Kouwenhoven built a plantation at what is now Kings Highway, and by 1651 Governor Peter Stuyvesant had also purchased a large piece of land in the area. Colonists grew corn, squash, beans, and tobacco. Farmers raised cattle, and clams were harvested from Jamaica Bay. In 1661 Stuyvesant granted the residents of New Amersfoort the right to local rule. This sense of autonomy was interrupted, however; in 1664 the English conquered New Netherland, and the town's name was changed to Flatlands.

August 1776 was a momentous month in the history of Flatlands. As the British prepared to land at Gravesend Bay, word came from the Provincial Convention of New York that farms in Kings County were to be destroyed in order to prevent descendants of the Dutch landowners, who largely took the British side, from helping the enemy. Fields and farms burned as residents fled in terror: Flatlands was among the most ravaged of the areas overtaken by British forces.

Flatlands remained agricultural until the 1830s, when with only 700 residents, it was the second-smallest town in Kings County. Blacks, who had farmed the land as slaves for their colonial owners, made up 20 percent of the population when New York State abolished slavery in 1827.

After the Brooklyn City Railroad Company extended horsecar service to Kings Highway in 1875 and Flatbush Avenue was completed, Flatlands residents gained access to downtown Brooklyn's stores and businesses, and the area began to grow, albeit slowly. In 1893 the Flatbush Avenue streetcars were electrified, and developers began building suburban houses that attracted a diverse population. In 1896 the town was the last to be annexed by the City of Brooklyn.

Between 1900 and World War II, the area continued to develop. The Inter-

Interwar development spread housing through Flatlands' fields in the 1930s (Brian Merlis Collection)

NEIGHBORHOOD FACTS

■ The landmarked Hendrick I. Lott House still stands on East 36th Street. The east wing of the house was built after 1719, and the main section and west wing were built in 1800. A traditional Dutch Colonial home, its small windows were designed to protect against Indian attack. The Historic House Trust has listed the Lott House as an official acquisition site. The landmarked John and Altje Baxter House, also called the Stoothoff-Baxter-Kouwenhoven House, still stands on East 48th Street. The small wing of this house was built in 1747, and the larger, main house was constructed in 1811. Around 1900, the entire house was reoriented on the property to match the position of other homes on the block.

■ One of the earliest settlers in the area was Joost Van Nuyse, who is said to have drowned in his well in 1792. The Joost and Elizabeth Van Nuyse House, sometimes called the Coe House, was once on an 85-acre farm. Still standing at 1128 East 34th Street, it is a New York City historic landmark.

■ In 1654 the Flatlands Dutch Reformed Church was formed by order of Peter Stuyvesant, at the intersection of Kings Highway and East 40th Street. The original church was housed in an octagonal building covered with spruce shingles and stood until 1794. The church that stands at that corner today, a Greek Revival building from 1848, is the third church building erected at the same site. It is surrounded by maple trees and a seventeenth-century cemetery, in which are interred many of Brooklyn's early Dutch landowners—the Wyckoffs, the Lotts, and the van Kouwenhovens—as well as some of the earliest freed African Americans. In 1973 the church was designated a historic landmark.

borough Rapid Transit line of the subway reached Flatbush and Nostrand Avenues, and by first traveling by trolley or bus to the Flatbush subway, residents of Flatlands could still reach Manhattan in a little more than an hour. But it was not the subway that transformed the area; it was the automobile.

Because Flatlands was not connected directly to any of the borough's subway lines, the neighborhood truly developed only after people were able to buy cars. When automobiles became affordable, change was swift. After Kings Highway was extended beyond Flatbush Avenue in the 1920s, brick row houses with garages were constructed in the fields of Flatlands: many of these still stand. Flatlands and Flatbush Avenues developed with locally owned businesses, some of which are run by descendants of the original owners. Although Flatlands has remained mostly Jewish, Italian, and

Futurama Homes built in the late 1950s, shown here today

Irish, during the 1980s immigrants from Jamaica, Haiti, and Guyana also settled in the neighborhood.

In the late 1950s, primarily 1959 and 1960, a section of Flatlands was developed with new attached, brick homes, known as the Futurama homes. Residents coined their neighborhood name, **Futurama**, when the Civic Association was formed.

The lots on which the Futurama homes were built are two feet wider than typical lots in Flatlands. Most of the original Futurama home owners remained until recently, but now many new families are moving into the area, remodeling the homes and filling the local, newly rededicated Jacob Joffe Park with young children.

Commerce along Flatbush Avenue

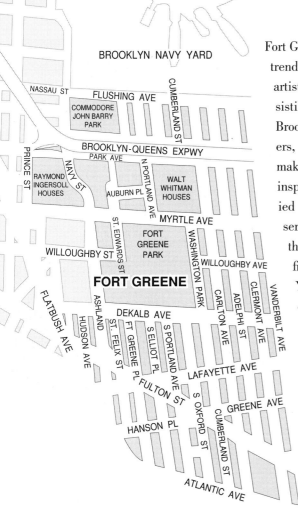

Fort Greene is an effervescent, trend-setting neighborhood that artists, in particular, find irresistible. In perhaps no other Brooklyn community can writers, musicians, designers, film makers, and visual artists draw inspiration from a rich and varied history that is so well preserved, or engage more fully in the animated debate that defines tomorrow's avant-garde. Young entrepreneurial and creative African Americans recognize a special tie to this unique community, for freed slaves once gained a step up into Brooklyn society by working as skilled shipbuilders and seamstresses there. (African Americans make up two-thirds of the residents today.) And residents of all ethnicities from throughout New York City are drawn to Fort Greene each fall for the trendsetting Next Wave Festival at the Brooklyn Academy of Music.

The neighborhood is named for Nathanael Greene, a colonial general and Revolutionary War hero who in 1776 supervised construction of Fort Putnam, on a hill that gave a clear view of the bay. But Greene lacked the ability that today's residents seem to have to foresee and guide Fort Greene's future: although the fort survived the Battle of Brooklyn, it was abandoned during George Washington's retreat across the East River.

Peter Caesar Alberti, the first Italian to arrive in Brooklyn, established a tobacco plantation in 1639 in what is today Fort Greene near Wallabout Bay. In 1781 the plantation became a shipyard, beginning a legacy of shipbuilding in the area. Construction of the Brooklyn Navy Yard followed; it was commissioned in 1801 and by the 1840s provided skilled work to many

Williamsburgh Savings Bank Tower (1929), still Brooklyn's tallest building (Brian Merlis Collection)

Fort Greene

128 African Americans, among others. In response to the shift in population, Colored School No. 1 opened in 1847 at St. Edwards Street and Park Avenue, where Public School 67 now stands. By 1870 more than half the African American population of Brooklyn lived in the area, alongside Irish, German, and English immigrants.

Fort Greene began drawing all of Brooklyn to the neighborhood when members of the Philharmonic Society of Brooklyn founded the Brooklyn Academy of Music (BAM). First opened in 1859 on Montague Street near Court Street, BAM, the oldest performing arts center in America, was destroyed by a fire in 1903 and was rebuilt at its current location on 30 Lafayette Avenue in 1908. Famous performers who have enthralled audiences at BAM include Sarah Bernhardt, Edwin Booth, Charles Dickens, Booker T. Washington, Henry Ward Beecher, Mark Twain, Philip Glass, Gustav Mahler, Enrico Caruso (he gave his last performance at BAM), Sergei Rachmaninoff, Gertrude Stein, Martha Graham, Paul Robeson, and Ezio Pinza. Today dance, theater, music,

NEIGHBORHOOD FACTS

■ Completed in 1860 at 88 Hanson Place, Hanson Place Seventh Day Adventist Church, formerly the Hanson Place Baptist Church, was an Underground Railroad station in the 1850s and is now a New York City landmark. Another Fort Greene architectural find is the former Joseph Steele House at 200 Lafayette Avenue. Sometimes called the Steele-Brick-Skinner House, it was built in the early 1850s, although the east side of the house may date back to 1812.

■ Richard Wright lived on Carlton Avenue, and it is said that he wrote sections of *Native Son* (1940) sitting in Fort Greene Park. Fort Greene is home to jazz singer Betty Carter, musicians Wynton and Branford Marsalis, and trumpeter Terence Blanchard.

■ From the mid- to late 1950s the Paramount Theatre, at Flatbush and DeKalb Avenues, shook with the music of Alan Freed's rock and roll shows. In 1962 the Paramount was converted into a gym (although its theater organ remains intact), and it is now a part of Long Island University's Brooklyn campus. During its heyday, the theater was filled each weekend night with more than 4,500 teenagers screaming to hear more of the music of the Moonglows, Fats Domino, Chuck Berry, the Penguins, the Shirelles, LaVern Baker, and Bo Diddley. The nearby Brooklyn Fox Theater's shows were hosted by radio disc-jockey Murray the K. An office building now stands on the site.

■ Film director Spike Lee once lived in Fort Greene, and the neighborhood was once home to his production company, 40 Acres and a Mule. In the early and mid-1990s, Spike Lee also had a store in Fort Greene, Spike's Joint.

■ Mollie Fancher, a famous late nineteenth-century psychic, lived at 160 Gates Avenue. When she was 16 an accident damaged her nervous system; thereafter Mollie was said to have developed powers that enabled her to read sealed letters, see colors in the dark, and tell time by listening to the ticking of a clock. Thousands traveled to Fort Greene to see her.

Merce Cunningham Dance Company in performance at the Next Wave Festival, 1997 (Dan Rest)

The Brooklyn Academy of Music, a cultural center for all of Brooklyn and beyond

● **Prison Ship Martyrs' Monument**
After running out of jail space during the American Revolution, the British held American prisoners in cattle, supply, and hospital ships in Wallabout Bay. More than 11,000 prisoners died of food poisoning, disease, and starvation. Many of the dead were buried in shallow trenches near the water's edge. For more than 20 years after the end of the war—until 1808, when the bodies were reinterred on a private estate—bones frequently washed up on the shore.

The first official monument for these prisoners was built in 1844, and the prisoners' remains were transferred to a crypt beneath what is now the Prison Ship Martyrs' Monument in Fort Greene Park. The newest monument, dedicated in 1908 by William Howard Taft, is a single 148-foot Doric column designed by architects with the firm McKim, Mead and White.

and performance art enthusiasts from the five boroughs and beyond visit BAM's Majestic Theater and Opera House for artistic performances that range from the Royal Shakespeare Company and the Brooklyn Philharmonic, the resident orchestra, to the Next Wave Festival, a series of avant-garde works that are often world premieres. Film is also celebrated at BAM. The former Playhouse, now BAM Rose Cinemas, has become a four-screen movie complex that features new releases from independent and international film studios. The area around BAM has been designated the Brooklyn Academy of Music historic district.

In addition, Fort Greene has a lovely historic district with notable churches, brownstones, and apartment buildings, many built between 1855 and 1880. The brownstones that still stand on the street named Washington Park, which overlooks the east side of Fort Greene Park, testify to the affluence of the area in the late 1880s. The 30-acre recreational site, originally called Washington Park, was established in 1848 after the City of Brooklyn purchased it in 1847; it was designed by Frederick Law Olmsted and Calvert Vaux (designers of Central and Prospect Parks) and completed in 1850. (A redesign by Olmsted and Vaux was completed in 1867.) The park adopted its neighborhood nickname in 1897.

Prison Ship Martyrs' Monument honors more than 11,000 Americans who died as prisoners of war during the American Revolution (Brooklyn Historical Society)

● Brooklyn Navy Yard

From the time it began operations in 1801 through the end of World War II, the Brooklyn Navy Yard was one of the busiest naval stations on the eastern seaboard. During the Civil War, the navy yard fitted out 400 ships; the *Monitor*, built in nearby Greenpoint, was clad in iron here. The *Arizona, Maine, Missouri,* and four other battleships were built at the facility; and in 1918, 18,000 workers were assembling and repairing ships at the yard.

The Brooklyn Navy Yard's 260 acres are now an industrial center that is home to 200 companies, including Cumberland Packing Corporation (packagers of Sweet-N-Low), Brink's Armored Car, and the Circle Line, which runs cruises around Manhattan and up the Hudson. In addition, on June 18, 1998, New York Studios announced its plans to build a $160 million motion picture and television studio on 15 acres of the former naval facility.

Four of the navy yard's structures are New York City landmarks. The Commandant's House (1806), which is also a national landmark, is a large Federal-style home at the northwest corner of the navy yard. Dry Dock No. 1 (1840–51), which cost more than $2 million to build, is made of granite from Maine and Connecticut. The Surgeon's House (1863) is a Second Empire home built during the Civil War for the chief surgeon of the naval hospital. And the U.S. Naval Hospital (1838; wings 1840 and ca. 1862) is a marble structure with eight square stone piers at its main facade.

picted in its exterior relief symbolize saving and thrift.

In addition to serving art and commerce, Fort Greene accommodates the scientifically inclined. Brooklyn Technical High School, founded in 1922, boasted an innovative program in advanced mathematics, science, and engineering that had been launched in 1919 as a program at Manual Training High School, where its popularity outgrew the facility. An all-city school, Brooklyn Tech admitted students only after they passed a stringent entrance examination. The school moved to its present location at 29 Fort Greene Place in 1933, and from 1938 it hosted a radio station, WNYE—whose antenna, at 593 feet, is the tallest structure in Brooklyn—that was used by the

In the early twentieth century, Second Empire brownstones and neo-Grec, Romanesque Revival, Queen Anne, and Italianate townhouses continued to be built, filling the neighborhood with eclectic architecture. Among the notable structures is the Brooklyn Masonic Temple (1906) on Clermont and Vanderbilt Avenues, a Classical Revival brick building with polychromatic terra-cotta detail. Another hallmark of the area, the Williamsburgh Savings Bank Tower at 1 Hanson Place, was completed in 1929. Erected during the craze for skyscrapers (Manhattan's Chrysler Building was completed in 1930 and the Empire State Building in 1931), it is still, at 512 feet, Brooklyn's tallest building, and until 1962 it boasted the tallest four-sided clock tower in the world. Both the exterior and the interior of the Williamsburgh Savings Bank Tower are New York City landmarks. Bees, pelicans, and squirrels de-

USS *North Carolina* launching from the Brooklyn Navy Yard, April 9, 1941 (Brian Merlis Collection)

Paramount Theatre during its transformation into a gymnasium for Long Island University, 1962 (Brooklyn Historical Society)

Wood frame Federal-style homes at Adelphi Street and Lafayette Avenue

Fort Greene was once home to Spike Lee's production company, 40 Acres and a Mule (David Lee)

Board of Education. In 1970 the school became coeducational, and in 1984 renovations were begun that would bring facilities for high-technology programs. Among Brooklyn Tech's illustrious alumni are two Nobel Prize laureates, George Wald and Arno Penzias; Harvey Lichtenstein, dancer and later president of the Brooklyn Academy of Music; and screenwriter Marshall Brickman.

During World War II, more than 71,000 navy personnel and civilians worked at the Brooklyn Navy Yard, the largest naval construction facility in the United States. In 1944 the New York City Housing Authority (the first such local authority in the United States) built the high-rise Walt Whitman and Raymond V. Ingersoll Houses close to the navy yard to house the enormous wartime workforce. The 3,500 units, on 38 acres (about 20 percent of the neighborhood), accommodated 14,000 people. Within the complex stands the landmarked Church of St. Michael and St. Edward at 108 St. Edwards Street. Until 1966, when the Brooklyn Navy Yard closed, a great proportion of Fort Greene residents made their living building and repairing ships.

Although for a brief time in the 1970s it seemed that Fort Greene might be losing residents and businesses, a strong community spirit pervaded the neighborhood. Residents of the housing complexes worked with police and elected officials to make public housing a success. In the southern part of Fort Greene, brownstone enthusiasts began moving in during the 1980s to renovate reasonably priced historic homes and settle in the area. Leading the effort to keep Fort Greene strong are the Fort Greene Community Coalition and the Fort Greene Community Leaders Against Drugs, whose programs focus on youth outreach, senior citizens, and neighborhood crime watches.

In 1997 a retail complex opened in the area: the Atlantic Center, a 70,000-square-foot shopping mall, one of the largest in Brooklyn. Further redevelopment continues around the center. Full blocks of new houses, for example, were completed at the south edge of Fort Greene (on Cumberland and Claremont Streets at Fulton Street) as a part of the Atlantic Center project.

Today, Fort Greene is vibrant and spirited, and new businesses and restaurants seem to open every week. Residents in the historic district sit on their stoops to visit with neighbors and friends, while some Fort Greene residents host private salons and discussion groups in their parlors and living rooms. Boutiques sell clothes made by local designers, and cafes feature readings and open-mike performances. In addition, the area is home to some of Brooklyn's finest African and Italian restaurants. No wonder *Essence* magazine tapped Fort Greene as "The Happening 'Hood."

High-rise apartments built in 1944 for Brooklyn's wartime labor force

Gerritsen

With its narrow streets, waterside houses, and local fishermen, Gerritsen Beach, part of the original town of Gravesend, has the allure of a quaint New England fishing town. The beautiful community remains one of Brooklyn's seaside secrets.

The neighborhood is named for Wolfert Gerritsen van Kouwenhoven, who in 1629 was among a group of people offered a total of 15,000 acres of land, including today's Gerritsen Beach, from the Dutch West India Company. In 1665 Hugh Gerritsen, a farmer and a descendant of Wolfert's, built a house and tidewater mill on Gerritsen Creek (now part of Marine Park). A hundred years later, Hugh's descendants are said to have used the mill to grind flour for George Washington's troops. (Another version of the story has the owners sinking the millstones to avoid having to grind flour for the British.) The mill stood until the mid-1930s, when it was destroyed by fire.

In the late 1800s, Gerritsen Beach was still primarily rural, but some prescient investors recognized its po-

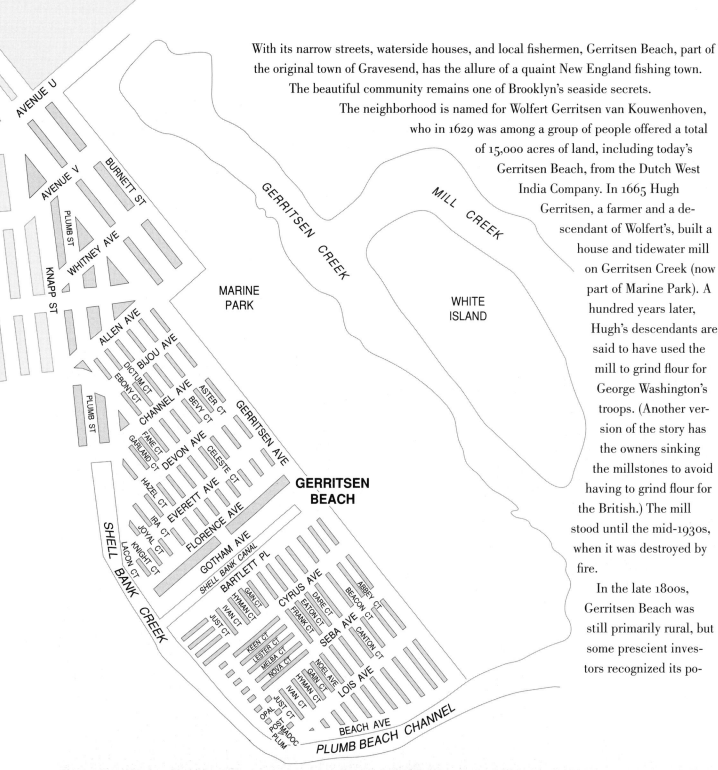

Beach

tential for other uses. In 1899 William C. Whitney, secretary of the navy under President Grover Cleveland, bought 67 acres of land in Gerritsen. He renovated a 150-year-old mansion and used it as a racing lodge. The lodge is difficult to identify after almost a hundred years of further renovations, but it still stands on Burnett between Avenue V and Whitney Avenue. In addition, in 1920 a land speculator bought 1,100 lots near the Shell Bank Creek and in 1923 doubled his $300,000 investment by selling them to the development firm Realty Associates.

Realty Associates transformed what once consisted of a few squatters' bungalows at the foot of Gerritsen Avenue into the Gerritsen Beach of today. In 1923 the company began to create the 1,700-foot Shell Bank Canal and to construct roadways, curbs, and sidewalks. This section of Gerritsen, south

NEIGHBORHOOD PROFILE

Boundaries: from Knapp Street and the Shell Bank Creek on the west to Burnett Street and Gerritsen Avenue on the east, from Avenue U on the north to the Plumb Beach Channel on the south.
Bus: B3: Avenue U B31: Gerritsen Ave.
Libraries: Brooklyn Public Library Gerritsen Beach Branch (Gerritsen Ave. at Channel Ave.)
Community Board: No. 15
Police Precinct: 61st Precinct (2575 Coney Island Ave.)
Fire Department: Engine 321 (2165 Gerritsen Ave.)

A small stable at Joyal Court

of the Shell Bank Canal, was subdivided into building lots, some as small as 34 by 52.5 feet, with alphabetically named streets. The area became a summer resort for Irish Americans filled with one-story bungalows featuring peaked roofs and no backyards.

By the late 1920s, Gerritsen was so

Boats docked at Shell Bank Creek marina

NEIGHBORHOOD FACTS

■ In 1922 the Gerritsen Volunteer Fire Department was chartered by New York State. More than 50 years later, the Gerritsen "Vollies," based at 32 Seba Avenue in Gerritsen Beach, comprise the only volunteer fire department in Brooklyn. Fire fighters, 50 volunteers who range in age from 18 to 70, respond to more than 600 fire, rescue, and emergency medical calls a year.

■ The Gerritsen Beach Branch of the Brooklyn Public Library, housed in a recently completed $2 million building on Gerritsen Avenue at Channel Avenue, is one of only two waterfront libraries in New York City.

■ Every year since 1987 the neighborhood has hosted the Great Gerritsen Beach Rowing Race on the Saturday after Labor Day. Residents race their human-powered boats (rowboats, canoes, kayaks, and paddleboats) around White Island in Marine Park's Gerritsen Bay back creek. Although only residents can enter, the public is invited to attend.

popular that owners of some bungalows winterized them so that they could live there year-round. Larger, two-story homes with backyards were built, and by the 1930s Gerritsen had more than 1,500 homes. The area north of the Shell Bank Canal is often referred to as New Gerritsen. On the northern blocks, which are also alphabetized, there are many red-brick houses and some small stores.

1920s beach bungalows converted to year-round homes

Rowboats, motorboats, sailboards, and sailboats abound in today's Gerritsen Beach, and four local yacht clubs accommodate boat owners. Neighborhood families—who for many years have been primarily of Irish, German, and Italian descent—play at Kiddie Beach, purchased in 1965 by the Gerritsen Beach Property Owners Association. Open to residents only, the beautiful beach has a concession stand, lifeguards on duty, a stage for summer performances, and an annual parade on July 1.

Gowanus

"Brooklyn don't seem to be like any other place on earth. Once let a man grow up amidst Brooklyn's cobblestones, with the odor of Newton Creek and Gowanus Canal ever in his nostrils, and there's no place in the world for him except Brooklyn. And even if he don't grow up there; if he is born there and lives there only in his boyhood and then moves away, he is still beyond redemption."—Senator George Washington Plunkitt, Tammany politician, 1905

The Carroll Street Bridge is one of four remaining retractile bridges in the country

If Plunkitt is right, no matter how much the surrounding communities of Boerum Hill, Park Slope, and Carroll Gardens encroach upon it, Gowanus will always live as a separate and unique neighborhood in the hearts of its residents. Many longtime Gowanus home owners have passed down through the generations row houses tucked between commercial buildings, creating enduring small communities that share a bond with the larger neighborhood. Tied to this strong allegiance by residents is the promise that what is important about Gowanus is not what the neighborhood has been, but what it will be, especially after the Gowanus Canal has been cleaned and revitalized.

Named perhaps for a man named Gowane, identified variously as a sachem of the Canarsee Indians and a member of the Mohawks, Gowanus was settled by the Dutch in the 1640s when the land was rural and home to Native Americans, wild animals, overgrown plants, and waterfowl. Some of the earliest and most brutal skirmishes of the Revolutionary War's Battle of Brooklyn took place between today's Gowanus and Park

Slope: 256 American soldiers from Maryland, for example, were killed at the Old Stone House at Gowanus, and more than a hundred others were wounded or taken prisoner by the British.

N E I G H B O R H O O D   P R O F I L E

Boundaries: from Hoyt Street between Wyckoff and 5th Streets and Smith Street between 5th Street and the Gowanus Expressway on the west to 4th Avenue on the east, from Wyckoff Street or Baltic Street on the north to the Gowanus Expressway (underneath Hamilton Avenue) on the south.
Subway: <u>IND F</u>: Smith/9th St.
<u>BMT 4th Avenue N and R</u>: Union St., 9th St.
Bus: <u>B71</u>: Union St./3rd St. <u>B75</u>: Smith St./9th St. <u>B77</u>: 9th St. <u>B37</u>: 3rd Ave.
Community Board: No. 6
Police Precinct: 76th Precinct (191 Union St.), 78th Precinct (211 Union St.)

In the early 1800s developers realized that the Gowanus Canal, an artificial waterway, was a perfect outlet into the Gowanus Bay, and they began to offer industrial plots along its banks. After the Gowanus Canal was enlarged in the 1840s, the population of the area grew enormously. In the late 1800s the canal was more than 5,000 feet long and up to 15 feet deep at high tide. By the end of the nineteenth century, the area was known as the Gashouse District after a household heating and gas company. In one 12-block section of Smith Street there were 23 taverns and many rooming houses for the seamen and laborers who passed through the area to work short-term jobs at the canal.

In its heyday the Gowanus Canal was edged by coal and lumber yards, brick and stone yards, paint and ink manufacturers, and flour, paper, and plaster mills. But the introduction of containerized shipping in the 1970s made the canal less attractive to large industries, many of which closed or moved away. Since the late 1980s the area around the Gowanus Canal has housed new, smaller industries, including a bagel company, beverage companies, bakeries, and a large furniture repair shop. Its residents have predominantly been blue-collar Italian Americans, Hispanics, and blacks, although white-collar workers are being drawn to the cooperative apartments.

Gowanus is a mixed-use neighborhood where warehouses and old factories are

Gowanus Canal looking north

One can buy a house, rent a garage, or notarize papers along the Gowanus Canal

being renovated as cooperative apartments and studio space for a growing number of resident artists. A former soap factory that was converted to arts space in 1983, for example, houses a large community arts organization, private art and performance spaces, and sound studios. Unfortunately, some magnificent buildings remain vacant, such as the New York City landmark Public Bath No. 7. Built on 4th Avenue from 1906 to 1910, it is faced in brick and terra cotta with glazed white surfaces and ornamented with fish, tridents, and shells.

Brooklynites tend to believe that the Gowanus Canal was polluted recently, not knowing that as early as 1880 complaints about the stench were being lodged, that in 1893 the *Brooklyn Eagle* called the waterway an open cesspool, and that not long after that it was referred to as Lavender Lake. As businesses grew, waste was dumped into the water—both accidentally and on purpose—and the natural tides could not keep the canal clean. In 1911 the Gowanus Flushing Tunnel was installed, but it closed in the 1960s because of damage by workmen.

Since then neighborhood activists have devoted their time to advocating for cleanup of the canal. Nearby sewage treatment plants have helped, but Gowanus enthusiasts say that what will change the water forever is the reactivation of the Flushing Tunnel, which was due to be rehabilitated by 1988. Although it has yet to be reactivated, when it begins functioning it will quickly start to move clean water through the canal. A year and a half later, fish could be swimming in the waters of Gowanus, and if the optimists are right, ten years after that residents may be jumping in for a dip themselves.

NEIGHBORHOOD FACTS

■ Legend has it that General George Washington visited the Vechte-Cortelyou House, built in 1699 and sometimes called the Old Stone House at Gowanus because it was the first stone house constructed in the neighborhood. The house was rebuilt in 1935 in James J. Byrne Memorial Playground, in nearby Park Slope. The stones used to build the house are said to be from the foundation of the original house. The house was reopened in 1997 as the First Battle Revival Center, dedicated to the history of the Battle of Brooklyn.

■ The tallest subway station in New York City is the F line stop at Smith and 9th Streets. The station stands 87.5 feet above the Gowanus Canal.

■ The wood-planked Carroll Street Bridge (1889) over the Gowanus Canal is the oldest of four remaining retractile bridges in the United States, and it is a New York City landmark. To allow boats to pass, the retractile bridge does not raise: it slides back onto the western shore of the canal. The bridge was restored in 1989 through the efforts of neighborhood groups in Carroll Gardens, Gowanus, and Sunset Park.

■ The Brooklyn Center for the Urban Environment sponsors a boat tour of Gowanus Canal. The hope of the sponsors is that this tour will help spark activism to get the canal cleaned up.

Gravesend

sens, and pastry shops, which once flourished in a more homogeneous neighborhood. And houses that were subdivided during the Depression are being restored to their original single-family luster by enthusiastic new home owners.

Although Gravesend was once almost entirely Italian American and Jewish, the neighborhood is now a multiethnic community where newcomers live side by side with families that have been there for generations. Russians began moving to the neighborhood in the early 1980s, and many of Gravesend's newer residents are Indian and Haitian immigrants and settlers of Asian and Irish descent. A Sephardic Jewish community settled into the area around East 3rd, 4th, and 5th Streets during this same period, close to the large synagogues and yeshivas of Ocean Parkway. During the summer, however, the longstanding Italian American community makes its presence known: the Roman Catholic Church of Sts. Simon and Jude, in partnership with Our Lady of Grace Catholic Church, sponsors an annual bazaar with rides for children, as well as tag sales.

Lady Moody House, also known as the Hicks-Platt residence, built in the mid-1600s

Gravesend, one of the original six towns of Brooklyn, is a neighborhood where faintly visible remnants of the past underlie the shapes of future dreams. Strolling toward the neighborhood's original center, at the intersection of McDonald Avenue and Gravesend Neck Road, you can discern the outlines of the initial four-square, 16-acre town plan, created by Lady Moody, Gravesend's pioneering founder. Chinese restaurants, which have popped up near Caribbean ice stands and Italian bakeries, inhabit buildings that echo with the voices of Italian owners of salumerias, delicates-

Gravesend originally included an enormous expanse of land: it encompassed Coney Island, Sheepshead Bay, Bensonhurst, Brighton Beach, and Manhattan Beach. Settled in 1643 (chartered 1645) by a group of English Anabaptists led by Lady Deborah Moody, the neighborhood was a haven for religious dis-

Church of Sts. Simon and Jude

senters. Lady Moody, a wealthy widow with a baronetcy inherited from her husband, left England in about 1639 and moved to New England. But the New Englanders did not welcome her radical Protestantism, so in 1643 she moved to New Amsterdam, founded Gravesend, and became the first woman to charter land in the New World. The only English settlement of Brooklyn, Gravesend was organized under a Dutch rule that allowed freedom of worship and self-government. By the 1650s Gravesend was also known as a refuge for Quakers.

The name Gravesend rightly blends the two influences, Dutch and English, that shaped its early development. Probably named by the Dutch authorities from the Dutch words *Grafes* and *Ande,* which together mean "end of the grove," or "count's beach," it is likely that Lady Moody's wishes were also consulted: Gravesend is a city at the mouth of the Thames River.

During the American Revolution the invading British came ashore at Gravesend from Staten Island on August 22, 1776, and legend has it that Lady Moody's house—which still stands at 27 Gravesend Neck Road—was used as a hospital during the Battle of Brooklyn. Until 1875 Gravesend was primarily rural; farmers of Dutch and German descent joined their English counterparts to work the land. The bucolic landscape remained mostly unchanged for the next 20 years, despite the development of resorts, hotels, and three racetracks at nearby

Family housing built in the 1940s and 1950s on Bay 43rd Street between Harway and Bath Avenues

NEIGHBORHOOD PROFILE

Boundaries: from Bay Parkway and Belt Parkway or, for local traffic, Shore Parkway on the west to Ocean Parkway on the east, from Avenue P on the north to the Belt or Shore Parkway on the south.
Subway: <u>IND F</u>: Avenue P, Kings Highway, Avenue U, Avenue X <u>BMT N</u>: Kings Highway, Avenue U, 86th St. <u>BMT West End Line B</u>: Bay 50th St.
Bus: <u>B82</u>: Kings Highway <u>B3</u>: Avenue U <u>B1</u>: Avenue X <u>B4</u>: Stillwell Ave./86th St./Avenue Z <u>B64</u>: Stillwell Ave. <u>B36</u>: Ocean Parkway
Libraries: Brooklyn Public Library Gravesend Branch (Avenue X near West 2nd St.), Highlawn Branch (West 13th St. at Kings Highway)
Community Board: No. 15
Police Precinct: 60th Precinct (2951 West 8th St.)
Fire Department: None

Coney Island. Even though more than 100,000 people flocked to the area on weekends and holidays, the local population stayed steady at about 6,000.

After Gravesend was annexed to the City of Brooklyn in 1894, however, the area began to be transformed. The electrification of the Sea Beach (1898) and Culver (1899) rail lines meant that those who settled in Gravesend could reach Manhattan in 45 minutes. A large Italian American community formed, most likely made up of railroad workers who had discovered the lovely neighborhood. Residential development in the area boomed.

Most of Gravesend's current houses were built after the 1920s. During the Depression, many were converted into two-family dwellings, but recent Gravesend residents have been busy restoring them to their original forms. The neighborhood also has some three- and four-family houses and a few small scattered apartment buildings. Some larger apartment buildings sit on Ocean Parkway and Coney Island Avenue; and between Kings Highway and Avenue U on Gravesend's eastern side, Spanish villas dot the side streets. A large number of Gravesend's residents live in the Marlboro Houses, a New York City housing project.

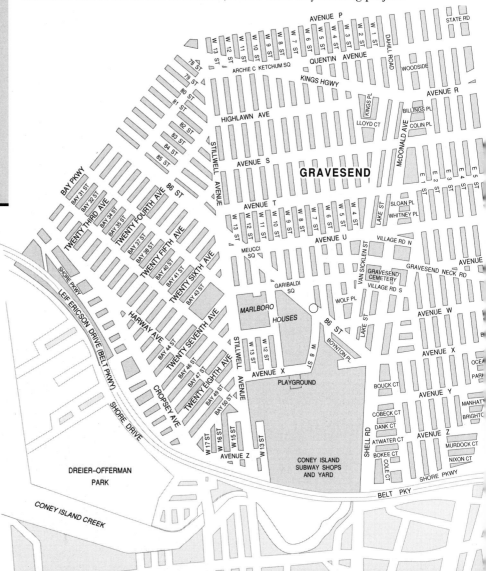

Greenpoint

The spin of the potter's wheel, the shipbuilders' five o'clock whistle, two young women chatting in Polish on a well-swept stoop: Greenpoint has always been a blend of industrial and residential, of people at work and at play. Well-maintained brownstones, flats, and tenement buildings, as well as three- and four-story row houses and aluminum-sided low-rise homes, invite immigrants to partake in America's history. In response, Italian, Hispanic, Irish—and in record numbers, Polish—immigrants have settled in this northwesternmost Brooklyn neighborhood, lending the sounds and aromas of their native countries to busy Manhattan Avenue.

Greenpoint, also called the "garden spot of America" by the *Brooklyn Eagle,* is one of the few Brooklyn neighborhoods that has retained its original name. The

NEIGHBORHOOD FACTS

■ For many decades, Eberhard Faber manufactured its signature yellow Mongol pencils in a factory on West Street, near Kent Street.
■ Young and old residents of Greenpoint enjoy visiting McCarren Park, a 35-acre oasis at the southern edge of the neighborhood where on summer weekends crowds cheer for their favorite softball teams. The park also has one of four swimming pools in Brooklyn built by the Works Progress Administration.
■ Greenpoint was the birthplace of actress Mae West.
■ During Poland's 1990 elections, more than 5,000 absentee ballots were postmarked Greenpoint.

Vista along Greenpoint Avenue

Dutch acquired the area from the Keskachauge Indians in 1638 and named it for a grassy stretch of land on the East River. During the eighteenth and early nineteenth centuries, Greenpoint, like much of the rest of the town of Boswijck (Bushwick), was used primarily for farming.

After 1840 Greenpoint became a center for shipbuilding. The neighborhood is known as the birthplace of the famous ironclad Civil War ship *Monitor*, launched in 1862. (A 1939 monument to the *Monitor* stands in Monsignor McGolrick Park, formerly known as Winthrop Park.) As development of the area around the piers became more formal in the late 1800s, streets and lots were carefully planned; as a result, almost all of the streets that run parallel to the river are in alphabetical order from north to south.

Kent Street, one block north of Greenpoint Avenue within the Greenpoint historic district, is still one of the best places to go to experience nineteenth-century Brooklyn. The street is filled with early flats, wooden frame houses, and masonry row houses. The cast-iron work on Greenpoint's older buildings was all produced in local foundries.

Indeed, Greenpoint's historic district contains a variety of buildings that reflect the diversity of the neighborhood's history. Among these is the Oliver H. Perry School, Public School 34, located on Norman Avenue. Built in 1867 with additions in 1870 and 1878, it is one of the oldest schools in continuous use in New York City. Another is the imposing Russian Orthodox Cathedral of the Transfiguration of Our Lord, at North 12th Street and Driggs Avenue. Completed in 1921, the distinctive onion-domed church has since been an ornate part of Greenpoint's landscape. Two more unusual landmarks are the Shelter Pavilion in Monsignor McGolrick Park (1910), and the freestanding cast-iron sidewalk clock in front of 752 Manhattan Avenue (early twentieth century).

In 1939 the Kosciuszko Bridge opened in Greenpoint at the site of a former drawbridge called Penny Bridge. Tadeusz Kosciuszko, a Polish military tactician and volunteer in the Continental Army, was instrumental in the American victory at Saratoga during the Revolutionary War and rose to the rank of colonel. The Polish community, already settled in Greenpoint in the 1930s, embraced this recognition of their contributions to America's independence.

By the late nineteenth century, Greenpoint was home to immigrants from En-

Eberhard Faber Pencil Company in 1920 (Brooklyn Historical Society)

N E I G H B O R H O O D
P R O F I L E

Boundaries: from the East River on the west to the Queens County line on the east, from Newtown Creek on the north to North 11th Street east to Richardson Street, south on Grandparent Avenue, and west on Frost Street or Maspeth Avenue on the south.
Subway: IND Crosstown G: Greenpoint Ave., Nassau St.
Bus: B24: Meeker Ave. B48: Nassau Ave. B24: Greenpoint Ave. B43: Manhattan Ave. B61: Manhattan Ave.
Libraries: Brooklyn Public Library Greenpoint Branch (Norman Ave. at Leonard St.)
Community Board: No. 1
Police Precinct: 94th Precinct (100 Meserole Ave.)
Fire Department: Engine 238 Ladder 106 (205 Greenpoint Ave.)
Hospitals and Clinics: Greenpoint Health Center (960 Manhattan Ave.)

gland, Ireland, Russia, Poland, and Italy. Both Greenpoint and Williamsburg became well known for what came to be called the five black arts: printing, pottery, petroleum and gas refining, glassmaking, and iron making. Some of the better-known companies include Charles Cartlidge and Company and Union Porcelain Works, which produced porcelain china. Brooklyn Flint Glass, which had been in Brooklyn since 1823, left Greenpoint in 1868 for Corning, New York, where it became Corning Glass Works. And Greenpoint's Bedi-Rassy Foundry, at 227 India Street, is famous for casting the Iwo Jima statue, which stands at the edge of Arlington National Cemetery.

In 1867 Charles Pratt founded Astral Oil Works, a petroleum refinery whose kerosene, Astral Oil, was so widely known that it was touted as the fuel that lit the holy lamps of Tibet. This success made Pratt a millionaire and allowed him to endow Pratt Institute (see Clinton Hill). Pratt even built housing for his employees and other workers, the Astral Apartments, which still stand on the east side of Franklin Street, between Java and India Streets. Now New York City landmarks, the Astral Apartments were unusual for their time: they were designed with a window in every room, as well as adequate kitchens and bathrooms. In

later years more than 50 oil refining companies were located in Greenpoint. The Brooklyn Union Gas tanks along Newtown Creek are reminiscent of this period in the neighborhood's history.

Greenpoint struggled through the early twentieth century as the demand for shipbuilding, light manufacturing, and warehousing declined in Brooklyn. Architectural remnants of this period include the main office of the Greenpoint Savings Bank at Manhattan and

One of many Polish restaurants on Greenpoint Avenue

Italianate masonry row houses with cast-iron lintels along Kent Street

Calyer, where the bank opened for business in 1908. The Depression years were especially rough. But from World War II to the present, the area has been invigorated again and again by immigrants, many of whom have worked at local factories. Newcomers from Puerto Rico, Guyana, the Dominican Republic, Colombia, Ecuador, Asia, and Pakistan have all settled in Greenpoint alongside their Polish neighbors.

Recent figures suggest that as many as 200,000 Polish Americans live in Greenpoint, making it the largest Polish American community in New York, New Jersey, and Connecticut combined. Polish American runners in the New York City Marathon look forward to the stretch of the race that winds through Greenpoint because there they are greeted by crowds cheering in their native language. And worshipers at St. Stanislaus Kostka Vincentian Fathers Church, who make up the largest Polish congregation in Brooklyn, take pride in the fact that Karol Cardinal Wojtyla, Archbishop of Cracow (now Pope John Paul II), visited Greenpoint in 1969.

Kensington &

If Brooklyn is a banquet of international sights, sounds, and flavors, Kensington and Parkville are its bouillabaisse—an eclectic, appealing potpourri of cultures and traditions. With Kensington's schoolchildren speaking more than 50 home languages, and with both neighborhoods' diverse array of housing, shops, and activities, Kensington and Parkville have become renowned as two of the most ethnically mixed neighborhoods in the borough.

The neighborhoods were not always so diverse. Like much of Brooklyn, Kensington and Parkville, along with Kensington's smaller neighborhoods **Dahill** and **Albemarle,** were originally colonized by Dutch farmers, in this case as part of the town of Flatbush. The area remained rural until 1850, when construction of the Coney Island Plank Road, which connected the City of Brooklyn to Coney Island, made the area more accessible and thus attractive to entrepreneurs. In 1851 the United Freeman's Association initiated development by buying the Ditmas and Tredwell family farms and laying out streets at an angle to the north-south grid. The first residences were built where Albemarle is today (at the northern end of Kensington, just south of Windsor Terrace), and the area was named **Greenfield.**

In 1870 Greenfield became Parkville, and after Ocean Parkway was completed in 1876, development accelerated. Around the turn of the century, the middle section of the neighborhood was renamed Kensington, after the western borough of London.

Much of the housing was built in the 1920s, in particular the freestanding

Parkville

● Ocean Parkway

Ocean Parkway is just one aspect of Frederick Law Olmsted and Calvert Vaux's dream to extend the natural beauty of Prospect Park into Brooklyn's neighborhoods. The design team also hoped eventually to connect this and a number of other parkways to Central Park, their crown jewel in Manhattan. When Ocean Parkway was completed in 1876, it featured a central drive, landscaped malls, a bridle trail, and pedestrian paths. The Coney Island Bicycle Path was added in 1895. The grand and lovely stretch of Ocean Parkway between Church and Sea Breeze Avenues has been designated a New York City scenic landmark. In the 1950s its northernmost section was replaced by the Prospect Expressway.

houses in Albemarle, Kensington's row houses, and all the five- and six-story apartment buildings. In later years higher apartment buildings were built, especially along Ocean Parkway. By this time the area had become a vibrant, middle-class neighborhood, home to many Jewish and Italian American families. Church Avenue, called simply "the avenue" by local residents, was a lively commercial strip that featured the Beverley movie house, candy stores, fine clothing shops, bakeries, and kosher butchers. Family names graced the local store awnings, and a public market enlivened 18th Avenue.

Kensington remained quiet and residential, and still largely Italian American and Jewish, until the early 1980s, when many older residents moved, either to be near their children or to relocate to warmer retirement communities. Although some of the thirty-, forty-, and fifty-year residents remained, many apartments and houses became available to new owners. Pakistani, Asian, East Indian, Polish, Indonesian, Turkish, Mexican, Haitian, Guyanese, Dominican, and Jamaican immigrants, sensing Kensington's warmth toward newcomers, settled in the area. In addition, in both Albemarle and central Kensington, many Russian immigrants live in the larger apartment buildings. A Muslim community has enriched the area around Coney Island and Foster Avenues. And working professionals of

Art Deco apartment building on Ocean Parkway

N E I G H B O R H O O D   P R O F I L E

Boundaries: <u>Kensington</u>: from 36th Street and McDonald Avenue on the west to Coney Island Avenue on the east, from Fort Hamilton Parkway and Caton Avenue on the north to Foster Avenue on the south. <u>Parkville</u>: from McDonald Avenue on the west to Coney Island Avenue on the east, from Ditmas/18th Avenue on the north to Foster Avenue on the south. <u>Dahill</u>: the triangle formed by 36th Street on the west, Dahill Road on the east, and Fort Hamilton Parkway on the north. <u>Albemarle</u>: from McDonald Avenue on the west to Coney Island Avenue on the east, from Caton Avenue on the north to Church Avenue on the south.

Subway: <u>IND F</u>: Church Ave., Ditmas Ave., 18th Ave.

Bus: <u>B35</u>: Church Ave. <u>B23</u>: Cortelyou Rd. <u>B8</u>: 18th Ave. <u>B67</u>: McDonald Ave. <u>B68</u>: Coney Island Ave. <u>Bx29</u>: Coney Island Ave.

Libraries: Brooklyn Public Library Kensington Branch (Ditmas Ave. near East 5th St.)

Community Board: No. 12

Police Precinct: 66th Precinct (5822 16th Ave.)

tion can strain relations among residents, in Kensington this new growth is seen as a strength, something to celebrate at the twice-yearly Church Avenue Fair, sponsored by Church Avenue merchants.

Growth in the local business community has also been nurtured. Although some of the old family businesses are struggling, the community has made an effort to help these businesses expand and survive the onslaught of national chain stores. For in Kensington, diversity, in businesses as well as in residents, is cherished.

Mansion converted to medical office on Ocean Parkway at Newkirk in Parkville

many ethnicities are busy renovating their beautiful, affordable Kensington homes.

More Orthodox Jewish residents are moving into Kensington as well, some of whom are relocating from Borough Park. On the eastern side of the neighborhood, near Avenue F, houses are being enlarged and renovated; some homes also house *shtieblech*, small synagogues with a rabbi's residence upstairs.

Kensington is a growing neighborhood, and its public schools are expanding to meet the new demand. But whereas in some communities a burgeoning popula-

N E I G H B O R H O O D   F A C T S

■ At the turn of the twentieth century, farms south of Green-Wood Cemetery were purchased by William Micieli. He laid out streets and named them after his children, Clara, Louisa, Minna, and Chester. Later streets were named Bill's Place and Micieli Place.

■ McDonald Avenue does not, as tradition has it, have any connection to the song "Old McDonald's Farm." It is named for John R. McDonald, chief clerk of the Kings County Surrogates Court. McDonald Avenue was formerly Gravesend Avenue.

Manhattan

"So many prosperous people in one place. . . . The straw hat with its blue or striped ribbon, the flannel suit, with its accompanying white shoes, light cane. . . . What a cool, summery, airy-fairy realm!"—Theodore Dreiser, The Color of a Great City, *1923*

Manhattan Beach, once an exclusive, grand, oceanfront resort, has matured into an inviting neighborhood of comfortable single-family homes on tree-lined streets named after venerable English seaside towns: Hastings, Dover, Pembroke. Small children in swimsuits frolic in the sand at the 40-acre Manhattan Beach Park, once the site of the spectacular Oriental Hotel, while families enjoy picnics on its sprawling fields. With no home farther than eight blocks from the beach, the neighborhood remains a sea lover's paradise.

Up to the mid-1800s, the area was known as Sedge Bank, a rural, largely unsettled farming section of what was later Coney Island and part of the original English town of Gravesend. Not until the 1820s, when Brooklynites first began to

Beach

NEIGHBORHOOD PROFILE

Boundaries: from West End Avenue on the west to Seawall Avenue and the Atlantic Ocean on the east, from Shore Boulevard on the north to the Esplanade, Manhattan Beach, and Oriental Beach on the south.
Bus: B1: Oriental Blvd. B49: Oriental Blvd./West End Ave.
Community Board: No. 15
Police Precinct: 61st Precinct (2575 Coney Island Ave.)
Hospitals and Clinics: Menorah Home and Hospital, Manhattan Beach Division (1516 Oriental Blvd.)

Dignified home on Coleridge Street

Footbridge across Sheepshead Bay from Manhattan Beach

visit Coney Island in significant numbers, did a demand for lodging and entertainment fuel growth in the island's development.

Manhattan Beach was the brainchild of Austin Corbin, a wealthy New York banker who in the nineteenth century made the peaceful sandy shore into a playground for New York's rich. Originally looking for a healthy home for his sickly infant son, Corbin spotted 500 acres of seaside land for sale and concocted his elaborate dream. With a savvy sense of what upscale New Yorkers wanted in a summertime escape, Corbin built two breathtaking hotels—the Manhattan Beach, which boasted 306 rooms for both day and seasonal guests, and the higher-priced Oriental, which catered to patrons wishing to spend the season. A pavilion welcomed day trippers.

Corbin also built the New York and Manhattan Beach Railway in 1876–77 and provided ferry service via the East 23rd Street ferry, which connected to the Man-

hattan Beach train at Brooklyn's 69th Street ferry slip. (Later Corbin became president of the Long Island Railroad, which linked with the Manhattan Beach line.) These new, expedient routes meant that it took only an hour for rich Manhattan businessmen to reach their vacationing families.

The Victorian interest in the exotic and the historic inspired extravagant entertaining at the Manhattan Beach Hotel, which was dedicated at its opening in 1877 by former president Ulysses S. Grant. In lavish "panorama" productions, hundreds of actors, acrobats, clowns, and dancers reenacted for

152 guests such dramatic historic episodes as the destruction of Pompeii, the storming of the Bastille, or battles of the Spanish-American War. Firework displays and live musical performances by John Philip Sousa (whose "Manhattan Beach March" was commissioned by the hotel) were also commonplace at both the Manhattan Beach and the Oriental Hotel, which was dedicated at its 1880 opening by President Rutherford B. Hayes.

New tastes in entertainment in Manhattan Beach and beyond, as well as an increased interest in creating a year-round community, led to a shift in how the area was used. At the turn of the twentieth century, the popular amusement parks opened in Coney Island; other neighborhoods of Brooklyn were developed as suburbs; and by 1910 Coney Island's three racetracks had closed. The Manhattan Beach Hotel closed and was demolished in 1911; the Oriental Hotel followed in 1916.

Permanent residential development began in 1908, when the Manhattan Beach Improvement Company, owned by realtor Joseph P. Day (who had bought out Austin Corbin, Jr.'s share when the Manhattan Beach Hotel folded), divided land north of the hotels into building lots. Several houses built during this

Main gate of Kingsborough Community College at end of Oriental Boulevard

Oriental Hotel (1880), ca. 1905 (New York Historical Society)

period remain standing today, as does St. Margaret Mary Roman Catholic Church (1920) on Oriental Boulevard, which was built to serve an early Irish congregation.

Manhattan Beach residents have been passionate about maintaining single-family homes in their community. Except for one building, which slipped in when a zoning variance lapsed in the early 1930s, apartment house construction has been prohibited in the neighborhood on all but West End Avenue. The classic look of Manhattan Beach has been altered with recent construction of large, modern homes.

Since houses began being built in Manhattan Beach, the residents have been mostly Italian American and Jewish. Manhattan Beach is now predominantly Jewish, and many of its newest residents are emigrants from the former Soviet Union, some of whom first settled in Brighton Beach.

Manhattan Beach has only a few small stores. Although most residents own cars, many walk to the busy shopping areas in nearby Brighton Beach or venture to Sheepshead Bay via a pedestrian path over the Ocean Avenue Bridge (1882).

On a summer evening in Marine Park, laughter spills out of open windows as neighbors prepare for a barbecue on a side street that has been closed for the event. Children skip inside the giddy twirl of a jump rope or toss free throws into driveway basketball hoops. Across Fillmore Avenue, in Brooklyn's largest green space—also named Marine Park—the *thwap* of a cricket bat and rowdy cheers announce that a Brooklyn Cricket League game is under way. With 800 acres of backyard to play in—including Brooklyn's largest golf course; bocce, tennis, basketball, and handball courts; a one-mile running track; fields for softball, football, cricket, and soccer; and a nature trail and environmental center—it's no wonder that many Marine Park families stay in the neighborhood for generations.

■ When in 1937 Flatbush Avenue was extended to connect Brooklyn to Jacob Riis Park in the Rockaways, Marine Parkway Bridge, now Gil Hodges–Marine Parkway Bridge, had the longest highway bridge lift span in the world (540 feet).
■ The Brooklyn Cricket League has been playing continuously in Brooklyn for more than 60 years, and in Marine Park for more than 20.
■ Each Halloween, Marine Park's children revel in a "haunted" twilight walk hosted by the 63rd Precinct Community Council.
■ More than 100 species of birds have been sighted in Marine Park.

Single-family houses at Avenue U and East 38th Street

Marine Park

Marine Park, part of the original town of Flatlands, retained its sleepy, bucolic character much longer than neighboring communities like Gerritsen Beach. It was not until the beginning of the twentieth century that developers began to buy land in the Jamaica Bay area in anticipation of the building of a major port. At about the same time, philanthropists Alfred T. White, who built experimental housing that still stands in Brooklyn Heights and Cobble Hill (see Cobble Hill), and Frederic B. Pratt, the son of Charles Pratt, founder of Pratt Institute (see Clinton Hill), bought 140 acres in the Marine Park area. In 1920 the William C. Whitney family donated their land to the city, conditional on its being used as a public park. Although Mayor John F. Hylan initially declined the gift, he eventually relented. Plans made in 1931 for the park included pools, a canal, marina, stadium, hockey rink, theater, and athletic fields. In 1939 a scaled-down Marine Park opened, its original grandiose plans having fallen victim to the Depression.

Housing construction began in earnest during the 1920s and 1930s, after a sewer system was built for the proposed port, which never materialized. Most of Marine Park's early homes were single-family houses with driveways, to accommodate residents with cars. (Even though a proposed bond approved an IRT subway extension to Avenue U, the neighborhood remained beyond the subway lines.) More construction followed in the 1930s, as the Belt Parkway was completed and developers filled in marshland. During this period, Flatbush Avenue was extended south of Avenue U, and the Marine Parkway Bridge was opened to connect Marine Park to the Rockaways.

NEIGHBORHOOD PROFILE

Boundaries: from Nostrand Avenue and Gerritsen Avenue on the west to Flatbush Avenue on the east, from Flatlands Avenue or, sometimes, Kings Highway, on the north to Avenue U and Avenue V on the south.
Bus: B7: Kings Highway B2: Avenue R/Avenue S B100: Fillmore Ave. B3: Avenue U B31: Gerritsen Ave. B44: Nostrand Ave. B9: Flatbush Ave. BQ35: Flatbush Ave. B41: Flatbush Ave. B46: Flatbush Ave.
Community Board: No. 18
Police Precinct: 63rd Precinct (1844 Brooklyn Ave.)

RYDER ST

KINGS HGWY

FLATLANDS AVE

AVENUE P

QUENTIN RD

NOSTRAND AVE

HENDRICKSON ST

FLATBUSH AVE

COLEMAN ST

KIMBALL ST

RYDER ST

E 38 ST

E 37 ST

E 36 ST

E 35 ST

E 34 ST

E 33 ST

E 32 ST

E 31 ST

AVENUE R

MARINE PARK

MARINE PKWY

MADISON PL

BURNETT ST

FILLMORE AVE

AVENUE S

AVENUE T

AVENUE U

AVENUE V

TO MARINE PKWY BRIDGE →

STUART ST

GERRITSEN AVE

MARINE PARK

MARINE PARK

MARINE PARK GOLF COURSE

GATEWAY NATIONAL RECREATION AREA

● Floyd Bennett Field

Marine Park is connected to what was once Floyd Bennett Field, New York City's first municipal airport. Built on 1,500 acres of reclaimed marshland, the field was dedicated in 1930 by Mayor James J. Walker and named for the pilot who in 1926 flew Admiral Richard Byrd over the North Pole. The airport was enlarged in 1936 as a project of the Works Progress Administration and was used by Amelia Earhart and Howard Hughes, among others. On July 17, 1938, Douglas (Wrong Way) Corrigan took off from Floyd Bennett Field and into the history books for an outrageous mishap. After announcing that he would fly to California, the pilot set off in a dense fog, crossed the Atlantic, and landed in Dublin. Corrigan's sense of direction may have failed him, but his instinct for publicity was right on target: the flight brought fame to Corrigan and Brooklyn. He even starred in the 1939 film of his exploit, *The Flying Irishman*. In 1942 Floyd Bennett Field was sold to the navy, and as Naval Air Station New York it provided air cover for convoys leaving from the Port of New York during the U-boat offensive of 1942. In 1972 the airfield was taken over by the National Park Service, and today it is part of the Gateway National Recreation Area.

Shops on Marine Parkway and Quentin Road

Single-family houses along Avenue R and Burnett Street

Today most homes in Marine Park are still single-family dwellings with driveways and garages, although the neighborhood also offers some attached and semi-attached houses, as well as smaller apartment buildings. A predominantly Italian American, Irish American, and Jewish neighborhood, Marine Park has a strong sense of community.

Midwood

Neighborhoods, like people, can have charisma—a magnetic charm that transcends the accoutrements of appearance, the idioms of a single era. Midwood is just such a neighborhood. Although its history is layered with distinctive moments, its strength lies in its timelessly attractive homes and its residents' enduring devotion to higher education and diversity. From its days as a sleepy suburb whose street lamps were illuminated by a lamplighter on his bicycle, to its role in the silent movie industry, to its current incarnation as the home of a large Hasidic and Orthodox Jewish community and many faculty members from nearby Brooklyn College, Midwood has always been a special place to live.

NEIGHBORHOOD FACTS

■ Legend has it that while the Vitagraph studios were being used to film silent movies, neighborhood residents and even passersby were occasionally asked to be extras. Lev Trotsky was also a bit player in a Vitagraph movie. The company stored its film in a warehouse in East Flatbush. The building had an early ventilation system on the roof that was designed to keep stored film cool in the days before air conditioning.

■ One of Midwood's best-known former residents is actor and director Woody Allen, who graduated from Midwood High School and Brooklyn College. Actress Marisa Tomei, who graduated from Edward R. Murrow High School in 1982, is also from Midwood.

Pakistani businesses on Coney Island Avenue near Cortelyou Road

158 Midwood lies between the original Dutch town of Flatbush and English town of Gravesend. Because the area was covered with thick forests, the Dutch called it the Midwout (middle woods). The neighborhood is still renowned for its 18,000 or so shade trees and for having one of the largest selections of single-family detached houses in Brooklyn. One of the most famous of these is the Johannes Van Nuyse House (1803), sometimes called the Van Nuyse–Magaw House, which has been landmarked by New York City. In 1916 the Dutch Colonial farmhouse was moved from its original site farther south to its current location on East 22nd Street, between Avenues I and J. Johannes Van Nuyse was the son of early settler Joost Van Nuyse, whose house still stands in Flatlands (see Flatlands).

In 1906 the largely underdeveloped neighborhood attracted the Vitagraph film company, which opened a studio at

Elegant single-family homes of Midwood

NEIGHBORHOOD PROFILE

Boundaries: <u>Midwood</u>: from McDonald Avenue on the west to Nostrand Avenue on the east, from around Avenue H on the north to Avenue P on the south. <u>East Midwood</u>: from Ocean Avenue on the west to Bedford Avenue on the east, from Brooklyn College campus on the north to Avenue L on the south. <u>Nottingham</u>: in flux, but generally from East 21st Street on the west to East 29th Street on the east, from Avenue L on the north to Avenue N on the south.
Subway: <u>IND F</u>: Avenue I, 22nd Avenue and Bay Pkwy., Avenue N, Avenue P. <u>Brighton Line D and Q</u>: Avenue J, Avenue M
Bus: <u>B11</u>: Avenue I/Avenue J/Bedford Ave. <u>B6</u>: Avenue J/Bedford Ave. <u>B9</u>: Avenue L/Avenue M/Avenue N <u>B7</u>: Kings Highway <u>B82</u>: Kings Highway <u>B68</u>: Coney Island Ave. <u>Bx29</u>: Coney Island Ave. <u>B49</u>: Ocean Ave.
Libraries: Brooklyn Public Library Midwood Branch (East 16th St. near Avenue J)
Theaters: Brooklyn Center for the Performing Arts at Brooklyn College (154 Gershwin Hall), George Gershwin Theater (Brooklyn College), Walt Whitman Hall (Brooklyn College), Sam Levenson Recital Hall (Brooklyn College), New Workshop Theater (Brooklyn College)
Community Board: No. 14
Police Precinct: 66th Precinct (5822 16th Ave.), 70th Precinct (154 Lawrence Ave.)
Fire Department: Engine 250 (Flatbush, 126 Foster Ave.), Engine 255 Ladder 157 (Flatbush, 1367 Rogers Ave.), Engine 281 Ladder 147 (Flatbush, 1210 Cortelyou Rd.)
Hospitals and Clinics: The New York Community Hospital of Brooklyn (2525 Kings Highway)

Locust Avenue and East 15th Street, off Avenue M. The studio was most active between 1906 and 1915 making silent movies and cartoons, and for a brief time Midwood welcomed Cecil B. DeMille and movie stars like Rudolph Valentino, comedian John Bunny, and Norma Talmadge. In 1925 Vitagraph opened a second studio in Hollywood, then was bought out by Warner Brothers. During the 1950s, NBC television purchased a portion of the studios and, beginning in 1953, used them to produce favorite shows like *The Steve Allen Show* and *The Perry Como Show* and the live special *Peter Pan*, starring Mary Martin. In the 1980s, the old Vitagraph studios were used to film live telecasts of *The Cosby Show*, and for more than 30 years, the popular daytime drama *Another World* has been shot there. A large portion of the studios was renovated in 1962 and now houses a Jewish girls' day school.

The neighborhood was discovered by would-be residents shortly after the turn of the century, after the Brooklyn-Manhattan Transit line of the subway opened in 1908 and the Interborough Rapid Transit line was extended there in 1920. The area became densely settled and heavily developed. As subdivisions and small groups of houses were created, neighborhood organizations were formed. Two areas delineated by these organizations, East Midwood and Nottingham, are still considered small neighborhoods within Midwood.

The history of **East Midwood**, which lies near the northeastern corner of today's Midwood, began in the first decade of the twentieth century. During this period, the area bounded by Ocean Avenue, Bedford Avenue, the Long Island Railroad recessed track (called "the cut"), and Avenue L was sold in 40-by-100-foot parcels, zoned for single-family detached houses. Streets were planned,

sidewalks laid out, roadways paved, and in 1923 a neighborhood organization was founded. **Nottingham** remained largely undeveloped even after 1921, when its neighborhood organization was founded by Joe Dorman, a New York City fire commissioner. The Nottingham area covered only nine square blocks then, from East 21st Street to East 29th Street, between Avenues L and

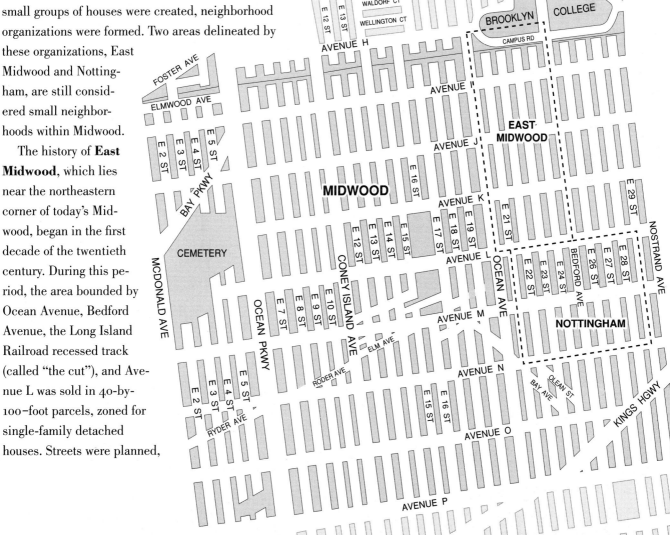

M, but as houses were built in the 1920s, the neighborhood's boundaries stretched to include areas north and south. Both Nottingham and East Midwood have no large stores and few small ones. Residents work to keep the areas noncommercial, and their efforts have kept property values rising. There are no large apartment buildings within these small neighborhoods.

In the 1920s and 1930s, and even into the 1940s, most Midwood residents were Italian American and Jewish. Since the 1980s, however, more Orthodox Jews have been moving into the neighborhood; today they make up approximately half of Midwood's population. Many of the residents of Midwood are Hasidic Jews. Both Ashkenazi Jews from northern Europe and Sephardic Jews from the Middle East and southern Europe live in Midwood.

The new conservative religious believers have had a profound effect on the look of Midwood. Houses that were already large are being renovated and expanded to accommodate families with many children. Synagogues have been built along Ocean Parkway, and within the neighborhood, on the residential streets, many homes have been converted to *shtieblech*, which serve as small synagogues and as homes for the rabbis who conduct services there. The neighborhood hosts religious schools. And many stores along the main commercial streets—Avenues

A Pakistani food shop

A kosher meat market

● Brooklyn College

In 1910 what became Brooklyn College opened in Manhattan as an extension of City College for Teachers. The school was enlarged in 1917 and began to offer evening freshman classes for men who had completed high school. When the school was enlarged a second time, it moved to Downtown Brooklyn and became a two-year college. In 1930 the Board of Higher Education authorized the school to become a four-year institution called Brooklyn College. In 1937 the current campus, which in fact lies within the neighborhood boundary of Flatbush, opened on the site of the Flatbush Golf Course. President Franklin D. Roosevelt laid the cornerstone in 1936.

Brooklyn College now has around 16,000 full-time students. Its faculty has included the Beat poet Allen Ginsberg and the violinist Itzhak Perlman, and it counts among its notable alumni former congressional representative Shirley Chisholm, writer Irwin Shaw, and filmmaker Paul Mazursky.

The Brooklyn College campus is undergoing a $500 million renovation, including the new Brooklyn College Library (2002). The facilities are open to all New York City residents who qualify.

J and M, Kings Highway, and Flatbush, Nostrand, and Coney Island Avenues —observe the sabbath by closing early on Friday and remaining closed on Saturday.

Meanwhile, immigrants from China, Haiti, Guyana, Jamaica, Iran, and India have also been moving into Midwood. In 1982 a large mosque opened on Coney Island Avenue. And so many immigrants from Pakistan have moved into the community that a section of stores along Coney Island Avenue is sometimes referred to as "Little Pakistan." Currently more than 70 Pakistanis own businesses in the area, rejuvenating a commercial district that had fallen into disrepair in the

1970s. Each August, Pakistan's Independence Day is celebrated with a street festival.

The new library at Brooklyn College (John Ricasoli)

Mill Basin

It seems that only the sea has been constant for Mill Basin. Not long ago, the waves of Jamaica Bay lapped onto wharves where refineries hummed with activity and busy tugs guided stately laden ships to their docks. Today, the same currents sweep yachts by million-dollar homes, past a shore where more than 200 private docks extend from carefully manicured lawns. Some of the posh houses of Mill Basin's waterfront along National Drive and Indiana Place may be worth $4 million or more and boast indoor swimming pools, elevators, and multicar garages.

In 1664 John Tilton, Sr., and Samuel Spicer of Gravesend acquired much of the area from the Canarsee Indians, who had named the place Equendito (broken lands) because of the incursion of tide pools and rivulets from Jamaica Bay. In the seventeenth century, Mill Basin, part of the original Dutch town of Flatlands, became known for its many tidal mills, which used the motion of the tides to grind grain. After 1675 the land was owned by Jan Martense Schenck, who foresaw the development of Jamaica Bay into a transatlantic port, and then, from 1818 to 1870, by the family of General Phillip S. Crooke.

Most of Mill Basin (then called Mill Island) was rural until 1890, when Robert L. Crooke built a lead-smelting plant. His company, Crooke Smelting, was bought out by the National Lead Company in 1900, and Crooke sold the remainder of his land to McNulty and Fitzgerald, which built the bulkheads that filled in the area's marshes. Until the first quarter of the twentieth century, Mill Basin's main resource continued to be shellfish—crabs, oysters, and clams pulled from Jamaica Bay. Clammers lived in shacks on stilts near the beach.

Large homes along East 66th Street overlooking the East Mill Basin

In 1906 the Flatbush Improvement Company bought the marshland and hired the Atlantic, Gulf and Pacific company to dredge the creeks and fill in the open meadows. After the company finished this work and laid out streets, 332 acres were ready for industrial development. Within ten years, National Lead, Gulf Refining, and other large industrial firms had opened plants in Mill Basin. Atlantic, Gulf and Pacific bought its own land in 1909, built three dry docks, and employed a thousand workers. Although companies in the area campaigned to promote Jamaica Bay as New York City's newest harbor, they were unable to attract much shipping business.

From 1913 to 1923, Flatbush Avenue was extended to the Rockaway Inlet. An additional 2,700 feet of dock facilities were built, and the extension allowed for a roadway along the marshes. At the same time a channel to Jamaica Bay was dredged and bulkheads and wharf platforms were built on the mainland side of Mill Creek. By 1919 Mill Basin had at least six manufacturing and commercial companies. During the

Boats docked at Mill Basin with Kings Plaza Shopping Center and its marina in the background

NEIGHBORHOOD PROFILE

Boundaries: Mill Basin: from Flatbush Avenue on the west to Veterans Avenue and East 68th Street on the east, from Avenue T up Ralph Avenue and east on Veterans Avenue on the north to East Mill Basin and Mill Basin on the south. Old Mill Basin: from Flatbush Avenue on the west to Mill Avenue on the east, from Avenue T on the north to Kings Plaza Shopping Center on the south.
Bus: B78: Avenue U/Ralph Ave. B3: Avenue U B100: Avenue T/Mill Ave./East 66th St.
Libraries: Brooklyn Public Library Mill Basin Branch (2385 Ralph Ave.)
Community Board: No. 18
Police Precinct: 63rd Precinct (1844 Brooklyn Ave.)

U is called **Old Mill Basin**. Most of Old Mill Basin's houses were built from the 1920s to the 1940s, when semidetached frame houses were built on 20-by-100–foot lots. Many of these houses, once home to Atlantic, Gulf and Pacific's thousand workers, have been beautifully renovated.

It was after World War II that the land south of Avenue U, surrounded by East Mill Basin and Mill Basin, changed radically. This area is often called Mill Island, in recognition of its geography before the area was connected to Brooklyn with landfill. During this time, Atlantic, Gulf and Pacific sold the land between Avenue U, East 68th Street, East Mill Basin, Bassett Avenue, and Strickland and Mill Avenues to Flatbush Park Homes. Mill Basin in general grew as landfill was added. Brick bungalows were constructed from East 65th Street to Mill Avenue, and a two-story cooperative apartment building was built in 1954 with a federal subsidy. Houses that sold for $10,000 to $12,000 when they were built in the late 1940s and early 1950s now sell for more than $300,000. Indeed, the land itself has become so desirable that the area's residents, mainly of Italian and Irish descent, have torn down the original bungalows on East 63rd, East 64th, and East 65th Streets and custom built new houses there.

In 1970 Mill Basin became home to the first suburban mall in Brooklyn, Kings Plaza Shopping Center, which opened on the south side of Avenue U, east of Flatbush Avenue. But as with the rest of the neighborhood, the lure of the sea is paramount: the shopping center is adjacent to an active marina.

1920s and 1930s, the docks were often rented to different small industrial firms. Until the late 1940s, Mill Basin remained industrial, but when plans dissipated for trains that would connect the area with the rest of Brooklyn's transportation systems, industry lost interest in the neighborhood. During this period, much of the land on the inland side of Avenue U still had small farms.

The area to the north of Avenue

Park Slope

In the late 1800s Park Slope became a magnet for Brooklyn's well-to-do, a retreat for those who wished to live lavishly as well as in close proximity to Brooklyn's lovely historic landmarks, the green expanse of Prospect Park, and quick commuter routes to Manhattan. But the appeal of today's Park Slope lies in its people as well as its places. Within its blocks of beautiful brownstones, Park Slope is home to a diverse and ever-changing community of residents who cherish the neighborhood's unique history and architecture.

Since its beginnings as "Prospect Hill," Park Slope has been divided into two smaller neighborhoods, **North Slope** and **South Slope**. Although real-estate prices and immigration have continued to keep these communities separate, the distinction is becoming blurred. The North Slope, for example, adjacent to Grand Army Plaza (see Prospect Heights) and the

Elegant row houses of Park Slope

166 7th Avenue shopping area, offered the only stores or restaurants in "the Slope" until the 1990s. But nowadays shops and dining areas are opening in South Slope as well.

Park Slope is named for its nearness to Prospect Park and its location on a gradual incline from the Gowanus Canal to the park. From the time of its colonization by the Dutch in the 1600s until the middle of the nineteenth century, the land was used primarily for farming, except for a brief, explosive moment during the Revolutionary War. On August 27, 1776, at the start of the Battle of Brooklyn, the outflanked American soldiers faced approximately 4,000 British troops at Battle Pass, which is today within Prospect Park, just north of the rebuilt Wildlife Conservation Center.

Even though Flatbush Road (now Flatbush Avenue) was well traveled, Park Slope was not developed until the 1870s, when Prospect Park was completed and horse-drawn rail cars reached the area. During this period the first row houses, most of which were four stories tall, were constructed, and the earliest mansions were built north of 9th Street. Two of these early buildings have been designated New York City landmarks. One, the William B. Cronyn residence at 271 9th Street between 4th and 5th Avenues, was built from 1856 to 1857 and later housed the Charles M. Higgins india ink company. The other, Public School 39, also known as the Henry Briston School, was erected in 1877 and can be found at 417 6th Avenue.

When a cable railway began crossing the Brooklyn Bridge in 1883, professionals and entrepreneurs were drawn to the area because of the easy commute to Downtown Brooklyn and Manhattan. Brownstone construction kept pace with this new demand.

During the late 1800s Prospect Park West (then 9th Avenue) from Grand Army Plaza to 1st Street was known as the Gold Coast of Brooklyn. Mansions were constructed whose splendor matched that of the 5th Avenue mansions in Manhattan. Park Slope magnates included George Tangeman, who produced Royal and Cleveland Baking Powder and whose house, built in 1891, still stands at 274–276 Berkeley Place; Thomas Adams, Jr., who conceived of Chiclets chewing gum and lived at 119 8th Avenue (1888); and William Childs, inventor of Bon Ami cleanser. Childs's home, at 53 Prospect Park West, was built in 1901 and now houses the Brooklyn Ethical Culture Society.

Magnificent mansions still exist in the rest of the landmarked historic district of Park Slope as well, and some of the finest Romanesque Revival and Queen Anne residences in the United States still grace its streets. The houses on Carroll Street and Montgomery Place are among the most notable. The Venetian Gothic Montauk Club, which opened in 1891, offered private membership and a luxurious interior for enter-

---

Map labels:

PACIFIC ST, DEAN ST, BERGEN ST, ST MARKS PL, WARREN ST, PROSPECT PL, BALTIC ST, PARK PL, BUTLER ST, STERLING PL, DOUGLASS ST, ST JOHN PL, DE GRAW ST, LINCOLN PL, SACKETT ST, BERKELEY PL, UNION ST, PRESIDENT ST, CARROLL ST, GARFIELD PL, 1 ST, 2 ST, 3 ST, 4 ST, 5 ST, 6 ST, 7 ST, 8 ST, 9 ST, 10 ST, 11 ST, 12 ST, 13 ST, 14 ST, 15 ST, 16 ST, 17 ST, 18 ST

FLATBUSH AVE, FOURTH AVE, FIFTH AVE, SIXTH AVE, SEVENTH AVE, EIGHTH AVE, PROSPECT PARK WEST, PLAZA ST WEST

POLHEMUS PL, FISKE PL, MONTGOMERY PL, WEBSTER PL, JACKSON PL, WINDSOR PL, PROSPECT AVE

PROSPECT EXPWY, 17 ST

NORTH SLOPE, PARK SLOPE, SOUTH SLOPE, PROSPECT PARK, GREEN-WOOD CEMETERY

167

North Park Slope house at Union Street
and Plaza Street West (Brooklyn Historical
Society)

NEIGHBORHOOD FACTS

■ In 1881 the Ansonia Clock factory at 7th Avenue and 12th Street was the largest clock factory in the world, employing many Polish and Irish immigrants. In 1982 the building that housed the factory was converted to cooperative apartments. It is now called Ansonia Court.

■ The Brooklyn Blades, New York City's only all-women's traveling ice hockey team, was launched in 1993 as an offshoot of a "learn to play" hockey program in Prospect Park.

■ Following a longstanding tradition in Park Slope, residents have frequent "stoop sales": on mild spring, summer, or fall weekends, they set out unwanted wares on their steps for sale.

■ Park Slope loves celebrations. The neighborhood's Irish American Day parade in March is the largest in Brooklyn; in October the community sponsors a children's Halloween Parade on 7th Avenue; and Prospect Park's New Year's Eve fireworks are spectacular.

■ On December 16, 1960, a commercial airliner collided with another airplane and after attempting an emergency landing in Prospect Park, crashed at 7th Avenue and Sterling Place. Eighty-four passengers and six persons on the ground were killed. A memorial garden now occupies the site of the crash.

taining. It remains a private club, but its upper floors have been sold and are now rented as apartments.

Three historic churches also stand in this section of Park Slope: St. John's Episcopal Church (1889; nave, 1885), Grace United Methodist Episcopal Church, originally Grace Methodist Episcopal Church (1883; parsonage, 1887), and Brooklyn Memorial Presbyterian Church (1883; chapel, 1888). The Brooklyn Conservatory of Music is housed in what was once the Park Slope Masonic Club (1881), which was originally a private residence on 7th Avenue at Lincoln Place.

At the turn of the century more-

168 unassuming, less-expensive row houses and apartment buildings were put up west of 7th Avenue and south of 9th Street as homes for workers at local factories and at the nearby Gowanus Canal. But grand structures were still being conceived, such as the now-landmarked, imposing Classical Revival synagogue Beth Elohim (1910; temple house, 1928), which stands at 8th Avenue and Garfield Place.

Construction in Park Slope slowed after World War I because subway lines had been built to reach areas farther south of the park that were still untouched and thus more desirable to developers. Between the world wars, the working-class sections of South Slope were home to predominantly Irish and Irish American residents.

After World War II, wealthier Park Slope residents moved to the suburbs, and working-class residents moved into North Slope. Some of the luxurious brownstones were turned into rooming houses and later demolished for new apartment buildings. Other buildings were abandoned. Only in the 1960s and 1970s did

Farmers' market on Prospect Park West

A United airliner collided with another plane on December 16, 1960, crashing near 7th Avenue and Sterling Place (Brian Merlis Collection)

residents begin to work to recover the value of these lovely homes, and they initiated a national movement in the process. Affordable row houses bought at that time are either still being enjoyed by their original buyers or have been sold at great profit, as the neighborhood is once again thriving.

For much of the 1970s and 1980s, wealthy upper-middle-class Park Slope residents lived only in the North Slope, whereas the South Slope was known as the home of newer immigrants from Puerto Rico, Latin America, the Dominican Republic, Jamaica, and Ireland. But South Slope residents have been busy beautifying, organizing, and revitalizing their section of the neighborhood, and the division between north and south has become less distinct. Indeed, investing in a South Slope home has been a wise choice for many. As ever more couples stay in Brooklyn to raise families, even today's upscale young professionals are unlikely to be able to afford a home in North Slope.

Park Slope has a vocal and supportive lesbian community, and since 1993 the Lesbian Herstory Archives, one of the largest collections of lesbian research materials in the United States, has been housed in the neighborhood. Park Slope is also noted for its large number of writers, editors, academics, and lawyers. Some joke that almost everyone in Park Slope is a recent transplant from the Upper West Side of Manhattan. It is true that unlike some Brooklyn neighborhoods, where most residents are Brooklyn natives, Park Slope contains few residents who grew up in the borough.

170

While the statue (built in 1895) still remains, the 14th Regiment Armory of New York National Guard has been turned over to the city and is now the Park Slope Armory.

Park Slope's sites and attractions are as varied as its residents. A popular annual attraction is the Seventh Heaven Street Fair. Sponsored by local merchants, the fair draws residents and visitors to 7th Avenue, Park Slope's main shopping thoroughfare, which features popular craft stores, jewelry shops, cafes, and restaurants. Both 5th and 4th Avenues have new stores and restaurants as well. Since 1998 food connoisseurs have delighted in the neighborhood's seasonal green market Saturdays at the 5th Street entrance to Prospect Park, and enjoy shopping at one of the largest food cooperatives in the United States, a Park Slope favorite since 1973.

NEIGHBORHOOD PROFILE

Boundaries: <u>Park Slope</u>: from 4th Avenue on the west to Prospect Park West on the east, from Flatbush Avenue on the north to 17th Street on the south. <u>North Slope</u>: from 4th Avenue on the west to Prospect Park West on the east, from Flatbush Avenue on the north to 9th Street on the south. <u>South Slope</u>: from 4th Avenue on the west to Prospect Park West on the east, from 9th Street on the north to 17th Street on the south.

Subway: <u>BMT Fourth Avenue N and R</u>: Union St., 9th St. <u>IND F</u>: 4th Ave., 7th Ave./Park Slope, 15th St.

Bus: <u>B41</u>: Flatbush Ave. <u>B75</u>: 9th St. <u>B63</u>: 5th Ave. <u>B67</u>: 7th Ave. <u>B69</u>: 8th Ave./Prospect Park West <u>IRT Line 2 and 3</u>: Atlantic Ave., Bergen St., Grand Army Plaza <u>IND D and Q</u>: Atlantic Ave., 7th Ave.

Libraries: Brooklyn Public Library Park Slope Branch (6th Ave. near 9th St.)

Community Board: No. 6

Police Precinct: 78th Precinct (65 6th Ave.)

Fire Department: Engine 220 Ladder 122 (530 11th St.), Engine 239 (395 4th Ave.)

Hospitals and Clinics: New York Methodist Hospital (506 6th St.), Park Slope Family Health Center (220 13th St.)

Mayor John Lindsay at Prospect Park bicycle race, April 1967 (Brian Merlis Collection)

Young girl contemplates life, a wonderful pastime in Prospect Park (Prospect Park Alliance)

● **Prospect Park**

Prospect Park, a New York City scenic landmark, offers residents of Brooklyn 526 acres of fields, woods, lakes, and trails for running, biking, and relaxing. (The Brooklyn Botanic Garden is technically in Prospect Heights and will be discussed in that entry.) Many think that the park, designed by Frederick Law Olmsted and Calvert Vaux, is even more beautiful than the team's first effort, Manhattan's Central Park.

Although the creation of a Brooklyn park was authorized in 1859, planning was delayed by the Civil War. Finally, in 1865 Olmsted and Vaux designed naturalistic Prospect Park, and its construction was completed by 1873. Their plan divided the park into three areas: meadows, forests, and bodies of water. The park's landmarked classical entrances, which are more formal than most of the other architectural features in the park, were designed by McKim, Mead and White and crafted by prominent sculptors, including Brooklyn-born Frederick MacMonnies, between 1889 and 1907. Among the sculptures is MacMonnies's statue of James S. T. Stranahan (1891), the founder of Brooklyn's park and boulevard system and the head of the commission for creating Prospect Park. (Stranahan was also a strong advocate for the building of the Brooklyn Bridge and the consolidation of the City of Brooklyn with New York City.) Prospect Park Boathouse (1904), which was restored in 1984, and the Croquet Shelter (1904) are other New York City landmarks that are well worth a visit. Near the boathouse stands the Camperdown Elm, the gift of A. G. Burgess in 1872, which inspired Brooklyn resident Marianne Moore to write "Camperdown Elm" (1967). Several brownstones in Park Slope were landmarked specifically to preserve the elm from north winds. At the southern extreme of Long Meadow is the Quaker Cemetery (1846), a fenced-in private cemetery that contains the grave of actor Montgomery Clift, among others.

Prospect Park has a skating rink and a carousel. The first carousel was erected in 1874; the present one is a composite construction built in 1990 from two Coney Island carousels that were created by Charles Carmel in 1915 and 1918. The carousel is one of 12 remaining Carmel designs. The Flatbush Toll Gate, removed from Flatbush Turnpike in 1889, stands near the carousel. A children's fishing contest, an annual tradition for more than 50 years, draws young anglers and their parents from throughout the borough. A mansion once owned by the Litchfield family, known as Litchfield Villa, has been retained as an elegant architectural complement to the lush outdoor space; today it houses the Brooklyn headquarters of the New York City Department of Parks and Recreation. The Italianate villa, considered one of the finest in the United States, was constructed in the mid-1850s by Edwin Clarke Litchfield, a railroad financier, on an estate situated near what is today Prospect Park West. Another significant building has also been given new life in the park. The Lefferts Homestead, an eighteenth-century Dutch farmhouse transported to Prospect Park from Prospect-Lefferts Gardens in 1918, is a New York City landmark that now serves as a children's museum. The revamped Prospect Park Wildlife Conservation Center (1993) has a free petting zoo that includes farm animals, exotic species like wallaby, emu, and red panda, and wildlife familiar to urban children—pigeons, mice, and hamsters.

Brooklyn Botanic Garden, Palm House
with lily pond (Christine M. Douglas)

The boathouse is now the Prospect Park
Audubon Center

Summer fun on the meadows and lake of
Prospect Park

On Rustic Bridge, Prospect Park, 1907
(Brian Merlis Collection)

PROSPECT PARK

Detail of sculpture atop Soldiers' and Sailors' Memorial Arch at Grand Army Plaza

Prospect Heights

A Prospect Heights artist at work

Prospect Heights is a homeowner's dream. After a period of decline and foreclosures, the neighborhood has bounced back—and then some. Government incentives offered in the 1980s to refurbish the community have reawakened developers and would-be residents to the beauty, intimacy, and tremendous investment potential of Prospect Heights. The small neighborhood features a wide array of homes, many with large gardens and yards hidden in back, including brownstones from the 1880s, limestones from the 1890s, and even—tucked among homes built around the turn of the century—brick row houses

Brownstones at Carlton Avenue and Bergen Street

NEIGHBORHOOD PROFILE

Boundaries: from Flatbush Avenue on the west to Washington Avenue on the east, from Atlantic Avenue on the north to Eastern Parkway, the Prospect Park Wildlife Conservation Center, and the Brooklyn Botanic Garden on the south.
Subway: <u>IRT 2, 3 and 4</u>: Grand Army Plaza
Bus: <u>B45</u>: Atlantic Ave./Washington Ave. <u>B65</u>: Dean St./Bergen St. <u>B71</u>: Eastern Pkwy. <u>B41</u>: Flatbush Ave. <u>B67</u>: Flatbush Ave.
Libraries: Brooklyn Public Library Central Branch (Grand Army Plaza)
Community Board: No. 8
Police Precinct: 77th Precinct (127 Utica Ave.)
Fire Department: Engine 219 Ladder 105 (735 Dean St.), Engine 280 Ladder 132 (489 St. John's Pl.)
Hospitals and Clinics: Nephrology Foundation of Brooklyn, North Unit (342 Flatbush Ave.)

Mural at a recycling center

from the earlier 1860s and 1870s. The community also has a smattering of carriage houses and freestanding mansions.

Residents within Prospect Heights have played an important role in their neighborhood's renewal by keeping the needs of their low- and moderate-income neighbors in focus. Many buildings have been restored with these inhabitants in mind. With middle- and upper-middle-income residents purchasing apartments in lavishly renovated buildings, the result has been a mixed-income neighbor-

Forty-foot bronze screen designed by Thomas Hudson Jones at entrance to library (Randy Duchaine)

One of a few area homes with a mansard roof

Soldiers' and Sailors' Memorial Arch at Grand Army Plaza (Brian Merlis Collection)

Engine No. 219 at 735 Dean Street in 1915 (Brian Merlis Collection)

hood in which all benefit from the community's rich diversity.

Most of the area was developed in the 1870s after Prospect Park was completed; by the 1890s, the neighborhood was being called Prospect Heights. Brownstones and townhouses were built on the side streets, and at the turn of the century, apartment buildings began to go up on the avenues. Although most of these apartment buildings have been converted to condominiums and cooperative apartments, they still tower over Grand Army Plaza and Prospect Park and from the outside look very much as they did when they welcomed their first occupants.

Until World War II the population was mostly middle class, and residents—many shop owners and workers in nearby factories—were primarily Jewish or of Italian or Irish descent. After the war the neighborhood became predominantly African American as an economic slump in the city caused many longtime residents to relocate.

Looking at Prospect Heights today, it is hard to imagine how difficult the 1960s

● Grand Army Plaza

Grand Army Plaza, the traffic circle where Prospect Park West, Flatbush Avenue, and Eastern Parkway meet, has one of the largest sculptures in Brooklyn, the Soldiers' and Sailors' Memorial Arch (1892). The arch, a New York City landmark that honors the Union troops of the Civil War, was built according to a design by John H. Duncan, the architect of Grant's tomb, who won a competition for the memorial. Two years after its completion, Stanford White planned alterations so that sculpture by Brooklyn-born Frederick MacMonnies could be added—as a result, today's arch has heroic bronze reliefs, bronze groups, and carved spandrel figures. Visitors can view this art close up in the spring and fall, when the parks department opens a stairway to the roof of the arch. Wedding parties like to pose in front of the imposing Bailey Fountain (1932), decorated with Tritons and Neptunes, despite the fact that it is seldom working because the pipes need repair. The plaza also contains the John F. Kennedy Memorial (1965), the only Brooklyn memorial to the late president, with a bust by Neil Estern.

Brooklyn Public Library (Ingersoll Memorial Library), off Grand Army Plaza

N E I G H B O R H O O D
F   A   C   T   S

■ The availability of clean water has been an important political issue for Brooklynites. The Mount Prospect Reservoir and Tower (early 1860s), part of Flatbush Water Works, originally supplied water from Ridgewood Reservoir for Brooklyn's higher elevations. Although the tower and reservoir were razed to make way for Institute Park and the Botanic Garden, a former retaining wall still separates the Brooklyn Public Library from the Botanic Garden. As Brooklyn's population grew, its wells became contaminated with sea water—one reason why consolidation with New York City seemed so attractive in 1898. Although Ridgewood water was still used until the 1960s, consolidation gave Brooklyn access to the Croton reservoir system.

■ Two public schools in Prospect Heights are New York City landmarks. Public School 9 (now P.S. 340) and the P.S. 9 Annex (now apartments) are across the street from each other on Sterling Place. Public School 9 was completed in 1868, and its annex was built in 1897 when the school became overcrowded. The composer Aaron Copland, who grew up in Prospect Heights, attended P.S. 9.

■ Both the movie *The Tenant* (1970) and the 1990s television show *Brooklyn South* were filmed in Prospect Heights.

were for residents of the neighborhood. During this transitional period, buildings were abandoned, and rioting on Washington Avenue led to arson and vandalism. The neighborhood lost a large percentage of its housing in the 1970s when many homes were foreclosed on and became city property. According to the 1980 census, Prospect Heights' income levels were below Brooklyn's.

During the early 1980s, however, New York City began selling groups of abandoned buildings to encourage redevelopment in Prospect Heights. Restoration began in the area near Prospect Place and moved east to Washington Avenue. The results were tremendous. Park Slope was becoming overcrowded, new jobs were being cre-

ated in Brooklyn, and housing was in demand. Over the next eight years, more than a third of the buildings were renovated, and the middle-class presence in Prospect Heights grew, lured by condominiums and cooperatives that were inexpensive relative to other areas of Brooklyn. Important to every new resident was the neighborhood's proximity to Prospect Park and mass transit.

Today renovated apartments sell for

PROSPECT HEIGHTS

SIXTH AVE
ATLANTIC AVE
PACIFIC ST
CARLETON AVE
DEAN ST
VANDERBILT AVE
BERGEN ST
ST MARKS AVE
FLATBUSH AVE
PROSPECT PL
UNDERHILL AVE
PARK PL
WASHINGTON AVE
STERLING PL
PLAZA ST WEST
PLAZA ST EAST
ST JOHNS PL
LINCOLN PL
EASTERN PKWY
PROSPECT PARK
BROOKLYN BOTANIC GARDEN

Brooklyn Museum of Art on Eastern Parkway

● **Three Cultural Giants: The Brooklyn Museum of Art, the Brooklyn Botanic Garden, and the Brooklyn Public Library**

Three of Brooklyn's greatest treasures are located in and adjacent to Institute Park (now a little-used name), which was created because Calvert Vaux, co-designer of Prospect Park with Frederick Law Olmsted, recommended that the entire park be located west of Flatbush Avenue to make room for cultural institutions. The resulting triangular green space, bounded by Eastern Parkway, Washington Avenue, and Flatbush Avenue, was designated the site of the Brooklyn Institute of Arts and Sciences (1843), which originally included the Brooklyn Academy of Music (see Fort Greene); it expanded during the 1890s to encompass the Brooklyn Museum of Arts and Sciences, Brooklyn Public Library, and Brooklyn Children's Museum (see Crown Heights). The name was retained until the institutions parted ways in the 1940s.

The Brooklyn Museum of Art (1897) was actually the first institute to grace Institute Park, although the museum's facade on Eastern Parkway was not completed until 1906. Only one-quarter of Stanford White's design was realized; had the building been completed as planned it would have been larger than the Metropolitan Museum of Art or the Louvre. The museum, a New York City historic landmark, boasts one of the country's finest art collections and is particularly well known for its American, Egyptian, and African holdings. In 2004, the Eastern Parkway entrance was restored with a new public plaza added. The Brooklyn Botanic Garden, behind the museum, opened in 1911. Since then Brooklynites have flocked there year-round, especially in springtime to see the cherry trees and to celebrate Forsythia Day, in honor of Brooklyn's official flower. In 1912 ground was broken for the Central Library of the Brooklyn Public Library (1897). Because funds for the library were raised in stages, the building, later redesigned to look from above like an open book, was not completed until 1941, when it was dedicated and named Ingersoll Memorial Library (after the borough president in office at the time). Although neighborhood bragging rights for the Brooklyn Museum of Art and the Botanic Garden may be in dispute, the library, a New York City landmark, sits clearly within the boundaries of Prospect Heights.

as much as 20 times their purchase price in the early 1980s. But residents have remained committed to not allowing gentrification to push out those who stayed through the hard times—working-class and low-income renters and home owners. Prospect Heights now has a wonderful Brooklyn mix of ethnicities and income groups; new immigrants from Jamaica, Haiti, Guyana, Trinidad and Tobago, the Dominican Republic, Barbados, and Panama continue to reinvigorate the neighborhood, and all enjoy sampling ethnic fast food and shopping for crafts on Washington, Flatbush, Vanderbilt, and Underhill Avenues.

Prospect-

Have you ever wondered whether neighborhood organizations can really make a difference? To those who might question the efficacy of grassroots initiatives, Prospect-Lefferts Gardens offers dramatic testimony. Here, in a neighborhood both lovingly preserved and artfully restored, neighborhood organizations have long initiated positive change and galvanized the community. Guidelines for the community's initial buildings ensured an attractive, enduring streetscape. Mandates in the early days against the construction of certain kinds of factories kept the neighborhoods quiet and residential. And during the early 1980s, homeowners became landlords of some apartment buildings in the area. The continuing work of these homeowners, and their willingness to use their own resources to assist neighbors in need, have been heralded as exemplars for other Brooklyn neighborhoods.

In 1977 the New York City Landmarks Preservation Commission noted that the Prospect-Lefferts Gardens historic district, which includes parts of Prospect-Lefferts Gardens and **Lefferts Manor,** the neighborhood's oldest development, remained "one of the finest enclaves of nineteenth-century and early twentieth-century housing in New York City." Restrictions in the Lefferts Manor neighborhood have kept many of the homes single-family residences. For this reason, the

Two- and three-family row houses with large front stoops

Lefferts

interiors of neighborhood houses, unlike those of many of Brooklyn's other fine homes, which have been converted into condominiums or cooperatives, have remained largely unchanged.

The legacy of this remarkable neighborhood began in the seventeenth century. In 1660 a Dutch immigrant named Leffert Pietersen van Haughwout founded a farm at the northern edge of Flatbush, at what is today Lefferts Manor. His farm stayed in the family for many generations, and the land surrounding it remained largely rural until the 1800s.

By 1873 nearby Prospect Park had been completed, and by the late 1800s the town of Flatbush was being built up. A direct descendant of van Haughwout's, James Lefferts, realized the residential value of the Lefferts farmland; in 1894 he subdivided the homestead into 600 separate lots and sold them to builders.

Most of the row houses built in Brooklyn during the 1890s were meant to accommodate more than one family, but Lefferts restricted Lefferts Manor by covenant to single-family residences in the hope of attracting a stable, middle-class population. To ensure that the homes would be attractive to these buyers, Lefferts set guidelines for the builders who bought plots in his development: each house had to cost at least $5,000 to build, be constructed of brick or stone, be at

least two stories high, and be set back from the street at least 14 feet.

The earliest houses still standing in the neighborhood are on Rutland Road and Midwood Street between Flatbush and Bedford Avenues, and on Midwood between Bedford and Rogers Avenues. Many of these buildings, constructed

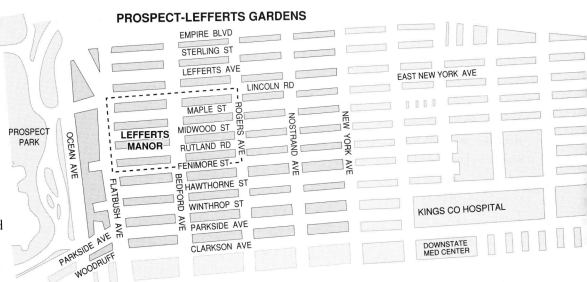

PROSPECT-LEFFERTS GARDENS

Gardens

182 in dark brick and stone, are distinguished by facades ornamented with garlands and wreaths. Parkside Avenue features wrought iron lanterns, and many individuals in Lefferts Manor have installed their own gas lamps in front of their homes.

Between 1905 and 1911, more than 500 houses were built in Prospect-Lefferts Gardens. Most of these houses are made of white limestone, with the

Police Department murals near Bedford Avenue and Empire Boulevard

exception of some lovely row houses on Maple Street. Built by Brooklyn architect Axel Hedman, these distinctive homes in Lefferts Manor have Spanish red-tiled roofs. Soon afterward, in 1913, the New York City–landmarked Brooklyn Central Office, Bureau of Fire Communications for the New York City Fire Department was built on Empire Boulevard. In 1919 the Lefferts Manor Association was formed by residents to ensure compliance with Lefferts Manor's rules. Still active, it is one of the oldest homeowners' associations in New York City.

Outside the boundaries of the original Lefferts Manor there were no building restrictions, so two-family row houses were built. Many still stand on Lefferts Avenue between Bedford and Rogers Avenues and on Sterling Street between Flatbush and Bedford Avenues. A shared front door and entryway make these row houses appear to be single-family dwellings. Between 1915 and 1925, approximately 85 more homes were built in the area. Many feature turrets, balconies, and porches.

As in so many other neighborhoods of Brooklyn, the 1920s and 1930s brought larger apartment buildings to Prospect-Lefferts Gardens. But these have been as well maintained as the row houses, and their Georgian facades still hint at the high ceilings and rich woodwork within.

Black, white, Caribbean American, and Asian American residents of Prospect-Lefferts Gardens are proud that their neighborhood has been peacefully integrated since the 1950s. Throughout that period and the turbulent 1960s the area remained mostly stable, racially mixed, and predominately middle class.

Then as now, businesspeople, lawyers, shop owners, artists, schoolteachers, and doctors filled the row houses and apartments. Maple Street gained its reputation as "Doctors Row" at this time.

Two large, 16-story apartment buildings, called Patio Gardens, were built in the early 1960s on the site of the former Patio movie theater. The more than 450 apartments in these buildings were donated to the National Kidney Foundation of New York and New Jersey by real-estate developer Donald Trump.

In the late 1960s, brownstone enthusiasts from surrounding areas adopted the Lefferts Manor name, extending the boundaries of this once small community. In 1969 the name of the neighborhood evolved further, into Prospect-Lefferts Gardens. The Prospect-Lefferts Gardens Neighborhood Association, from which the neighborhood name was derived, was formed by new residents who were buying brownstones. Prospect was chosen in honor of Prospect Park, Lefferts for the land's original owner, and Gardens for the nearby Brooklyn Botanic Garden. Although the association no longer exists, its spirit continues with the work of other neighborhood organizations.

Prospect-Lefferts today has wide blocks shaded by sycamore and maple trees, although immigrants from the West Indies during the 1980s have brought a new look to small shops and restaurants on Flatbush Avenue.

Apartments and shopping along Flatbush Avenue

NEIGHBORHOOD FACTS

■ The Peter Lefferts House, also known as the Lefferts Homestead, is a New York City historic landmark. Originally built on what is now Flatbush Avenue between Maple and Midwood Streets, it was burned by the British as American troops retreated in 1776. The rebuilt building (1783) was moved to Prospect Park (see Park Slope) in 1918 so that it would be saved from destruction.

■ For several decades, residents of the neighborhood's historic homes have dressed up their unique dwellings for an annual Prospect-Lefferts Gardens house tour.

■ James Lefferts's original specifications for Lefferts Manor included the requirement that the neighborhood have no pig pens, glue factories, or breweries.

Prospect

Stepping past the planter-topped brick gateposts engraved with the initials PPS, visitors to Prospect Park South will find an elegant, serene, and fraternal community, a living portrait of turn-of-the-century Brooklyn. Grand homes represent a wonderfully eclectic mix of different styles: neo-Tudors, French Revivals, Queen Annes, Italian villas, Colonial Revivals, and Missions stand stately and beautiful against a backdrop of towering shade trees and lush front lawns. The historic district of Prospect Park South, a New York City landmark bounded by Stratford Road on the west, East 17th and East 18th Streets on the east, Church Avenue on the north, and Beverley Road on the south, preserves some of the city's finest freestanding homes.

Prospect Park South shares its early history with the town of Flatbush. Neigh-

Park South

borhood land, once owned by the Dutch Reformed Church of Flatbush, remained bucolic until its development in 1899, after rail service reached south of where Prospect Park stands today.

In 1899 Dean Alvord, a developer, bought 40 acres of land from the church and launched a new community, one that was to avoid the row houses already prevalent in Brooklyn. Alvord's unique neighborhood, one "patronized almost entirely by people of intelligence and good breeding" was to offer *rus in urbe*, the country in the city. The later Brooklyn developments of Ditmas Park, South Midwood, Rugby, and Fiske and Manhattan Terraces (see Flatbush and East Flatbush) modeled their neighborhoods after Alvord's successful design.

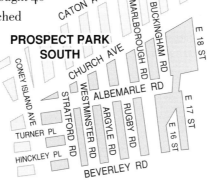

PROSPECT PARK SOUTH

Streets with highbrow British names like Stratford, Westminster, and Buckingham hid buried utility lines and were paved before a single housing plot was sold. Alvord hired a landscaper to design the entire neighborhood's layout, and he established restrictions for construction. Houses were required to be set back 39 feet from the sidewalk, and eight feet of land were to be left between the street and the sidewalk for trees and grass. Buckingham and Albemarle Roads were planned with center malls for trees. To give the neighborhood both short-lived and long-lasting shade, trees that would mature and age quickly were planted between longer-lived trees that would grow large. On many streets, trees were actually planted just within property lines, creating the illusion of streets that are even more expansive than they are (in the early days, this strategy also prevented tethered horses from eating the leaves).

NEIGHBORHOOD FACTS

■ Prospect Park South's neighborhood association, founded in 1905 with the support of 53 families, is one of the oldest continuously running neighborhood groups in the country, and it originally paid for the local subway station. The association's annual house-to-house New Year's dinner is a favorite event of today's members, who number 203 families.

■ The large homes of Prospect Park South have been featured in such movies as *Sophie's Choice* (1982) and *Reversal of Fortune* (1990).

■ Not to be missed is the Japanese House (1902), a pagodalike palace in the heart of Brooklyn, at 131 Buckingham Road.

■ The official residence of the president of Brooklyn College is 115 Westminster Road.

■ Newspaper journalist Nellie Bly (Elizabeth Cochrane Seaman), famous for her exposé of conditions in mental institutions, once lived in Prospect Park South.

A tree-lined vista in Prospect Park South's historic district

NEIGHBORHOOD PROFILE

Boundaries: from Coney Island Avenue on the west to about East 18th Street on the east, from Church Avenue on the north to Beverley Road on the south.
Subway: <u>Brighton Line D</u>: Church Ave., Beverley Rd.
Bus: <u>B</u>35: Church Ave.
Community Board: No. 14
Police Precinct: 70th Precinct (154 Lawrence Ave.)

Shingle-style house at 115 Buckingham Road built for William H. McEntee, 1900

Landmarked villa in the historic district

Prospect Park South, landmarked in 1979, is still a neighborhood of large, single-family houses, with carefully clipped shrubs and English gardens. In 1907, when the two-track Brighton line added two more tracks, many homes on Buckingham Road lost large portions of their backyards, a reminder that this little oasis is in the middle of Brooklyn. Today, new cars and satellite dishes also update the neighborhood's look. For the most part, however, Prospect Park South retains an aura of the past.

Farmers' market at southwest corner of Prospect Park, just north of the neighborhood

By 1905 almost all of the building plots had houses, and the development was nearly completed. The new neighborhood was considered the height of elegance, and many of Brooklyn's top businessmen, including the chief executives of Gillette, Fruit of the Loom, Sperry-Rand, and the *Brooklyn Eagle*, moved in with their families. The house built for the president of Fruit of the Loom, Jack Daniels, at 1215 Albemarle Road, even had a bowling alley in the basement. Today, highly paid professionals continue to make their home in this beautiful community.

Red Hook

On a starry night in Red Hook, near the renovated west side called "the Back," light from a sculptor's studio casts a warm glow across piers extending into upper New York Bay. Once one of the busiest harbors in the nation, Red Hook has been challenged in recent decades to recast its future, to overcome changes in the shipping industry and the isolation of being surrounded on three sides by water. But the persistence and inventiveness of Red Hook residents are ensuring the neighborhood's comeback. Like the newly resown community gardens along Red Hook's western piers, such neighborhood initiatives as a subsidized housing program and a commitment to local youth have nurtured revitalization in the area.

For 200 years after it was settled in 1636, "Roode Hoek," so called because of the color of its soil and the shape of its land, was marshy and rural. In the 1840s, however, the opening of the Atlantic Basin led to rapid growth throughout the neighborhood. Piers in the Atlantic Basin were developed by the Atlantic Dock Company, and wharves in the Erie Basin were built up by William Beard, a railroad contractor.

The peninsula quickly became one of the busiest shipping centers in the United States. By the beginning of the Civil War, ships from all over the world docked at Red Hook to receive and unload cargo and to be repaired and serviced. Warehouses that were used to store supplies for the Union army are still standing in the neighborhood. In later years, until the decline in grain traffic in the 1950s, scores of grain barges from the Erie Canal clustered at the opening

of the Gowanus Canal, waiting for a turn at the active piers.

The neighborhood was still bustling at the turn of the century and well into the 1930s and 1940s. It was also renowned as a tough section of Brooklyn;

Members of the Red Hook team of the United Football League, in front of Red Hook housing project

Hudson Waterfront Museum, with the
Statue of Liberty in the distance

Al Capone got his start as a small-time
criminal there, along with the wound
that led to his nickname, "Scarface."
Residents in those years were mostly
Italian American dockworkers, but a
small colony of Puerto Rican immigrants shared the neighborhood as
well. The ambience of these years is
well captured in Arthur Miller's play *A
View from the Bridge* (1955), Elia Ka-
zan's *On the Waterfront* (1954; filmed in
Hoboken, N.J., but set in Red Hook),
and H. P. Lovecraft's short story "The
Horror at Red Hook" (1925).

Originally built for the families of
dockworkers, the Red Hook Houses,
opened in 1938, were one of the first

NEIGHBORHOOD FACTS

■ In the 1920s wealthy patrons docked their yachts and had them repaired in
Tebo Yacht Basin. The financier J. P. Morgan dry-docked his yacht, the
Corsair, at Tebo.

■ A Guatemalan soccer league has been playing on Red Hook's fields for
more than 25 years.

■ The independent movie *Straight Out of Brooklyn* (1991) was filmed in Red
Hook. Its director, Matty Rich, was only 19 years old when the film was completed. *Last Exit to Brooklyn* (1989), a gritty movie about life on the waterfront based on the 1964 novel by Hubert Selby, Jr., was also filmed there.

■ Hudson Waterfront Museum is housed in Lehigh Valley Barge No. 79, a
wooden-covered cargo barge (1914). The barge, the only surviving example
of its kind, is anchored at Garden Pier at the foot of Conover Street. The
museum sponsors circus acts and sunset music series.

■ The Brooklyn Historic Rail Road Association runs the Trolley Museum,
where visitors can view three trolleys, one from the 1890s and two others
that were in use during the 1950s. The association is currently laying track
between Pier 41 and Beard Street Pier.

■ A local car-repair shop has grown to become the largest provider of movie
cars in the United States. Picture Cars East, founded in 1970 on Huntington
Street between Hicks and Henry Streets, was discovered when a supplier of
movie cars spotted an antique car that the owner was restoring. The company employs local residents and has supplied cars for more than 900 movies, including *Batman* (1989), *Ghostbusters* (1984), *Annie* (1982), *Eraser*
(1996), and *Godzilla* (1998).

and largest housing projects in the city. The Red Hook Recreation Center (1936) opened during this same era, and its outdoor, Olympic-size swimming pool, renovated in the mid-1980s, is still a favorite warm-weather hangout. Today more than 7,000 residents live in the Red Hook Houses. On sunny spring and summer days, when residents of the houses sit outside on the green "Mall" in benches and lawn chairs, the area feels both lively and homey.

During the early 1950s, residents began to drift away, because unlike adjacent neighborhoods, Red Hook was inaccessible by subway. By the 1960s the population of the community had declined sharply: it seemed that as quickly as new immigrants arrived, others moved on. Moreover, many buildings and warehouses built in the 1800s were crumbling because no money was available to renovate them. Exacerbating the problem was the popularity of containerized shipping since the early 1970s, which caused Red Hook shippers to move their business to newer ports in New Jersey.

The first flicker of renewal began in the 1970s on the west side of Red Hook, near the waterfront. Here in the Back, painters and sculptors found that they could buy row houses very inexpensively through a city program that subsidized housing for artists. The influence of these new residents is celebrated each spring: in May and June, a warehouse at the end of historic Beard Street Pier houses an annual Pier Show featuring exhibitions, performances, and films. Another historic pier, Pier 41, features glass blowing, glass etching, and carpentry busi-

nesses. Propelled by the efforts of the Pier 41 Association, whose mission is to open the waterfront to the public, a July artist series offers free entertainment and concerts to residents and visitors. New residents of the Back call it an enchanting place where the stars twinkle like nowhere else in Brooklyn, and where picture-perfect views of the Statue of Liberty inspire all. Natives

NEIGHBORHOOD PROFILE

Boundaries: from the Buttermilk Channel on the west and north to Hamilton Avenue and the Gowanus Expressway on the east to Erie Basin and Gowanus Bay on the south.
Bus: <u>B61</u>: Van Brunt St. <u>B77</u>: Dikeman St./Lorraine St. <u>Bx27</u>: Brooklyn Battery Tunnel <u>Bx28</u>: Brooklyn Battery Tunnel <u>Bx29</u>: Brooklyn Battery Tunnel
Libraries: Brooklyn Public Library Red Hook Branch (Wolcott St. at Dwight St.)
Community Board: No. 6
Police Precinct: 76th Precinct (191 Union St.)
Fire Department: Engine 202 Ladder 101 (31 Richards St.), Engine 279 Ladder 131 (252 Lorraine St.)

who have never left Red Hook have welcomed the artists and hope more new residents will move in. Everyone, it seems, wishes for a waterfront revitalization that will include much-needed commercial redevelopment, new housing, or both.

Red Hook mourned in 1992 when Patrick Daly, the principal of Public School 15, an elementary school in Red Hook, died after being caught in drug-related crossfire. Daly was universally respected for his willingness to deal directly and individually with the parents and students of the Red Hook Houses, and his death brought the eastern side of Red Hook closer together. Concerned about the effects on community morale of negative publicity about Daly's death, residents joined with the New York City Police Department, city planners, and business leaders to establish community groups that would promote neighborhood development.

The residents' hard work has had encouraging results. A new, large community garden has opened, plans have been developed for commercial use of the Red Hook waterfront, and the necessity of building more affordable homes for working families has been discussed more openly. Local groups now run programs for escorting the elderly home at night and plan activities for Red Hook youth. And residents who have worked to persuade businesses to open in the community feel proud that a Home Depot opened in 1998 and that a branch of the Independence Savings Bank now offers its services to Red Hook residents.

These 1900 frame houses are still typical of the neighborhood

A seaside residence on Beach 38th Street

Point, where Sea Gate lies today. Over the next 20 years Norton's Point, also called the West End of Coney Island, developed an unsavory reputation as the stomping ground of gamblers, thieves, and pickpockets. Most of the land remained undeveloped for many years. In 1871 William Marcy (Boss) Tweed, leader of Tammany Hall, hid out in Sea Gate after escaping from prison.

In 1888 a portion of the land in the area was bought by William K. Ziegler, president of the Royal Baking Powder Company, to whom Aldrick Man, president of the Sea Beach Railroad, proposed a plan to develop Sea Gate as an

After passing through one of Sea Gate's two secured entrances, residents of this tiny, exclusive neighborhood enjoy meandering on winding roads to their single-family, detached houses, which replaced early mansions that dotted the peninsula. Sea Gate, a private beachfront enclave governed by the 8,000-member Sea Gate Association, has only 43 blocks, 900 homes, and no stores. Most of the neighborhood's residents are Jewish, and recently they have been joined by Hasidic Satmar Jews, some from Russia.

Until the mid-1600s, what is today Sea Gate was the tip of the Canarsee Indian village of Narriockh. In 1645, when Lady Moody received the charter for the town of Gravesend, she and her followers acquired from the Indians land that included both Coney Island and Sea Gate.

During the mid-1840s, Michael Norton, a corrupt politician known by the nickname "Thunderbolt," opened Norton and Murray's Pavilion at Norton's

191

NEIGHBORHOOD PROFILE

Boundaries: from Gravesend Bay and the Atlantic Ocean on the west to West 37th Street on the east, from Oceanview Avenue and Bay View Avenue on the north to the Atlantic Ocean on the south.
Bus: B36: West 37th St. B74: West 37th St. Bx29: West 37th St.
Community Board: No. 13

Sea Gate

upper-class neighborhood. In 1892 the Norton's Point Land Company bought land intending to start a residential community. But in 1899 a large number of local people who already owned

land or houses—including the Vanderbilt, Morgan, and Dodge families—founded the Sea Gate Association and bought out the Norton's Point Land Company's holdings. The association oversaw the construction of a restricted community, ironically, in view of its current population, one that did not allow Jews to buy homes in the neighborhood. Gates were erected at Surf, Mermaid, and Neptune Avenues (the Mermaid and Neptune Avenue gates have limited access), and a 12-foot-high fence was installed to the water's edge to keep outsiders from entering the neighborhood from Coney Island. The private community was officially born.

New York City police do not watch over Sea Gate; since 1940 Sea Gate police have had the exclusive authority to enforce laws in the neighborhood. The force consists of approximately 20 offi-

Typical home on Sea Gate Avenue

Norton's Point Lighthouse, the last manned lighthouse on the East Coast, on Beach 47th Street

Entrance to Sea Gate, Neptune Avenue and West 37th Street

cers, two police cars, a van, a holding cell, and an independent radio system. At entry gates members of the Sea Gate police check residents' photo identification cards and keep track of all incoming cars' destinations within the neighborhood.

The exclusivity of Sea Gate has often caused clashes with city policies. Until the mid-1980s, the city sanitation department would not pick up the neighborhood's garbage because residents wanted the sanitation workers to carry their trash cans to and from their backyards, rather than pick them up at the curb. And at times city officials have declared Sea Gate's beaches open to the public, whereas Sea Gate residents have fought to keep them private.

During bad storms, Sea Gate homeowners who live closest to the shore sometimes seek help at emergency shelters: one is in Sea Gate at the men's club, the other is outside the gates in the local school. But although these storms have been eroding Sea Gate's beach, residents still enjoy their proximity to the water, their private beach, and rising property values.

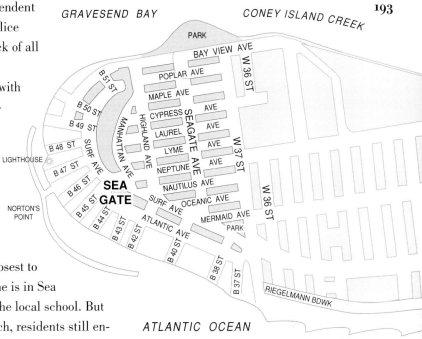

The spray of ocean water, the whir of line spinning off of a reel, the flap of sails and the urgent call "Hard a-lee!"—the sounds of Sheepshead Bay remind all that the neighborhood still looks seaward for its sustenance and inspiration. Every summer, more than 20 party boats daily push off from Sheepshead Bay piers with as many as 200 novice and experienced fishermen looking forward to a day of deep-sea action. A bait and tackle shop on Emmons Avenue supplies residents with equipment and fish stories. And active local boat clubs, a sailing school, and scuba diving organizations help fuel Brooklynites' dreams of exploring the secrets of the bay.

Sheepshead Bay, named for a local fish, remained undiscovered by European colonists during much of Brooklyn's early development. Although Gravesend was settled nearby in 1643, Sheepshead Bay was inhabited mainly by Canarsee Indians until almost 150 years later. In the eighteenth century the Wyckoff and Lotts families held land grants and built farms in the area. Some stunning architectural examples still exist from this period. The Henry and Abraham

Fishing boats at Emmons Avenue pier

Sheepshead

NEIGHBORHOOD PROFILE

Boundaries: <u>Sheepshead Bay</u>: from Ocean Parkway on the west to Nostrand Avenue, Gerritsen Avenue, Knapp Street, and Shell Bank Avenue on the east, from Kings Highway or Avenue P on the north to Sheepshead Bay on the south. <u>Homecrest</u>: from Ocean Parkway on the west to East 16th Street on the east, from Kings Highway on the north to Avenue V on the south. <u>Madison</u>: from Ocean Avenue on the west to Nostrand Avenue and Gerritsen Avenue on the east, from Kings Highway on the north to Avenue U on the south. <u>Plumb Beach</u>: peninsula southeast of Sheepshead Bay, connected to Sheepshead Bay by the Belt Parkway.

Subway: <u>Brighton Line D</u>: Kings Highway, Avenue U, Neck Rd., Sheepshead Bay <u>Brighton Line Q</u>: Kings Highway, Sheepshead Bay

Bus: <u>B7</u>: Kings Highway <u>B82</u>: Kings Highway <u>B100</u>: Quentin Rd. <u>B2</u>: Avenue R <u>B31</u>: Avenue R <u>B3</u>: Avenue U <u>B36</u>: Avenue Z <u>B4</u>: Emmons Ave. <u>B1</u>: Ocean Pkwy. <u>B36</u>: Ocean Pkwy. <u>B68</u>: Coney Island Ave. <u>Bx29</u>: Coney Island Ave. <u>B49</u>: Ocean Ave. <u>B44</u>: Nostrand Ave.

Libraries: Brooklyn Public Library Kings Bay Branch (3650 Nostrand Ave.), Kings Highway Branch (2115 Ocean Ave.), Homecrest Branch (2525 Coney Island Ave.), Sheepshead Bay Branch (2636 East 14th St.)

Community Board: No. 15

Police Precinct: 60th Precinct (2951 West 8th St.), 61st Precinct (2575 Coney Island Ave.)

Fire Department: Engine 246 Ladder 169 (2732 East 11th St.), Engine 254 Ladder 153 (901 Avenue U), Engine 276 Ladder 156 (1635 East 14th St.)

Hospitals and Clinics: Coney Island Hospital (2601 Ocean Pkwy.), Nephrology Foundation of Brooklyn, South Unit (2651 East 14th St.)

left. The house is considered an extraordinary example of the Dutch Colonial style, and it is a New York City landmark. The landmarked Elias Hubbard Ryder House (1834), at 1926 East 28th Street, is also Dutch Colonial, although it is a very late example. The building was slightly altered when it was moved to its present site in 1929.

Settlers were eventually drawn to the Sheepshead Bay's cool summer breezes and beautiful shore. During the early nineteenth century, informal wooden cottages were built along the

Angel supervises Santa Claus on Avenue S and East 13th Street in Homecrest

Wyckoff House (1766), for example, also known as the Wyckoff-Bennett Homestead, stands on the corner of Kings Highway and East 22nd Street. Kings Highway was used by British troops as an approach during the Battle of Brooklyn, and the Wyckoff-Bennett Homestead was seized during the Revolutionary War and used to house Hessian officers, who carved graffiti into a glass door before they

Bay

rim of the Sheepshead Bay inlet, and a sheltered anchorage for small local boats was devised. Two hotels were built to accommodate tourists. Sam Leonard's Hotel was built in 1833, and Tappen's Hotel stood from 1845 until 1948. Local restaurants began to attract visitors with delicious fresh seafood, for which Sheepshead Bay's eateries remain famous.

The chef of Tappen's, Jacques Villepigue, later opened Villepigue's Inn (1879) on Ocean Avenue.

In 1877 the first privately owned farm in the area was sold for development, marking the beginning of a new trend to subdivide and build up farms and beachfront properties. Development accelerated during the 1870s, when New York railroad lines were extended into Sheepshead Bay.

As the numbers of residents and visitors increased, so did the incentive to create amusements that might profit from them. The Coney Island Jockey Club, founded in 1880 by such notables as August Belmont, Sr., Leonard Jerome (Winston Churchill's grandfather), William Vanderbilt, and Pierre Lorillard, was the governing body for the Sheepshead Bay Race Track. The 112-acre track, located on a 2,200-acre expanse along Ocean Avenue between Jerome Avenue and Gravesend Neck Road and extending east to the Shell Bank Creek (Knapp Street), introduced such well-known horse races as the Futurity and the Brooklyn Handicap, as well as jockeys like Irishman "Snapper" Garrison and African American Isaac Murphy, who were often adversaries. The track also lured Brooklyn and New York's wealthiest horse-racing aficionados, who frequented Sheepshead Bay's hotels, casinos, and restaurants.

A 1910 law making Brooklyn racetracks financially

The Wyckoff-Bennett Homestead (1766), at East 22nd Street and Kings Highway

responsible for bookies' losses dampened profits, so the Sheepshead Bay Race Track's owners welcomed other entertainments to the site. In 1911 Calbraith P. Rodgers took off from the racetrack in his plane, the *Vin Fiz*. The flight, sponsored by the makers of a popular soft drink, was the first transcontinental flight. In 1915 Harry Harkness transformed the racetrack into the Sheepshead Bay Speedway, which hosted auto races, motorcycle races, and, as a last resort, balloon races. In the end, however, the track was unable to draw enough spectators. It closed in 1919.

During the 1920s and 1930s, a flurry of new residential and commercial developments transformed Sheepshead Bay. Some of these improvements were sponsored by New York City, which took title to the area in 1931. The land occupied by the former speedway was sold for housing; buildings that stood on wooden stilts over the water were reconstructed and modernized; piers were built as a Works Progress Administration project; and Emmons Avenue was widened and paved.

The many new cars in Brooklyn during this period made the relatively undeveloped southern shore seem ever more attractive. The south side of Emmons Avenue, then as now, was a beautiful waterfront street. And during the 1940s, many owners of party boats tied their craft to adjacent docks, offering day fishing trips. Sheepshead Bay thus continued to draw new residents, especially after the Belt Parkway (originally named the Circumferential Highway) was created in 1939 (it reached the bay area in 1941) to speed traffic around the borough. The influx peaked in 1960s, when the bay was the fastest growing community in Brooklyn. The dynamic neighborhoods expanded quickly to accommodate new Jewish and Italian American immigrants to the area; six- to eight-story apartment buildings were added to Ocean and Nostrand Avenues, and summer waterfront cottages were winterized and enlarged.

Sheepshead Bay's newest residents are Russians who have moved from Brighton Beach. Also joining longtime Italian American and Jewish residents are immigrants from Haiti, Jamaica, Guyana, Korea, China, and Turkey. East 15th Street, a two-block street off Gravesend Neck Road, has been home to an African American community, descendants of racetrack workers, since the nineteenth century. First Baptist Church (1899) of Sheepshead Bay was founded by these residents.

In 1996 a zoning variance for the neighborhood's waterfront allowed in a large retail mall that attracts shoppers from throughout southeastern Brooklyn.

Today, Sheepshead Bay abuts on its northern edge two smaller neighborhoods, **Homecrest** and **Madison,** which share its early history. (Some who live on the streets adjacent to Kings Highway also use the unofficial moniker Kings Bay for their area.) During the heyday of the Sheepshead Bay Race Track, the land occupied by

MB
EACH

Civil War–era wood-frame house on Emmons Avenue

Homecrest and Madison remained mostly undeveloped, but at the turn of the century "Homecrest by the Sea" was created. The large, one-family Victorians in this development were advertised as being only 30 minutes from Manhattan and ten minutes from the shore. The Homecrest Presbyterian Church, which still graces the neighborhood, was founded at about the same time. Homecrest has also added two-family houses, townhouses, and low-rise apartment buildings to accommodate its residents, the newest of whom are immigrants of Chinese, Russian, Israeli, Korean, Italian, Syrian, Egyptian, and Lebanese descent.

Madison takes its name from the heart of the neighborhood, James Madison High School. The school has

NEIGHBORHOOD FACTS

■ From 1920 to 1979, Lundy's restaurant was one of the most famous draws of Sheepshead Bay. Until 1934, on its original location on a pier, patrons were treated to panoramic views of the Atlantic, then from 1934 to 1979 the restaurant was housed in a Spanish-mission-style stucco building on Emmons Avenue (at the site of the former McMahon Bayside Hotel, built in 1873). In its heyday, the Lundy's dining room could seat an astonishing 2,800 diners. The restaurant employed 220 waiters, who served more than 5,000 meals a day. In 1979 Lundy's was closed because of a labor dispute. But the restaurant was revived in 1995 in a newly landmarked part of the Emmons Avenue building. Now nearly 800 diners at a time can enjoy the food, hospitality, and history of Lundy's.

■ Methodist Episcopal (now United Methodist) Church of Sheepshead Bay was founded in 1845 on East 23rd Street. John Y. McKane, a local boy who became the "boss" of Gravesend (and who served five years in prison for election fraud in the 1890s), was the head of its Sunday School. The Lundy family were later members of the congregation. The church is now located on Ocean and Voorhees Avenues.

■ Each year on the fourth Sunday in June, Sheepshead Bay residents gather to celebrate the Blessing of the Fleet, a tradition since 1992.

A popular enterprise along the waterfront, circa 1998

Sea View Gardens in the 1920s (Brian Merlis Collection)

many graduates of renown, including Supreme Court Justice Ruth Bader Ginsberg, Brooklyn Dodgers outfielder Cal Abrams, singer Carole King, journalist Jane Brody, *Mad* magazine founder William M. Gaines, and playwright Garson Kanin. Frank Torre, brother of Yankees' manager Joe Torre, played baseball for Madison. Madison is considered by some to be a suburb within Brooklyn, with its elegant homes and treelined streets. In addition to its longtime Irish American, Jewish, and Italian American residents, the neighborhood is home to newer families with ties to Russia and China, as well as a growing community of Orthodox Jews, who have renovated a number of the large old houses to accommodate their families.

In addition to the neighborhoods of Homecrest and Madison, Sheepshead Bay encompasses the former island known as **Plum(b) Beach,** which was connected to the mainland of Sheepshead Bay by the Belt Parkway. Originally named for its indigenous beach plums and referred to as Plumb Island, Plumb Beach was bought by the U.S. government in the late 1890s as a site for mortar fortification.

When the project was abandoned, the area was leased on the condition that it be made into a beach resort.

Plumb Beach was a bungalow colony of squatters, although around World War I it had an army base and a hotel. Residents relied mostly on one another and on the ferry service to Sheepshead Bay, for there was no electricity, gas, or telephone service until 1939, when the Belt Parkway was completed. The area became part of the Gateway National Recreation Area in 1972.

Spanish and Dutch architectural styles along Avenue R at East 8th Street

199

Sunset

If diversity is a hallmark of a good community, Sunset Park, one of the most heterogeneous neighborhoods in Brooklyn, is a wonderful place to live. In Sunset Park, people of different nationalities and ethnicities are not partitioned into sections of the large neighborhood; they live next door to one another. As longtime residents know, the genuineness of Sunset Park's commitment to ethnic and racial inclusion is as clear as its distinctive view of the Verrazano Narrows Bridge.

Sunset Park is named for a local 24.5-acre park built in the 1890s. Because the City of Brooklyn used to end just short of 60th Street, much of what is today Sunset Park was (and still sometimes is) considered part of South Brooklyn. The neighborhood's once-busy working waterfront is now home to new businesses and parks. Its upland residential community contains the largest historic district on the Federal Register in the Northeast and is renowned for its many owner-occupied row houses.

Dutch settlers acquired portions of Sunset Park from the Canarsee Indians in the 1640s and began farming along the waterfront. Although streets were mapped during the 1830s, the land remained predominantly agricultural until the mid-1800s. Among the first wave of new settlers were Irish immigrants fleeing the 1840s potato famine. In the 1870s a local ferry pier and railroad terminal became popular as a transfer point for those traveling to Coney Island.

During the 1880s and 1890s, Polish, Norwegian, and Finnish immigrants settled in the area, and by the first half of the twentieth century, Sunset Park was known as a thriving Scandinavian community. During this early period, the newcomers introduced cooperative housing, long known in Finland. A section of Sunset Park from 45th to 60th Streets came to be called "Little Norway," and a small

Chinese fish and vegetable market at 8th Avenue and 58th Street

Park

area from 40th to 43rd Streets, between 5th and 9th Avenues, was known as "Finntown." Until the 1970s visitors to Finntown could relax in an authentic Finnish sauna, sample food in Finnish restaurants, and purchase Finnish crafts. In 1991, to honor this time in Sunset Park's history, 40th Street was officially renamed Finlandia Street.

Nearly all of the area's residential construction occurred during the late 1800s and early 1900s. Today brownstones and limestones, as well as brick and wood row houses, set the tone for the neighborhood. Two of Sunset Park's landmarked buildings were constructed during this

time. The Weir Greenhouse (1900), a large wood and brick structure with a distinctive octagonal dome, can be found on 5th Avenue across

GOWANUS BAY

UPPER NEW YORK BAY

BUSH TERMINAL DOCKS

BUSH TERMINAL WAREHOUSES

MARGINAL ST

THIRD AVE

FIRST AVE

SECOND AVE

GOWANUS EXPWY

FOURTH AVE

FINLANDIA ST

FIFTH AVE

L.I.R.R. YARD

BAY RIDGE YARD

LEIF ERICSON DRIVE (BELT PKWY)

PARK

SUNSET PARK

SIXTH AVE

SEVENTH AVE

EIGHTH AVE

PROSPECT EXPWY

17 ST
18 ST
19 ST
20 ST
21 ST
22 ST
23 ST
24 ST
25 ST
26 ST
27 ST
28 ST
29 ST
30 ST
31 ST
32 ST
33 ST
34 ST
35 ST
36 ST
37 ST
38 ST
39 ST
(40 ST)
41 ST
42 ST
43 ST
44 ST
45 ST
46 ST
47 ST
48 ST
49 ST
50 ST
51 ST
52 ST
53 ST
54 ST
55 ST
56 ST
57 ST
58 ST
59 ST
60 ST
61 ST
62 ST
63 ST
64 ST
65 ST
66 ST
67 ST

ENTRANCE

BMT YARD

GREEN-WOOD CEMETERY

from the main entrance to Green-Wood Cemetery. And the fortresslike former 68th (originally 18th) Police Precinct Station House and Stable (1892), which now houses the Sunset Park School of Music, is on 4th Avenue.

Wood row houses on 3rd Avenue and 42nd Street set the tone for this neighborhood

fire and police departments, and power plants. Some of the buildings in his complex have rooms that span three acres.

By the 1930s and well into the 1940s the neighborhood was in decline. The 3rd Avenue elevated line had ceased operation during the Depression, and the construction (and eventual widening) of the Gowanus Expressway in the early 1950s separated the industrial from the residential sections of the neighborhood. After World War II many older residents moved to the suburbs. Their homes and waterfront jobs were filled, in

The purchase by Irving T. Bush of oceanfront property that had once been Ambrose Park, a picnic area where in 1892 Buffalo Bill set up the tents for his Wild West show before his European tour, changed forever the landscape of Sunset Park—although no one would have believed it at the time. The idea that Bush could successfully compete with Manhattan's ports seemed so ludicrous that when he began building his terminal in 1890 it was called "Bush's Folly." His initial warehouse, single pier, tugboat, and old railroad engine developed into the Bush Terminal, a 200-acre complex of piers, warehouses, display rooms, and factory lofts. Many Italian dock workers settled in Sunset Park, drawn by the ample work. Bush's project was so successful that he expanded it in 1902 and eventually owned his own rail system,

Commerce along 4th Avenue

large part, by immigrants from Puerto Rico.

Even the spirit and resilience of new residents could not help the neighborhood, however, and the physical decline of Sunset Park continued. In the 1950s corruption in the Federal Housing Administration, as well as in the real-estate and banking industries, led to the abandonment of homes. Although the city did build a small container port, Northeast Marine Terminal, most of the maritime industry moved to the New Jersey shore. In 1960, during one of the many attempts to revitalize

the Bush Terminal, the legendary complex was renamed Industry City, and in 1965 it was bought by a group of investors led by Harry Helmsley. Five of Bush Terminal's 18 original piers are no longer standing. Happily for wildlife in the area, illegal dumping near the piers, which caused some problems for the community, also created land that could be reclaimed by nature. The fenced-off area where the piers once jutted out into Gowanus Bay is now an unofficial bird sanctuary where a mated pair of ring-necked pheasants lives and many other local and migrating birds visit.

In 1969 the Lutheran Medical Center needed more space than its location could provide. Hospital administrators, deciding to stay in the area, purchased an abandoned factory on 2nd Avenue and 55th Street from the city for one dollar and spent more than $70 million renovating the property. The medical center helped local nonprofit organizations renovate 500 housing units that are now federally subsidized. The revitalization of the neighborhood had begun.

During the 1980s and 1990s, Sunset Park rebounded. Immigrants from the Do-

NEIGHBORHOOD FACTS

■ Ralph Kramden, the New York City bus driver portrayed by Jackie Gleason in *The Honeymooners*, was supposed to have spent time in Sunset Park. In 1988 the 5th Avenue Bus Depot at 36th Street in Sunset Park was renamed the Jackie Gleason Bus Depot in the actor's honor.

■ During World War II, 80 percent of all supplies and soldiers heading for Europe were shipped from the Brooklyn Army Terminal.

■ Standing at the top of Sunset Park near 6th Avenue north of 44th Street, residents and visitors can take in the spectacular view of the tallest building in each of three boroughs, the Citibank Building in Queens, the Williamsburgh Savings Bank Tower in Brooklyn, and the Empire State Building in Manhattan.

■ Early Finnish immigrants to Sunset Park built a four-story cooperative apartment building in 1916, Alku I (Beginning I), between 8th and 9th Avenues. Alku I and other buildings erected later—two garages and a shopping complex—were the first cooperatives in the United States.

■ Topps Chewing Gum was manufactured in a factory loft in Bush Terminal; starting in 1951 the company began producing its famous baseball cards there as well.

Fatih Camii Mosque, converted from a movie theater

minican Republic, as well as from Guyana, Columbia, Ecuador, India, Vietnam, Jordan, and Poland, moved to the area. Chinese residents were made to feel especially welcome: local real-estate agents advertised homes in Chinese newspapers, made it known that they could negotiate sales in Chinese, and played up the existence of the N train, the neighborhood's direct and inexpensive link to Manhattan's Chinatown. As a result Sunset Park became home to a substantial Chinatown. Every year in late October, residents celebrate Sunset Park's diversity on 5th Avenue with the Sunset Park Parade of Flags.

Commercial revival increased when the Brooklyn Army Terminal, which had been deactivated in the 1970s, was reopened in 1987 as a center for light industry. Built in 1919, at 58th Street and 2nd Avenue, the building was designed by Cass Gilbert, designer of Manhattan's Woolworth Building.

During this same period, Bush Terminal was revived as an industrial park, and bodegas, restaurants, and retail stores owned by Latin Americans sprang up between 35th Street and 60th Street along 5th Avenue. The vibrant 5th Avenue Business Improvement District is a welcome sign of the neighborhood's comeback.

Imported Turkish tile in the interior of Fatih Camii Mosque

● **Green-Wood Cemetery**

Green-Wood Cemetery was commissioned in 1838 as a retreat where visitors could contemplate death as a reconciliation with nature. When churchyards were sold thereafter, the cemeteries were first moved to Green-Wood. Until Prospect Park was completed in 1873, the cemetery was used by Brooklyn residents for recreation. The grassy hills, shade trees, manmade lakes, and breathtaking views of New York harbor became such a popular playground that by 1844 a daily stagecoach shuttled visitors from the ferries to the cemetery. The success of Green-Wood as a tourist attraction fueled a competition to design a public park for New York City; indeed, the design submitted by Frederick Law Olmsted and Calvert Vaux for "Greensward" formed the basis for Central Park.

The cemetery's spectacular Gothic Revival gate, at 5th Avenue and 25th Street, is a New York City landmark. Its majestic pinnacled gables and adjoining pavilions are made from New Jersey brownstone, and above the entrance four panels depicting scenes of death and resurrection were carved by John Moffit. Among those buried across the 478 acres in Green-Wood's half-million graves are William Marcy (Boss) Tweed, De Witt Clinton, Lola Montez, Peter Cooper, Henry Ward Beecher, Nathaniel Currier, James Ives, Margaret Sanger, Leonard Bernstein, and notorious Mafia figures Albert Anastasia and Joey Gallo.

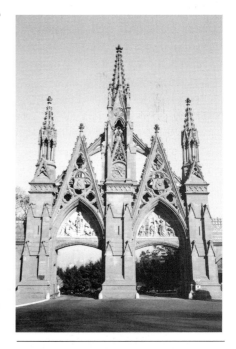

Main gate of Green-Wood Cemetery at 5th Avenue and 25th Street

Williamsburg

● Williamsburg Bridge

The Williamsburg Bridge, which spans the East River between Delancey Street on Manhattan's Lower East Side and Marcy Avenue in Williamsburg, was built to ease the congestion on the Brooklyn Bridge. When it was completed, Jewish residents of the Lower East Side saw it as a passageway to a new, less crowded life in Brooklyn.

The bridge, opened in 1903, was designed by Leffert L. Buck, but his creation was not well received. Buck was so criticized for the graceless form of the bridge that Henry Hornbostel was hired while the bridge was being built to add ornamental detail to its towers and to design the bridge's approach in Manhattan.

When it was built, the Williamsburg Bridge was the longest and heaviest suspension bridge in the world and the first with towers made entirely of steel. Even so, it took only seven years to build, half the time it took to construct the Brooklyn Bridge. The bridge is 7,308 feet long with a main span of 1,600 feet. The deck of the bridge carries two subway tracks and four traffic lanes.

In the 1970s, engineers found the bridge in such a state of neglect that they closed it down and discussed demolishing it, but the city decided to repair it so it lived to celebrate its centennial in 2003.

There's something for everyone in today's Williamsburg. Conservative and cool, Hasidic and hip, Williamsburg's Southside and Northside create an improbable but somehow just right balance for this unique neighborhood—and indeed, seem to represent Brooklynites' remarkable ability to accommodate distinct philosophies of life within close physical boundaries. Whether taking in the view (particularly spectacular at night) of the Williamsburg Bridge and the lower Manhattan skyline from a top-floor artist's loft, or dancing through the streets with Torah scrolls to celebrate Simchas Torah, residents of Williamsburg share the beauty of historic buildings, breathtaking sunsets, and a fundamental resolve to keep improving their wonderful community.

Williamsburg has long been home to light industry and warehouses. Although much of this warehouse space has been converted to popular residential lofts, the neighborhood still has many industrial areas: along the piers on the East

Hebrew school at Clymer Street and Lee Avenue

River, in what is sometimes called East Williamsburg, and on the shores of the Newtown Creek and English Kills.

Williamsburg was originally part of the Dutch town of Boswijck (Bushwick). Captain Kidd, an early visitor, often stopped by to see Jean Meserole, the first European settler (or squatter—he and his family lived on the 107-acre farm "without deed or patent") to the area. Meserole's farm was located between today's South 7th Street and North 1st Street. In the late 1600s Dutch, French, and Scandinavian farmers settled in the area with their African slaves. One of the isolated hamlets there was called **Cripplebush** until the 1820s, although during the American Revolution, British soldiers chopped down for fuel the many thick trees and bushes from which it derived its name.

Williamsburg remained rural until 1802, when Richard Woodhull arrived with his vision of a new residential area for those who worked in Manhattan. Woodhull began a ferry service from what is today Metropolitan Avenue to Corlear's Hook in Manhattan. He then purchased 13 acres around the ferry landing and in 1810

named it Williamsburgh, after Col. Jonathan Williams, who had originally surveyed the site. Few were interested, however, and Woodhull declared bankruptcy in 1811.

David Dunham, known as one of the fathers of Williamsburg, had better luck. (Another "father" was Noah Waterbury, who built Williamsburg's first distillery in the area in 1819.) Dunham opened a steam ferry and oversaw the incorporation of the village of Williamsburgh in 1827. Industry became attracted to the area, and soon the community's shore was lined with distilleries and sugar refineries. Foundries and shipyards bustled with activity. Some of the largest firms in America, including Pfizer Pharma-

208 ceutical and what is today the Domino Sugar Refineries, were all launched in the neighborhood during the mid-1800s. The population grew so large (31,000 in 1852) that Williamsburgh was chartered as a city in 1852. In 1855 the city was annexed by the City of Brooklyn and the "h" on Williamsburg was dropped.

During the mid-1800s, Williamsburg was a playground of the rich, a place where Commodore Cornelius Vanderbilt and William C. Whitney, secretary of the navy under President Grover Cleveland, visited resort hotels, beer gardens, and private clubs. German, Austrian, and Irish professionals and industrialists built mansions, established businesses, and enjoyed the fashionable suburb.

Many of the more lavish buildings of Williamsburg were constructed during this period. The original Williamsburgh Savings Bank building (1875), whose interior and exterior are landmarked, is at 175 Broadway. (The more famous, 1929 Williamsburgh Savings Bank Tower is in Fort Greene; see entry.) Two other buildings are landmarked as well: the Kings County Savings Bank building, at 135 Broadway, was built in 1868, and Public School 71K, at 119 Heyward Street, was completed in 1889. Now home to Beth Jacob School, P.S. 71K was designed to allow maximum light into each class-

Williamsburg Bridge and American Sugar Refining Company, seen from Kent Avenue and South 2nd Street

NEIGHBORHOOD PROFILE

Boundaries: <u>Williamsburg</u>: from the East River on the west to the Queens County border on the east, from North 15th Street south on Berry Street to North 12th Street, continuing east to Bayard Street and south at Manhattan Avenue to Richardson Street, going east to the Queens County border to Flushing Avenue on the south. <u>Southside/Los Sures</u>: from the East River on the west to Union Avenue on the east, from Grand Street/Avenue on the north to Division Avenue on the south. <u>Northside</u>: from the East River on the west to Union Avenue on the east, from North 15th Street on the north to Grand Street/Avenue on the south.
Subway: <u>BMT Canarsie Line L</u>: Bedford Ave., Lorimer St., Graham Ave., Grand Ave., Montrose Ave., Morgan Ave. <u>IND Crosstown Line G</u>: Metropolitan Ave./Grand St., Broadway <u>BMT Jamaica Line J and M</u>: Marcy Ave., Hewes St., Lorimer St., Flushing Ave. <u>BMT Jamaica Line Z</u>: Marcy Ave.
Bus: <u>B57</u>: Flushing Ave. <u>B60</u>: South 4th St./South 5th St./Meserole St./ Montrose Ave. <u>B54</u>: Grand St. <u>B59</u>: Grand St. <u>B24</u>: Metropolitan Ave./ Grand St./Kent Ave. <u>B40</u>: Broadway <u>B46</u>: Broadway <u>B48</u>: Wallabout St./ Middleton St./Lorimer St. <u>B61</u>: Bedford Ave./Wythe Ave. <u>B44</u>: Roebling St./ Bedford Ave./Lee Ave. <u>B43</u>: Graham Ave. <u>B18</u>: Graham Ave.
Libraries: Brooklyn Public Library Williamsburgh Branch (Division Ave. at Marcy Ave.), Leonard Branch (Devoe St. at Leonard St.)
Community Board: No. 1
Police Precinct: 94th Precinct (100 Meserole Ave.)
Fire Department: Engine 206 (1201 Grand St.), Engine 211 Ladder 119 (26 Hooper St.), Engine 212 Foam Unit 82 (136 Wythe Ave.), Engine 216 Ladder 108 (187 Union Ave.), Engine 221 Ladder 104 (161 South 2nd St.), Engine 229 Ladder 146 (75 Richardson St.), Engine 237 (43 Morgan St.)
Hospitals and Clinics: Woodhull Medical and Mental Health Center (760 Broadway), Woodhull Williamsburgh Health Center (279 Graham Ave.)

room. Williamsburg's oldest landmarked building was originally the New England Congregational Church, now the Light of the World Church. The church, a lovely Italianate brownstone located at 179 South 9th Street, was built in 1853.

The Williamsburg that was popular among the rich began to change in 1903 when the Williamsburg Bridge opened. The new link between boroughs allowed Eastern European immigrants—including Lithuanian, Polish, Italian, and Russian Orthodox newcomers—to leave the crowded Lower East Side of Manhattan for the relative expansiveness of Brooklyn. To accommodate the many new residents, the six-story tenements that are so prevalent in Williamsburg today were built, and many brownstones and wood-frame houses were quickly turned into multiple dwellings. By 1917 the population had more than doubled, and Williamsburg had the most densely populated blocks in Brooklyn.

In the late 1930s and early 1940s, Jewish immigrants fleeing Nazism came to Williamsburg and settled in what is today called **Southside**. They formed Hasidic synagogues and schools, and today there are more than 20 Hasidic sects in Williamsburg, including the larg-

est sect, the Satmar, whose members come primarily from Hungary and Romania. The Hasidic section of Williamsburg is just northeast of the Brooklyn Navy Yard, and its busiest commercial street is Lee Avenue. The area is busy with buses picking up and dropping off those who work in Manhattan and with families shopping at kosher markets and bakeries. The Hasidim dress in traditional clothing: men wear dark suits and dark hats; women keep their arms, legs, and heads covered; boys dress like their fathers; and girls wear dresses, not pants.

Southside Williamsburg is not entirely Hasidic,

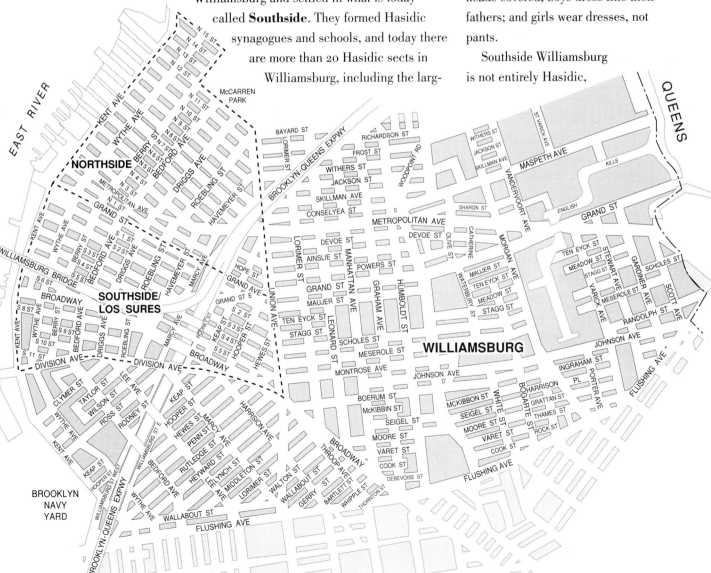

Produce stand at Division Avenue and
Roebling Street

however. African Americans live in
Williamsburg, and in the 1980s Dominicans and other Latin Americans
joined many Puerto Ricans who had
come in the 1960s. Because of the
Latin influence, the southern section of
Williamsburg, north of Division Avenue, is now known by the Spanish
name for Southside, **Los Sures**. In
1974 Boricua College opened one of its
campuses in Williamsburg. It was one
of the first bilingual colleges (Spanish
and English) in New York City to be
accredited.

Approximately 3,000 of Southside's
residents live in large apartment complexes. The Williamsburg Houses
(1938), for example, are a public hous-

Cultures blend at a neighborhood bodega

NEIGHBORHOOD FACTS

■ Since 1887 Peter Luger Steak House at 178 Broadway has been serving its famous steak dinners. Even earlier, starting in 1876, the proprietors had managed Charles Luger's Cafe, Billiards and Bowling Alley.

■ Twenty-seven streets in Williamsburg are named with the last names of signers of the Declaration of Independence. Look for Edward Rutledge of South Carolina, Caesar Rodney of Delaware, Josiah Bartlett of New Hampshire, and George Wythe of Virginia, among others. Also, keep an eye out for Keap Street. The signature of Thomas McKean of Delaware was incorrectly read as Thomas M. Keap.

■ Betty Smith's 1943 novel *A Tree Grows in Brooklyn* is set in Williamsburg.

■ From 1916 until 1976 Schaefer Brewing Company operated at South 10th Street and Kent Avenue, the site of Noah Waterbury's old distillery. The company closed briefly during Prohibition and reopened with the slogan "Our hand has never lost its skill." In 1995 the Brooklyn Brewery came to Williamsburg, the first brewery in the neighborhood in 20 years. The brewery operates at North 11th Street, where it produces more than 25,000 barrels of beer a year.

■ In 1998 Eastern District High School graduated its last class of seniors. Founded in 1900 and occupying at various times three different sites in Williamsburg, the high school counts writer Henry Miller, theater impresario Joseph Papp, and singer Barry Manilow among its alumni.

■ Comedian Mel Brooks, talk show host Geraldo Rivera, and the artist José Serene were all raised in Williamsburg.

■ In July many Northside streets are filled with Italians celebrating the giglio, a festival in honor of the South Italian saint Paulinus. Every year since 1903, when Italian immigrants from Nola founded the festivities, more than 200 men join together to parade a 65-foot-tall, multitiered tower through the streets.

ing complex of 20 apartment buildings spread across 25 acres of gardens and playgrounds. The original plan for the Williamsburg Houses was heralded for its pedestrian pathways and courtyards.

The **Northside** of Williamsburg was separated from the rest of Williamsburg when the Brooklyn-Queens Expressway was built in 1957. Today this section has an entirely different feel from the southern section. It is a mix of young artists and professionals, of Italian immigrants and Polish immigrants with relatives in nearby Greenpoint.

The Northside is full of young people who are hip and trendy, and because of this it is often listed as one of New York City's newest bohemias. Lamp posts and restaurant facades are filled with advertisements for studio space and sublets. (One such studio is located at 270 Union Avenue, in the landmarked building that used to house Colored School No. 3, built in 1879.) Brightly colored hair, retro clothes, antique shops, and buildings decorated by the artists who live within them are the norm. Many new restaurants and cafes have opened in the area, which derives part of its popularity from the fact that as the first stop in Brooklyn on the L train it offers a convenient commute to Manhattan.

Mural at North 10th Street and Kent Avenue in Northside

Windsor

PROSPECT PARK WEST

HOWARD PL

PROSPECT PARK SOUTHWEST

16 ST

FULLER PL

PROSPECT AVE

TENTH AVE

WINDSOR PL

SHERMAN ST

17 ST

18 ST

ELEVENTH AVE

PROSPECT PARK

20 ST

WINDSOR TERRACE

TERRACE PL

21 ST

GREEN-
WOOD
CEMETERY

TERRACE PL

SEELEY ST

18 ST

PROSPECT EXPWY

TERRACE PL

VANDERBILT ST

REEVE PL

SHERMAN ST

GREENWOOD AVE

PROSPECT
LAKE

VANDERBILT ST

E 7 ST

McDONALD AVE

GREENWOOD AVE

E 2 ST

E 3 ST

E 4 ST

E 5 ST

CATON PL

E 8 ST

CONEY ISLAND AVE

FORT HAMILTON PKWY

KERMIT PL

CATON AVE

The secret is out, thanks to some knowledgeable reporting a few years ago in the *New York Times:* Windsor Terrace offers lovely homes and tree-lined, gracefully curving streets, all in an enchantingly peaceful neighborhood tucked between Prospect Park and Green-Wood Cemetery. Along Terrace Place, Seeley Street, and Vanderbilt Street, in the heart of Windsor Terrace, two- and three-story frame and brick houses—some connected, some separated by small yards and driveways—welcome schoolchildren, working parents, and active retirees home each day. The neighborhood, only nine blocks wide, also features limestone and brownstone row houses, as well as newer condominiums in buildings that have undergone extensive internal renovations.

The area was first inhabited by the Canarsee Indians and then acquired by John Vanderbilt, a farmer. Upon his death the land was divided into two farms that were sold in 1849 to William Bell, a developer. Bell created 47 building lots, around which the village of Windsor Terrace was built and incorporated by 1851. The numbered blocks between Vanderbilt Street and Greenwood Avenue were developed in 1862. By 1876 Windsor Terrace could boast of having its own public school, and in 1888 a volunteer fire department was formed. Eventually a fire house was constructed as well. Engine Company 240, at 1307 Prospect Avenue, was built in 1896 of brick, limestone, and slate. The building has a stone lookout tower from which firemen spotted local fires.

Row houses were built on and near Prospect Park Southwest in the early 1900s, and further development began in Windsor Terrace in 1925, when two-family houses on Sherman Street and Terrace Place were constructed, followed by two large apartment buildings on Prospect Avenue, a number of stores on 11th Avenue at Sherman Street, houses on Terrace Place, and single-family houses on

Outside the Kensington Stables at East 8th Street and Caton Place

Terrace

Seeley Street. The construction of apartment buildings, even low ones, was big news in Windsor Terrace. As late as 1942, local papers squawked about their construction as if such large buildings were being seen in Brooklyn for the first time.

In the early twentieth century, Irish American workers moved into Windsor Terrace. For some time afterward, generations of Irish Americans were born and reared in the homes once owned by their grandparents and great-grandparents. These established families have recently been joined by a younger, more ethnically mixed group that moved to the neighborhood from Park Slope and similar areas, seeking larger apartments and lower rents.

Throughout the 1940s, 1950s, and 1960s, Windsor Terrace remained a quiet, isolated neighborhood treasured by its residents, although construction of the Prospect Expressway in the 1950s brought more traffic through the neighborhood. Because it was so small, the residents knew one another well; they usually sold their houses to friends and family, relying on personal connections and word of mouth rather than realtors.

NEIGHBORHOOD PROFILE

Boundaries: from McDonald Avenue on the west to Prospect Park Southwest and Coney Island Avenue on the east, from Prospect Park West on the north to Caton Avenue on the south.

Bus: B16: Caton Ave. B75: Prospect Park West B69: Prospect Park West B67: McDonald Ave. Bx29: Prospect Expressway B68: Prospect Park Southwest

Libraries: Brooklyn Public Library Windsor Terrace Branch (East 5th St. at Fort Hamilton Pkwy.)

Community Board: No. 7

Police Precinct: 72nd Precinct (830 4th Ave.)

Fire Department: Engine 240 (1307 Prospect Ave.)

The 1980s brought renewed interest in Windsor Terrace. New families who wanted to buy in town but could not afford more affluent neighborhoods like Brooklyn Heights or Park Slope discovered the neighborhood. In the late 1980s new, publicly assisted two-

Gracefully curving Windsor Terrace row houses

NEIGHBORHOOD FACTS

■ Farrell's, the neighborhood watering hole, has been in Windsor Terrace since 1933. Habitués claim that actress Shirley MacLaine stopped in to have a drink while she was filming *Desperate Characters* (1971) in the neighborhood. And Brooklynites watching *As Good As It Gets* (1997) will notice that the character played by Helen Hunt lives on Windsor Place and goes to Farrell's with her mother. Other films made in the area include *Smoke* and *Blue in the Face*, which was shot in a former post office across from Farrell's. Both 1995 movies featured actor Harvey Keitel.

■ Parkwest Commons at 279 Prospect Park West, one of Windsor Terrace's condominium buildings, was a paint factory warehouse in 1975 when it was used as the bank that Al Pacino tries to rob in the movie *Dog Day Afternoon*. Although the building was changed slightly for the movie and later renovated, it is still recognizable.

■ Authors Pete Hamill and Frank McCourt lived in Windsor Terrace.

family houses designed for moderate and middle-income families were built on Terrace Place and Seeley Street. Opportunities to buy these houses were determined by lottery.

In spite of this growth, Windsor Terrace retains much of its original charac-

Farrell's, a popular neighborhood bar since 1933

ter. A new pavilion multiplex theater with a cafe has revitalized the old Sanders Theater (1926) off Bartel Pritchard Square, but the traffic that rushes by on McDonald Avenue bypasses Windsor Terrace's quiet streets, where residents still live in family homes. And future generations will enjoy the same highly prized view of Prospect Park that their parents had, for the neighborhood was rezoned in the late 1980s to keep out high-rise buildings.

Brooklyn Timeline

JOHN B. MANBECK, BROOKLYN BOROUGH HISTORIAN

1524	Giovanni da Verrazano sails into New York Bay during exploratory cruise
1609	Henry Hudson lands on today's Coney Island, explores New York Bay and Hudson River
1614	New Netherlands Company assigned monopoly of trade with New Netherlands
1621	Dutch West India Company chartered, gaining control of the New Netherlands Company
1625	First superintendent of Brooklyn appointed
1636	Dutch make initial purchases in today's Brooklyn: tracts in Flatlands and near Gowanus Bay
1636–84	All Brooklyn lands are transferred to Europeans by the Indians in two dozen deeds enacted
1637	Joris de Rapelye, Flemish (Walloon) immigrant, founds Wallabout Bay settlement
1639	Earliest recorded property sale between settlers: land for a tobacco plantation in Gowanus
1640	Patent for land in South Brooklyn granted to Frederick Lubbertsen
1642	Cornelius Dircksen begins first ferry service across East River between Brooklyn and Manhattan
1642–45	Kieft's War between Dutch and Indians
1643	Lady Deborah Moody and her Anabaptist followers settle in Gravesend; Antony Jansen van Salee granted patent for parts of Gravesend and New Utrecht
1645	Gravesend town patent issued: only English-speaking original town
1646	Town of Breuckelen (Brooklyn) chartered by Dutch West India Company
1647	Town of New Amersfoort (Flatlands) chartered; Hans Hansen Bergen, a Norwegian settler, receives a grant of waterfront land in Brooklyn and Bushwick
1652	Town of Midwout (Flatbush) chartered; Pieter Claesen Wyckoff House built (the oldest house in New York State); Dutch West India Company acquires Yellow Hook (Bay Ridge) from Nyack Indians
1654	Flatbush Reformed Dutch Church founded at Flatbush and Church Avenues (the first church in Brooklyn; present building completed 1798); "Conye Island" purchased from Indians by town of Gravesend; Brooklyn, Flatbush, and Flatlands form militia against pirates and robbers on rivers
1655	Crime of stealing fences made punishable by whipping and branding for the first offense, death for the second

1656   Gravesend passes license law prohibiting sale of liquor to Indians; first taxes levied in town of Breuckelen, to pay the salary of the Rev. John Polhemus

1657   Town of New Utrecht chartered by Jacques Cortelyou; Thursday declared official Market Day by magistrates of Breuckelen

1660   Twenty-two house lots laid out in Bushwick; 14 Frenchmen and one Dutch translator arrive in Bushwick; Leffert Pietersen van Haughwout starts a farm in Lefferts Manor

1661   Town of Boswijck (Bushwick) chartered by Gov. Peter Stuyvesant

1662   First schoolmaster appointed in Bushwick

1663   Jean Meserole and family become squatters on a 107-acre farm in Bushwick without deed or patent

1664   English capture New Amsterdam, and the colony is renamed New York; "popular representation" principle established

1665   Hugh Gerritsen builds tidewater mill in Gerritsen Beach; decree that all land purchases from the Indians must be approved by governor

1668   Court of Sessions moves from Flatbush to Gravesend (until 1685); Robert Hollis granted exclusive privilege of selling hard drink in the village of Breuckelen

1670   First town record on highways recorded in Gravesend; the name Conye Eylant first appears on a map

1673   New York is recaptured by the Dutch, renamed New Orange

1674   English rule reestablished by Treaty of Westminster; Dutch flag flies in New Utrecht for the last time, for 22 minutes

1677   Gov. Edmund Andros grants a patent separating New Lots from Flatbush; New Lots village streets laid out; New Utrecht Reformed Church established (first building, 1699)

1683   Brooklyn, Bushwick, Flatbush, Flatlands, Gravesend, New Utrecht united under one jurisdiction, Kings County

1686   Gov. Thomas Dongan brings confirmation from James II of land patents granted to Brooklyn by Gov. Richard Nicolls in 1667

1687   Town of Brooklyn pays its first annual quitrent for the king of England to New York Colony: 20 bushels of wheat

1692   Court of Sessions orders every town to build a "good pair of stocks and a good pound" (jail) which must always be kept in good repair

1697   Common lands in Brooklyn divided among freeholders

1698   First census of Kings County taken: 2,017 total population (1,721 white, 296 black; Indians aren't counted)

1702   Boundaries of New Utrecht fixed

1704   Main Road (Fulton Street) laid out

1734   Beach Lane opens, the first road built on Coney Island

1772   Town of Brooklyn volunteer fire department founded; a weekly stagecoach begins runs between Brooklyn and Sag Harbor

1774   Colonial Assembly empowers Gowanus residents to widen and maintain the Gowanus Canal and to tax users; ferry service opens between Coentes Market in Manhattan and the foot of Joralemon Street; St. George Tavern opens by the Brooklyn wharf

1775   Representatives of all Brooklyn towns except Flatlands meet to choose a nominating committee for delegates to Second Continental Congress; Brooklyn deputies Henry Williams and Jerome Remsen are chosen to attend the provincial convention in Manhattan

1776   Battle of Brooklyn: Gen. William Howe arrives from Halifax, Nova Scotia, to lead the British; Gen. Charles Lee posts 400 Pennsylvania troops from Wallabout to Gowanus; after the British victory, an encounter at Old Stone House allows Gen. George Washington's troops to retreat from Brooklyn; British military occupation of Brooklyn begins, and prison ships are established in Wallabout Bay

1781   Ascot Heath in Flatlands opens as first flat racetrack in Kings County; establishment of a shipyard near the later site of the Brooklyn Navy Yard

1782   First Brooklyn "newspaper": *Brooklyne Hall Super-Extra Gazette,* one issue published June 8 (one page, three columns of text)

1783   Britain recognizes the independence of the United States; British supplies are auctioned at Kings Naval Brewery

1787   Erasmus Hall Academy (now Erasmus Hall High School) founded

1788   Idea of a bridge between New York and Brooklyn first broached

1790   First U.S. census taken: Kings County has 4,495 total population (3,017 white, 1,478 black); the town of Brooklyn has population of 1,603

1797   Town Clerk John Doughty frees his slave Caesar Foster, the first recorded act of manumission in Brooklyn

1799   *The Courier, and Long Island Advertiser* (later *The Courier, and New York and Long Island Advertiser*), Brooklyn's first newspaper (a weekly), begins; gradual emancipation of slaves in New York State begins

1800   John Jackson buys Vinegar Hill land

1801   U.S. Navy establishes the Brooklyn Navy Yard in Wallabout Bay

1807   Jamaica Plank Road (now Jamaica Avenue), a toll road, completed

1812   War of 1812 begins: fortifications built at Fort Greene

1814   Steam ferry service inaugurated between Brooklyn and New York

1816   Village of Brooklyn organized within the town of Brooklyn, John Garrison, first president

1818   Brooklyn, Jamaica and Flatbush Turnpike (now Fulton Street) incorporated; Bridge Street African Wesleyan Methodist Episcopal Church founded in

Downtown Brooklyn (Brooklyn's oldest black church; later moved to Bedford-Stuyvesant)

1819 John Bunce appointed first postmaster of the village of Brooklyn

1821 Union Course Race Track, in Queens near the Brooklyn border, opens for thoroughbred racing, leading to development in nearby Brooklyn

1822 Cornerstone laid for St. James Church (later St. James Procathedral), the first Roman Catholic church on Long Island (Downtown Brooklyn); Brooklyn auxiliary of the American Society for Meliorating the Condition of the Jews established

1823 Apprentices Library (forerunner of the Brooklyn Museum) established

1824 Coney Island Causeway (Shell Road), a toll road, opens in Coney Island; Terhune brothers open Coney Island's first public house, Coney Island House

1825 The marquis de Lafayette visits Brooklyn to lay the cornerstone of Apprentices Library at Henry and Cranberry Streets; first public performance by Brooklyn's first African-American comedian, John Hewlett; construction of Fort Hamilton begins

1827 Village of Williamsburgh incorporated within the town of Bushwick; slavery abolished in New York State; Weeksville settled by free blacks, named after settler James Weeks; Brooklyn Savings Bank chartered; the clerk of the village of Brooklyn announces the establishment of garbage collection; mutineers from the brig *Vineyard* land on Pelican Island in Jamaica Bay with treasure but are captured in Gravesend

1831 Kings County Hospital founded

1832 Chimney sweep William Thomas, the first black landowner in Brooklyn, buys 30 acres of farmland

1834 Town of Brooklyn (which includes the village of Brooklyn) becomes the City of Brooklyn, with George Hall as the first mayor: Kings County now consists of one city (Brooklyn) and five towns (Bushwick, Flatbush, Flatlands, Gravesend, and New Utrecht); Brooklyn and Jamaica Railroad Company (later Long Island Railroad; after 1944, Long Island Rail Road) charters route from Brooklyn to Greenport, R.I.; Long Island Insurance Company opens office on Front Street, the earliest surviving office building in New York City; John Pitkin buys land in New Lots to build a shoe factory

1835 Jonathan Trotter elected second mayor of Brooklyn

1836 Cornerstone of Brooklyn City Hall, now Borough Hall, laid (completed 1849); South Ferry operation begins service between Atlantic Avenue and Manhattan; Brooklyn and Jamaica Railroad Company opens a route from Brooklyn to Hicksville

1837 Revolutionary War hero General Jeremiah Johnson elected third mayor of Brooklyn

1838   Green-Wood Cemetery incorporated

1839   Brooklyn city plan adopted; grids for streets laid out

1841   The *Brooklyn Eagle* begins publication as the *Brooklyn Eagle and King's County Democrat;* Brooklyn Athenaeum established

1843   Brooklyn Board of Education established

1844   First monument and crypt to Revolutionary War prisoners (later Prison Ship Martyrs' Monument) erected in Fort Greene; Eddy and Hart's Coney Island Pavilion, a huge tent for dancing, with food and beer, opens; riots break out between nativists and Irish immigrants on Dean, Court, and Wyckoff Streets; Brooklyn Female Academy, later Packer Collegiate Institute, opens

1846   Walt Whitman is appointed editor of the *Brooklyn Eagle;* Richard Butts plans and develops Carroll Gardens; Kings County Penitentiary erected in Crow Hill (demolished 1907)

1847   Atlantic Basin completed; Henry Ward Beecher begins his pastorate at Plymouth Church (later Plymouth Church of the Pilgrims and known as the "Grand Central Terminal of the Underground Railroad") in Brooklyn Heights; Starin's Excursions begins a steamship route between Manhattan and Coney Island; Colored School No. 1 opens in Fort Greene

1848   Opening of Washington Park, now Fort Greene Park; gas power introduced to Brooklyn, followed by the first great fire; Cypress Hills Cemetery incorporated

1849   Members of Brooklyn bar meet to organize a law library; the Great Cholera Epidemic begins

1850   Coney Island Plank Road (later Coney Island Avenue), a toll road, opens; second great fire in Brooklyn; Frederick Law Olmsted and Calvert Vaux complete the design of Washington Park (redesigned 1867)

1851   Village of Williamsburgh secedes from town of Bushwick to become city of Williamsburgh (chartered 1852): Kings County now comprises two cities and five towns; Boerum Hill Cafe, now the Brooklyn Inn, opens at Hoyt and Bergen Streets; Dry Dock No. 1 completed at Brooklyn Navy Yard

1852   Town of New Lots organized

1853   Roman Catholic Diocese of Brooklyn established; Brooklyn Collegiate and Polytechnic Institute organized; Brooklyn City Railroad starts horse-car operation from Fulton Ferry Terminal

1854   City of Williamsburgh and town of Bushwick annexed by City of Brooklyn, to be known collectively as the Eastern District (takes effect 1855): Kings County now consists of one city and five towns

1855   Walt Whitman publishes *Leaves of Grass*

1856   Ground broken for Mt. Prospect Reservoir in the park between today's Brooklyn Public Library Central Library and the Brooklyn Museum of Art; yellow fever epidemic

1857   Metropolitan Police District created for City of Brooklyn; legislature authorizes Brooklyn to take over Nassau Water Company; Philharmonic Society of Brooklyn formed; Mercantile Library (a predecessor to the Brooklyn Public Library) founded in Brooklyn Heights to serve working people (later housed on Montague Street); Friends Meeting House on Schermerhorn Street founded (Downtown Brooklyn)

1858   National Association of Base Ball Players, baseball's first centralized organization, formed by delegates from Brooklyn and New York and includes 71 Brooklyn teams; water from Ridgewood Reservoir introduced into Brooklyn

1859   Brooklyn Academy of Music (BAM) incorporated; St. Francis Academy, now St. Francis College, founded in Brooklyn Heights; Dime Savings Bank of Brooklyn established; steam trains removed from Atlantic Avenue tunnel

1860   New York State Legislature establishes the first Thursday in June as "Anniversary Day" (now "Brooklyn Day") to celebrate the founding of the Brooklyn Sunday School Union; Hanson Place Baptist Church (now Hanson Place Seventh Day Adventist Church), a station on the Underground Railroad in the 1850s, completed in Fort Greene; U.S. census shows Kings County population at 279,122, making Brooklyn the third-largest city in the United States

1861   Henry Ward Beecher, in a rousing speech imitating a slave auctioneer, raises money from his Plymouth Church congregation to free a slave; mobs visit *Brooklyn Eagle* and other newspapers to force them to show their loyalty to the Union by displaying the flag; Brooklyn City Railroad Company Building opened on Old Fulton Street in Downtown Brooklyn

1862   The ironclad ship *Monitor,* outfitted at Brooklyn Navy Yard, is launched at Greenpoint; Alfred M. Wood, Brooklyn's first Civil War hero and later mayor of Brooklyn, is honored with a reception and parade; Brooklyn, Bath and Coney Island Railroad opens Gunther Line, a horse-car line, the first direct public transportation to Coney Island; Cypress Hills Cemetery is incorporated into the National Cemetery System, making it the only national cemetery in New York City

1863   Two grain elevators in Atlantic Basin set on fire by mob of 200 in an extension of the Civil War draft riots; Long Island (now Brooklyn) Historical Society is organized; Surf House, owned by Peter Tilyou, opens

1864   Brooklyn and Long Island Sanitary Fair (health fair) opens at Brooklyn Academy of Music, raising $390,000; Brooklyn, Bath and Coney Island's Gunther Line converted to steam, called the Dummy Line because its engine was disguised to look like a passenger car with the boiler mounted vertically

1865   Wechsler & Abraham (later Abraham & Straus) opens at 285 Fulton Street (now Cadman Plaza); Charles S. Brown buys land that he names Brown's Village (now Brownsville)

1867   The incomplete Prospect Park opens, designed by Frederick Law Olmsted
        and Calvert Vaux: park contains Endale Arch Bridge, a pedestrian bridge
        (Brooklyn's oldest bridge); Parade Grounds created south of Prospect Park for
        military events; the state legislature approves dredging Gowanus Canal; New
        York Bridge Company formed to build Brooklyn Bridge

1868   Brooklyn Common Council authorizes $3 million to construct the proposed
        East River (Brooklyn) Bridge; William A. Engeman purchases land for Brigh-
        ton Beach from William Stillwell; Eastern Parkway, designed by Olmsted and
        Vaux, is completed, the first six-lane parkway in the world

1869   John Augustus Roebling, designer and builder of the Brooklyn Bridge, dies as
        a result of a ferry accident before completion of the bridge; Adrian Martenses
        Suydam subdivides his Bushwick farm for development

1870   Ground broken for the Brooklyn tower of the Brooklyn Bridge; Citizens' Gas
        Company begins illuminating streets and houses of New Utrecht, Bath Beach,
        Fort Hamilton; *Brooklyn Eagle* protests disposal of dead cats, dogs, horses,
        goats, and cows in Coney Island waters

1871   Ice bridge forms over East River: thousands walk across to Manhattan;
        Feltman's restaurant opens in Coney Island

1872   East New York votes 3–1 for annexation by Brooklyn; Camperdown Elm
        planted in Prospect Park near the boathouse

1873   Brooklyn's new city charter passed by New York State Assembly; William
        Engeman opens Ocean Hotel in Brighton Beach; bust of John Howard Payne,
        composer of "Home, Sweet Home," unveiled in newly completed Prospect
        Park; New Lots Town Hall completed

1874   Municipal Union favors merger of Brooklyn with New York; the frankfurter is
        introduced in Coney Island by Charles Feltman

1875   Henry Ward Beecher tried and acquitted of adultery in sensational trial; Pros-
        pect Park and Coney Island Railroad opened by Andrew Culver; Flatbush
        Town Hall built; [Thomas] Cable's Ocean House, a family hotel, opens in West
        Brighton (Coney Island)

1876   Coney Island branch of New York, Bay Ridge and Jamaica Railroad opens;
        Coney Island property owners protest use of steam trains to replace horse-
        drawn cars on route from Prospect Park to the ocean; suffragist Victoria C.
        Woodhall lectures at the Brooklyn Academy of Music on "The Human Body:
        The Temple of God"; Brooklyn manufacturers are represented at Centennial
        Exposition in Philadelphia; ground broken for new Municipal Building in
        Downtown Brooklyn; E. F. Farrington, master mechanic, makes his first cross-
        ing in a bosun's chair over cables of Brooklyn Bridge from anchorages; Ocean
        Parkway, a toll parkway designed by Frederick Law Olmsted and Calvert
        Vaux, opens for travel between Prospect Park and Coney Island; Ocean Ave-

nue opens; Li Hung-Chang, prime minister of China (known as the "Bismarck of Asia") visits the Brooklyn Navy Yard and Union League Club; Horace Greeley's monument unveiled in Green-Wood Cemetery; great Brooklyn theater fire: 295 killed; Charles Luger's Cafe, Billiards and Bowling Alley opens; Charles Looff introduces the first carousel in Coney Island

1877 Two Brooklyn newspapers, the *Argus* and the *Union,* are consolidated into the *Argus-Union;* cornerstone of St. John's Hospital laid (later St. John's Episcopal; now Interfaith Medical Center); Manhattan Beach Hotel, owned by Austin Corbin, opened by former President Ulysses S. Grant; Sea View Railway, Brooklyn's first elevated railway, begins service between Brighton Beach and West Brighton (Coney Island)

1878 Manhattan Beach Railroad Company runs its first train from Bay Ridge to Manhattan Beach; Hotel Brighton, later the Brighton Beach Hotel, opens; Iron Tower (originally Sawyer Tower) transferred from Philadelphia Centennial Exposition to Coney Island by Andrew Culver: at 300 feet, it is the highest tower in Brooklyn and has two steam elevators; Brooklyn's first use of outside electric illumination, at Loeser's Department Store on Fulton Street

1879 New York and Sea Beach Railroad line opens; Louis Stauch opens a restaurant in Coney Island; William A. Engeman opens Brighton Beach Race Track; Charles M. Gage opens restaurant in Brooklyn Heights that in 1882 becomes Gage & Tollner

1880 Coney Island Jockey Club opens at Sheepshead Bay Race Track; Society of Old Brooklynites organized; Ansonia Clock factory damaged by fire with loss of $1 million; Surf Avenue opened from Brighton Beach to West Brighton (Coney Island)

1881 Seth Low elected mayor of Brooklyn; Long Island Historical Society opens new building on Pierrepont Street; Oriental Hotel in Manhattan Beach opened by President Rutherford B. Hayes

1882 Cornerstone of Seney Hospital (now New York Methodist Hospital) laid in Park Slope

1883 Fear of collapse causes panic on Brooklyn Bridge on May 30, a week after opening, leaving 12 dead, 30 injured; Brooklyn Baseball Association formed, organizing as a minor league team (later the National League Brooklyn Dodgers); the Lexington Avenue Line, Brooklyn's second elevated railway, is completed from Brooklyn Bridge to Broadway

1884 The Colossus, or Colossal Elephant, opens in Coney Island; Switchback Railway, the first roller coaster, started in Coney Island by LaMarcus Adna Thompson

1885 Magnolia Grandiflora tree planted on Fulton Street in Bedford; Brooklyn, Bath and West End Railroad completed from New Utrecht to Coney Island

1886 Town of New Lots annexed by City of Brooklyn without the governor's signature: Kings County now includes one city and four towns; Brooklyn Jockey Club opened by Dwyer Brothers (closed 1910); Girls High School opens (Bedford-Stuyvesant)

1887 Pratt Institute founded; tornado sweeps Brooklyn; Peter Luger Steak House opened on site of Charles Luger's Cafe; Electus Litchfield buys land that he develops as Blythebourne, later Borough Park

1888 Blizzard hits Brooklyn; Hotel Brighton moved inland by 12 locomotives; Anton Siedl, conductor of the Metropolitan Opera Orchestra, inaugurates Wagner concerts at Brighton Beach (discontinued 1896); Norton's Point, now Sea Gate, purchased by William Ziegler for development of exclusive community

1889 Flatbush Avenue purchased from Flatbush Plank Road Company for $10,000 and the old toll house abolished (now located in Prospect Park); bill introduced into legislature for a subway tunnel connecting Brooklyn to New York; Brooklyn City Railroad gains control of five more rail lines; Fulton Street Elevated Railway opens; Jim Jeffries knocked out by "Gentleman Jim" Corbett at Coney Island; Carroll Street Bridge, a retractile bridge, opened over Gowanus Canal

1890 Town of Flatbush votes against annexation by City of Brooklyn; electric trolley cars begin running to Coney Island; Brooklyn Dodgers win their first National League pennant; Charles Feltman opens Tivoli in Coney Island; City Works Department reports that Brooklyn has 69,000 shade trees; seven-foot man-eating shark captured in Jamaica Bay; E. Moody Boynton begins operation of Boynton Bicycle Railway, a monorail running between Bensonhurst and West Brighton (Coney Island); Norton's Point lighthouse built (Sea Gate); Irving T. Bush begins construction of Bush Terminal (derided as "Bush's Folly") in Sunset Park

1891 Museum of Brooklyn approved by the governor; Stepniak, the Russian nihilist, lectures at First Baptist Church (now the Baptist Temple, Boerum Hill) on Tolstoy's political ideas; toll on Brooklyn Bridge footpath lifted; statue of Henry Ward Beecher unveiled at City Hall Park; Brooklyn Central Post Office built on Tillary Street; Montauk Club opens in Park Slope

1892 Bay Ridge citizens oppose annexation to City of Brooklyn; Coney Island Athletic Club formed, site of future world championship boxing matches; Boys High School completed in Bedford-Stuyvesant; Soldiers' and Sailors' Memorial Arch dedicated at Grand Army Plaza; Brooklyn Fire Headquarters built on Jay Street; Henry Meyer purchases 65 acres of East Flatbush for his Germania Land Company

1893 Plan for Brooklyn Institute Museum (now the Brooklyn Museum of Art)

adopted; Ulmer Park opens in Bensonhurst, now Bath Beach; John Philip Sousa inaugurates concert seasons at Manhattan Beach Hotel; Eagle Warehouse and Storage Company of Brooklyn opens; John Y. McKane, Gravesend supervisor, sentenced for election fraud: serves five years in Sing Sing starting in 1894

1894 Consolidation of City of Brooklyn with New York City approved in plebiscite; towns of Flatbush, Gravesend, and New Utrecht annexed by City of Brooklyn: Kings County now comprises one city and one town (Flatlands); Brooklyn Heights Railroad threatened with legal action if more than 5 cents is charged for a fare; Mackay-Bennett transatlantic cable completed from Coney Island to Hudson River, linking telephones in America to Europe; Ferris wheel introduced to Coney Island by George C. Tilyou; Buffalo Bill appears with his Wild West show at Ambrose Park (now Bush Terminal in Sunset Park)

1895 Monthlong Brooklyn trolley strike: 5,500 men out at cost of $2 million; Sheepshead Bay and Gravesend Bay freeze over in severe blizzards; Brooklyn City Hall fire: big bell explodes from the heat; first three trains from Brooklyn Bridge terminus to Manhattan Beach Hotel: travel time of 40 minutes; Sea Lion Park, first enclosed amusement park, opened by Paul Boyton in Coney Island; Calvert Vaux drowns after a fall off a Gravesend pier; Coney Island Bicycle Path opens

1896 Town of Flatlands, last independent town, annexed by City of Brooklyn; the X ray receives its first demonstration at Adelphi Academy on Lafayette Street; free postal delivery begins in New Utrecht, Gravesend, Flatbush; euchre, a popular card game, at the height of its popularity: more than 400 women take part in a charity game at St. George Hotel in Brooklyn Heights; William Jennings Bryan, Democratic presidential nominee, campaigns for free silver at the Brooklyn Academy of Music, causing great disorder outside; Brighton Beach Music Hall and Iron Pier in Coney Island are washed away by a storm; construction begins on Williamsburg Bridge; Pratt Institute Free Library, Brooklyn's first free library, opens

1897 Brooklyn Public Library formed; the Brooklyn Institute of Arts and Sciences (the Brooklyn Museum of Art) opens on Eastern Parkway; Steeplechase Park opens in Coney Island

1898 City of Brooklyn (Frederick Wurster, last mayor) consolidated into Greater New York; alleged Spanish spy arrested at Fort Hamilton; pneumatic mail tubes between Brooklyn and New York under East River formally opens; Beverley Square East constructed in Flatbush

1899 Edward Grout elected Brooklyn's first borough president; the Brooklyn Children's Museum, the world's first children's museum, opened; Dean Alvord develops Prospect Park South; Jim Jeffries defeats Bob Fitzsimmons, world heavyweight boxing champion, at Coney Island, and his bout with Tom Sharkey, also at Coney Island Athletic Club, is filmed; electric cars substituted for steam trains on 5th Avenue elevated; the Gravity Steeplechase Race Course opened at Steeplechase Park in Coney Island

1900   Gov. Theodore Roosevelt signs bill incorporating Brooklyn Public Library; 17 barbers are arrested for working on Sunday; Eastern District High School opens (Williamsburg); remains of 110 recently discovered prison ship inmates from American Revolution interred in Fort Greene vault; Bergen Beach Yacht Club opens; Beverley Square West constructed in Flatbush; U.S. census shows population of Brooklyn to be 1,166,582

1901   Frederick MacMonnies sculpture *Spirit of the American Navy* placed on the marble arch at Grand Army Plaza; Coney Island Hospital opens; Brooklyn Law School opens

1902   Willis Haviland Carrier invents the air conditioner: installs the first one in the firm of Lithography and Publishing Company; Jan Kubelik, Czech violinist, performs at Brooklyn Academy of Music; permission to erect slaughterhouse on ground west of Wallabout Market granted by Board of Health; Brooklyn Heights Railroad Company's steel drawbridge over Coney Island Creek suddenly sinks to the bottom of the creek; cornerstone of new *Brooklyn Eagle* building laid at Washington Street; ground broken for Norwegian Hospital in Bay Ridge; Ditmas Park created in Flatbush; Caton Park started in Flatbush

1903   Williamsburg Bridge opens; Luna Park opens in Coney Island; street revision commission suggests name changes for 249 Brooklyn streets; powder magazine at Fort Lafayette in Bay Ridge blows up, killing four; New York mayor Seth Low drives first spike in construction of New York's first subway; polio epidemic in Brooklyn: 2,375 dead; bronze statue of Abraham Lincoln in Prospect Park blown from pedestal and broken in severe electrical storm; Montague branch of Brooklyn Public Library opens; first of 6 "comfort stations" (public restrooms) opened at Brooklyn Borough Hall; American Revolutionary prison ship *Jersey* discovered under 12 feet of rubbish and mud in Brooklyn Navy Yard; Pitken Avenue Public Baths open: showers free, soap and towels 5 cents; a young woman and her escort walk the cable of Williamsburg Bridge; Institute Park, adjoining Brooklyn Botanic Gardens, opens; BAM building on Montague Street burns, killing one; Mardi Gras parade begins in Coney Island; Topsy the elephant electrocuted at Luna Park for killing a man: event filmed by Thomas Edison's company; Highland Park opens

1904   Dreamland opens in Coney Island; Board of Health orders sheriff to shut down Raymond Street (now Ashland Place) Jail; statue to the *General Slocum* disaster (in which a steamboat sank after the boiler blew up) unveiled at Bedford Avenue and Eastern Parkway by President Theodore Roosevelt; work begins on Brooklyn extension of subway to Atlantic Avenue; Brooklyn Rapid Transit trolley cars begin service on Williamsburg Bridge; Majestic Theater opens on Fulton Street (reincarnated in 1988 as BAM Majestic Theater); West Midwood built by Henry Meyer

1905   New morgue on Willoughby Street opens; Havemeyer sugar plant, Brooklyn, shuts down, idling 2,000 workers; "Funny Face" logo developed by George Tilyou for Steeplechase; Fanny Crosby Day established in celebration of the blind hymn writer; Brooklyn's oldest Jewish congregation (now the Congregation Baith Israel Ashei Emes) moves into building of former Middle Dutch Reformed Church, establishing Kane Street Synagogue (Cobble Hill); electric locomotives succeed steam locomotives on Atlantic Avenue; Percy Williams Amusement Park opens in Bergen Beach

1906   Vitagraph film company opens in Midwood (closed 1915); Rapid Transit Commission approves extension of Fort Hamilton subway route to Coney Island; Jewish Hospital (now Interfaith Medical Center) dedicated in Bedford-Stuyvesant; mammoth bones found in tunnel excavation at foot of Joralemon Street, Brooklyn Heights; press renames the frankfurter the "hot dog"

1907   Thirty-five acres of Steeplechase Park burn (rebuilt the following year); Long Island Railroad station opens at Hanson Place and Flatbush Avenue; Golden City Amusement Park, Canarsie, opens; first trolley car runs on Livingston Street; Prison Ship Martyrs' Monument laid in Fort Greene Park; Brighton Beach Baths open; Dime Savings Bank built on Fulton Street; Brighton Beach Race Track converted to Brighton Motordome (closed 1915)

1908   New York's first subway, the Interborough Rapid Transit (IRT), is connected from Manhattan to Brooklyn Borough Hall by the Joralemon Street tunnel; Hoyt Street station opens with private entrance to Abraham & Straus; new BAM theater opens; cornerstone laid for Brooklyn College (later Brooklyn Preparatory School) in Crown Heights on site of old Kings County Penitentiary (later site of Medgar Evers College); elevated train service begins over Williamsburg Bridge; Midwood Park completed in Flatbush; Monument for the Prison Ship Martyrs, a tribute to the 1,000 victims who died in captivity on British prison ships in the American Revolution, dedicated in Fort Greene by Secretary of War William Howard Taft, later elected the 27th president

1909   Manhattan Bridge opens; Golden City Amusement Park, Canarsie, destroyed by fire; Sigmund Freud visits Coney Island during lecture trip; Jehovah's Witnesses establish headquarters in Brooklyn Heights

1910   Twenty-four-hour automobile race at Brighton Beach Race Track leaves one killed, three injured; 16 persons injured on Coney Island roller coaster known as the Rough Riders Switchback and 12 people injured on "double whirl" ride when axle breaks; new police precinct established at Avenues H and J for "better protection against burglars"

1911   Brooklyn Botanic Garden opens; Dreamland burns down; fire sweeps Barren Island, damaging 100 homes; Calbraith P. Rodgers takes off from Sheepshead Bay Race Track on first transcontinental flight: 82 hours, 4 minutes actual flying time; U.S. Postal Bank established in Brooklyn; Manhattan Beach Hotel demolished; New Utrecht Dispensary established by women of Borough Park (becomes Maimonides Medical Center in 1966)

1912   New ferry service begins between Bay Ridge and Staten Island

1913   Ebbets Field stadium for the Brooklyn Dodgers opens

1914   "Go to Church Day" inaugurated in Brooklyn; Brooklyn morgue moves from Raymond Street and St. Edmund's Place to Kings County Hospital; 50 men arrested at Coney Island for "topless" bathing

1915   4th Avenue subway opens officially; Sheepshead Bay Speedway opens on site of Sheepshead Bay Race Track (closed 1919)

1916   St. Joseph's College established; Brooklyn Dodgers lose World Series to Boston Red Sox four games to one; $100,000 raised for Jews in Europe; 400 Erasmus Hall High School boys "rush" teachers to protest lunchroom conditions; Oriental Hotel in Manhattan Beach demolished; Nathan Handwerker opens Nathan's in Coney Island; Eden Musee, a wax museum, opened in Coney Island; Howard E. and Jessie Jones home, in Arts & Crafts style, built in Bay Ridge; Margaret Sanger opens nation's first birth-control clinic, which is closed by police after a week (Brownsville)

1917   Sanger sentenced to Queens County Penitentiary for disseminating birth-control information; Port of New York sealed at the Narrows because of German blockade; five days of rioting break out over high price of food; 8,000 African Americans protest discrimination and oppression; Louis Chevrolet defeats Ralph DePalma for $10,000 Harkness Cup in motorcar race at Sheepshead Bay Speedway; Lev Tolstoy visits Brooklyn Civic Club in Downtown Brooklyn

1918   Malbone Street tunnel wreck on Brighton Line of BRT during railway strike: 94 killed, 100 injured—street name changed to Empire Boulevard as a result; Military Ocean Terminal (later Brooklyn Army Terminal) completed; 18 drowned when a storm upsets their canoes in Rockaway Inlet; Peter Lefferts Homestead transferred to Prospect Park from Prospect-Lefferts Gardens; Kenmore Terrace constructed in Flatbush

1919   Big fire in Greenpoint: 35 tanks of oil, gasoline, and naphtha burn

1920   Subway begins service to Coney Island; Brooklyn–Staten Island bridge first proposed; "Neighbors Day" observed in Brooklyn; Dodgers lose World Series to Cleveland Indians five games to two; Secretary of the Navy Franklin D. Roosevelt addresses Brooklyn Labor Day parade; gunpowder magazine found at Plumb Island in bomb search; Wonder Wheel, a Ferris wheel with sliding cars, opens in Coney Island; William C. Whitney donates his land to city for Marine Park

1921   A Brooklyn court rules that a reasonable rent is 10 percent of value of house; U.S. Marines ride Brooklyn mail trucks to protect them from "bandits"

1922   Gerristen Volunteer Fire Department chartered by New York State, the only volunteer fire company in Brooklyn; yachts fire on U.S. agents as they seize rum runners off Clinton Street; Brooklyn Technical High School established in Fort Greene

1923   Riegelmann Boardwalk opens in Coney Island; Brighton Beach Hotel demolished; Shell Bank Canal constructed

1924   Fulton Ferry service across the East River ends after 282 years; first bathing beauty contest held in Coney Island

1925   Earthquake shakes Brooklyn; 35,000–seat Coney Island Stadium on Surf Avenue and West 8th Street opens on land leased from Brooklyn-Manhattan Transit; experts oppose erection of Narrows bridge (Verrazano Narrows Bridge)

1926   Long Island University chartered; Municipal Building completed on Joralemon Street; Board of Education headquarters building completed on Livingston Street; Sanders Theater opens at Bartel Pritchard Square in Windsor Terrace (now Pavilion Theater)

1927   Half Moon Hotel opens in Coney Island

1928   Cyclone roller coaster ride opens in Coney Island

1929   Williamsburgh Savings Bank Tower, the tallest building in Brooklyn, completed at 1 Hanson Place; work on Floyd Bennett Field begins: height of swampland raised 16 inches above sea level, eliminating former Barren Island; Enduro's Sandwich Shop opened by Harry Rosen at Flatbush and DeKalb Avenues (known as Junior's Restaurant since 1950)

1930   Brooklyn College established as a four-year college; Floyd Bennett Field, New York's first municipal airport (after 1941 New York Naval Air Station), dedicated by Rear Adm. Richard E. Byrd; Loew's Pitkin Theater built in Brownsville; U.S. census shows that Brooklyn remains the city's most populous borough: 2,560,401

1932   Bailey Fountain in Grand Army Plaza completed

1933   Wiley Post takes off from Floyd Bennett Field for solo round-the-world flight: 7 days, 18 hours; Farrell's, a watering hole in Windsor Terrace, opens

1934   Lundy's restaurant opens on site of former Bay Side Hotel in Sheepshead Bay

1935   Ground broken for Brooklyn College on former Flatbush golf course (opens

1937): President Franklin D. Roosevelt lays the cornerstone for the
gymnasium

1936   Independent A train opens on Fulton Street; USS *Brooklyn* launched at
Brooklyn Navy Yard; 50-ton whale beached at Emmons Avenue and Knapp
Street in Sheepshead Bay

1937   Marine Parkway Bridge, now Gil Hodges–Marine Parkway Bridge, opens;
Williamsburg Houses, first federally subsidized housing project in Brooklyn,
opens; first conviction of a member of "Murder Inc.," a contract-killing organization founded in Brownsville

1938   Two famous flights from Floyd Bennett Field: Howard Hughes's record-
breaking round-the-world flight in 3 days, 19 hours, and Douglas (Wrong
Way) Corrigan's intended trip to California that ends in Ireland; New York
City Parks Department takes over administration of Coney Island from borough president

1939   Kosciuszko Bridge opens in Greenpoint; William Mangels opens the Ameri-
can Museum of Public Recreation, a collection of amusement memorabilia, in
Coney Island (lasted one year); Marine Park, largest park in Brooklyn, opens;
L & B Pizza opens its Spumoni Gardens in Gravesend

1940   Fulton Street elevated train service discontinued; Pres. Franklin D. Roosevelt
breaks ground for Brooklyn-Battery Tunnel; at the Half Moon Hotel in Coney
Island, Abe (Kid Twist) Reles turns state's evidence on his colleagues in
"Murder Inc.," helping to destroy the criminal organization; Reles subsequently "falls" from window to his death

1941   Cadman Plaza Civic Center plan presented; Central Library of Brooklyn Public Library opens at Grand Army Plaza; Circumferential Highway (Belt Parkway) opens; Dodgers lose World Series to New York Yankees, four games to
one; Parachute Jump transferred from Lifesavers exhibit at New York World's
Fair to Steeplechase Park

1942   New York Maritime Training Center at Sheepshead Bay opened on site of
Manhattan Beach Baths; Half Moon Hotel becomes U.S. Navy Convalescent
Hospital (later Sea Gate Naval Hospital); Brooklyn Terminal Market opens in
Canarsie

1944   Battleship *Missouri* launched at Brooklyn Navy Yard; elevated train service
over Brooklyn Bridge discontinued; first contingent of 30 enlisted Coast
Guard SPARS arrive at Manhattan Beach Coast Guard Station; Luna Park
destroyed by fire

1945   Cadman Memorial Center consecrated; 50 hurt as wooden trolley crashes on
Brooklyn Bridge; Coast Guard Station at Manhattan Beach closed down; Luna
Park closed

1946   New York City Technical College opens

1947   Jackie Robinson, the first African American player in the modern major leagues, joins Brooklyn Dodgers, who lose World Series to Yankees four games to three; annual Forsythia Day to honor borough flower inaugurated; Coney Island attendance tops 5 million

1949   Dodgers lose World Series to Yankees four games to one

1950   Fort Hamilton Veteran's Hospital dedicated; Brooklyn Bridge trolley ceases after 52 years; Tappen's Restaurant, on Emmons Avenue in Sheepshead Bay since 1845, destroyed by fire, rebuilt on Ocean Avenue; Brooklyn-Battery Tunnel opens; *Brooklyn Eagle* awarded scroll by Brooklyn Civic Council commending newspaper "for its crime exposé and 109-year-old fight for the betterment of Brooklyn"; Vanderveer Estates constructed in East Flatbush; U.S. census shows Brooklyn population at 2,738,175, its peak

1951   Sale of Trommer Beer and its Brooklyn brewery to Piel Brothers

1952   Ground broken for new branch of Brooklyn Public Library at Kings Highway and Ocean Avenue, first branch financed by the city; Dodgers lose World Series to Yankees four games to three

1953   New York City buys Brooklyn–Staten Island ferries from Brooklyn and Richmond Ferry Company rather than let service end; Dodgers lose World Series to Yankees four games to two; Brooklyn Museum acquires Crooke-Schenck House, which is rebuilt inside the museum

1955   Dodgers win World Series, beating Yankees, four games to three; *The Honeymooners*, a weekly 30-minute television series set in Bensonhurst, begins; *Brooklyn Eagle* shuts down after 114 years; Whitman Hall, Brooklyn College, dedicated; Brooklyn Bridge officially paid for: $25 million, plus $50 million in interest over 73 years

1956   Brooklyn's last trolleys cease operation; Dodgers lose World Series to Yankees four games to three (New York's Don Larsen pitches only perfect game in Series history); the Port Authority of New York begins to develop Brooklyn waterfront; Brooklyn Union Gas Co. absorbs Kings County Lighting and New York and Richmond Gas Company; Marvin Kratter buys Ebbets Field for $3 million to build enormous apartment house and a shopping center

1957   Brooklyn Dodgers win their last game at Ebbets Field, against the Pittsburgh Pirates, and move to Los Angeles; New York Aquarium opens at Coney Island; Brooklyn's 106th National Guard Infantry Regiment dissolves after 95 years; first public beach opens in Manhattan Beach

1958   Transit Authority requests 150 diesel buses to replace 175 trolleys now operating in Brooklyn

1959   Brooklyn Thoracic Hospital opens; Seacoast Towers completed in Brighton Beach; decision made to destroy historic Fort Lafayette, situated on an island off Fort Hamilton, to build Narrows Bridge

1960   "Demolition Day" at Ebbets Field; New York Senate approves bill to name Narrows Bridge after Giovanni da Verrazano; E. Quigley survives 133-foot leap from Brooklyn Bridge to win $100 bet; commercial airliner crashes in Park Slope, killing 90 persons

1962   Brooklyn Paramount Theater closes, is sold to Long Island University and converted to a gymnasium

1963   Astroland amusement park opens in Coney Island on site of Feltman's Restaurant

1964   Verrazano-Narrows Bridge, the longest suspension bridge in the world at the time, completed; Brooklyn Bridge declared national landmark; Steeplechase Park closes; Brooklyn-Queens Expressway (BQE, Rte. 278), a 10 mile elevated highway connecting Gowanus Expressway (1964) and the Belt Parkway (1941) to Queens, opens: carries 100,000 vehicles a day

1965   John F. Kennedy monument dedicated at Grand Army Plaza; Kingsborough Community College opens at Manhattan Beach on site of New York Maritime Training Center at Sheepshead Bay

1966   Brooklyn Heights historic district created, first such district under New York City Landmarks Preservation Law; Brooklyn Navy Yard closes

1967   Bedford-Stuyvesant Restoration Corporation established; a thousand Brooklyn College students clash with police in Vietnam War protest

1968   Hunterfly Road Houses in Weeksville named city landmark

1969   First West Indian Day Parade along Eastern Parkway; New York City takes possession of Brooklyn Navy Yard

1970   Kings Plaza Shopping Center opens in Mill Basin

1972   Gateway National Recreation Area created on site of former Floyd Bennett Field

1974   Starrett City housing project opens

1976   Rheingold and F. M. Schaefer beer companies leave Brooklyn; Afrikan Street Carnival (now African Street Festival) moves to present location at Boys and Girls High School in Bedford-Stuyvesant; First Häagen-Dazs shop opens on Montague Street in Brooklyn Heights

1977   Howard Golden elected Brooklyn borough president; Fulton Mall created; Brooklyn Children's Museum opens in current building

1979   Lundy's restaurant in Sheepshead Bay closes in labor dispute

1980   U.S. census shows Brooklyn population at 2,230,936

1981   Thunderbolt roller coaster in Coney Island closes; two cables snap on Brooklyn Bridge, killing a pedestrian

1983   First "Welcome Back to Brooklyn" day established by borough president Howard Golden; first Mermaid Parade in Coney Island; "Next Wave" festival inaugurated at BAM

1984   Centennial celebration of the 1883 opening of the Brooklyn Bridge: time capsule buried in Brooklyn anchorage

1987   MetroTech Center, 10-block office complex in Downtown Brooklyn, opens: cost $1 billion; new conservatory and education center opens at Brooklyn Botanic Garden

1989   Brooklyn Philharmonic Orchestra formed at BAM

1990   U.S. census shows Brooklyn most populous N.Y. borough at 2,300,664

1993   Prospect Park Zoo, closed after a tragic accident, reopens as Prospect Park Wildlife Conservation Center; Lesbian Herstory Archives opens in Park Slope

1995   First Brooklyn History Fair at Borough Hall; Lundy Bros. Restaurant (re)opens; Brooklyn Brewery opens in Williamsburg

1996   First Brooklyn History Awards, for preservationists, historians, and archivists of Brooklyn history, awarded at Borough Hall

1997   Howard Golden elected to last term as borough president: in 2002 will have served unprecedented 25 years; Atlantic Center, a shopping mall, opens in Fort Greene; President Bill Clinton visits Andries Hudde Junior High School in Flatlands to kick off a "Stop Smoking" campaign; Vinegar Hill Historic District created

1998   New York Marriott Brooklyn in MetroTech opens, the first new hotel in Brooklyn in 50 years; BAM Rose Cinemas open; Old Stone House, site of the Battle of Brooklyn, reopens after extensive renovations

1999   Controversial *Sensations* exhibit at the Brooklyn Museum of Art causes furor, and Mayor Giuliani withholds city funding; Senator-elect Hillary Clinton addresses Martin Luther King Day audience at the Brooklyn Academy of Music; Brooklyn time capsule buried at Brooklyn Children's Museum by Borough President Howard Golden to be opened 50 years later; West Brighton Carousel building (1879) dismantled from Brighton Beach Baths for eventual reconstruction as an information center within the New York Aquarium at Coney Island (the carousel had been removed from the building in 1959)

2000   Millennium ushered in with celebration at Grand Army Plaza; U.S. census lists Brooklyn's population at 2,465,326; Thunderbolt roller coaster, famed as a ride and featured in the movie *Annie Hall,* demolished by city; Department of Parks acquires Lott House (1720) in Marine Park, second-oldest Dutch farmhouse in Brooklyn

2001   Marty Markowitz, former New York state representative, elected Brooklyn borough president; 283 Brooklynites die in World Trade Center disaster; Keyspan Park opens for the Cyclones, a Mets farm team; Oceana opens in Brighton Beach on site of Brighton Beach Baths; new federal and state courthouses begin construction in Downtown Brooklyn; Battle of Brooklyn reenacted in Prospect Park and Old Stone House for 225th anniversary

2002   Memorandum of understanding signed by city and state to build 70 acre park along East River waterfront between Manhattan Bridge and Atlantic Avenue, borough's largest park; Gateway Center, new shopping mall in Canarsie, opens; Borough President Markowitz appears in Coney Island's Mermaid Parade as King Neptune; Brooklyn College opens its new library, the largest within the City University of New York

2003   Child's Restaurant (1923) on Coney Island boardwalk is the fourth Coney Island site landmarked (after the Parachute Jump, Cyclone, and Wonder Wheel); Brooklyn Historical Society reopens on Pierrepont Street after 3 years of reconstruction; Senator Charles Schumer opens Academic Village on campus of Kingsborough Community College; Bailey Fountain (1932) in Grand Army Plaza reopens after extensive reconstruction

Characteristics from the 2000 U.S. Census Bureau

TIMOTHY CALABRESE, RESEARCH ASSOCIATE, POPULATION DIVISION, NEW YORK CITY DEPARTMENT OF CITY PLANNING

Brooklyn's population is constantly shifting as people move into and out of neighborhoods. The data items presented in this section were taken from the 2000 Census Summary Files 1 and 3. Data from the Summary Files are available for a variety of geographic areas throughout the nation, including states, counties, and census tracts. New York City has 2,217 census tracts, small geographic areas that usually contain between three and five thousand persons. Census tracts were aggregated to approximate the boundaries of neighborhoods, as defined by the maps presented in this book. Census tract boundaries and neighborhood boundaries, while sometimes similar, are never exactly the same. (One neighborhood, Prospect Park South, was not included because no census tracts fit within the boundaries of the neighborhood.) Therefore, the data presented here are meant to give only a general picture of the size and characteristics of neighborhoods. Numbers have been rounded to the hundreds, so items with small values will round to zero. For more complete small-area data, please visit the Department of City Planning's website at www.nyc.gov/planning or the U.S. Census Bureau's website at www.census.gov.

Some data item descriptions were generalized in the tables. "Median age" represents the average of median age for census tracts in a neighborhood. Similarly, "Median household income" was calculated as the average of median household income for census tracts in a neighborhood and is in 1999 U.S. dollars. *Mutually Exclusive Race and Hispanic Origin* combines Hispanics (an ethnic group) as a separate additive category to create a combined race and Hispanic origin distribution. This is done by subtracting Hispanics from each race group to create "White, Non-Hispanic"; "Black or African American, Non-Hispanic"; "Asian, Non-Hispanic"; and "Some other race, non-Hispanic," in which were included the aggregate of races with extremely small representation; "Hispanic" is then given as a separate additive category. In addition, changes in 2000 permitted respondents to list more than one race. As a result, each of the major race groups are for single-responses only and a separate, "Two or more races, Non-Hispanic," category is included. Finally, in the *Region of Birth of Foreign Born*, Oceania was not included because of the very small numbers in that category.

BATH BEACH

	Number	Percentage
Total Population	28,600	100.0
Age		
Under 18 years	5,600	19.6
65 years and over	5,300	18.5
Median age (years)	39.2	—
Mutually Exclusive Race and Hispanic Origin		
White, Non-Hispanic	19,600	68.5
Black or African American, Non-Hispanic	200	0.7
Asian and Pacific Islander, Non-Hispanic	5,400	18.9
Some other race, Non-Hispanic	0	0.0
Two or more races, Non-Hispanic	900	3.1
Hispanic (of any race)	2,100	7.3
Marital Status		
Population 15 years and over	23,800	100.0
Never married	6,500	27.3
Now married, except separated	12,800	53.8
Separated, widowed or divorced	4,500	18.9
Housing		
Occupied units	11,200	100.0
Owner-occupied	3,800	33.9
Renter-occupied	7,400	66.1
Education		
Population 25 years and over	20,600	100.0
High school graduate or higher	14,600	70.9
Bachelors degree or higher	4,900	23.8
Region of Birth of Foreign Born		
Total foreign born	12,700	100.0
Europe	6,500	51.2
Asia	4,900	38.6
Africa	200	1.6
Latin America	1,000	7.9
Northern America	0	0.0
Language Spoken at Home		
Population 5 years and over	26,800	100.0
English only	10,900	40.7
Language other than English	16,000	59.7
Household Income		
Median household income (dollars)	36,400	—

BAY RIDGE AND FORT HAMILTON

	Number	Percentage
Total Population	82,800	100.0
Age		
Under 18 years	15,700	19.0
65 years and over	13,200	15.9
Median age (years)	38.3	—
Mutually Exclusive Race and Hispanic Origin		
White, Non-Hispanic	57,200	69.1
Black or African American, Non-Hispanic	1,100	1.3
Asian and Pacific Islander, Non-Hispanic	9,500	11.5
Some other race, Non-Hispanic	400	0.5
Two or more races, Non-Hispanic	4,700	5.7
Hispanic (of any race)	10,300	12.4
Marital Status		
Population 15 years and over	69,700	100.0
Never married	22,800	32.7
Now married, except separated	33,900	48.6
Separated, widowed or divorced	13,000	18.7
Housing		
Occupied units	36,300	100.0
Owner-occupied	10,700	29.5
Renter-occupied	25,600	70.5
Education		
Population 25 years and over	61,400	100.0
High school graduate or higher	49,400	80.5
Bachelors degree or higher	20,900	34.0
Region of Birth of Foreign Born		
Total foreign born	30,400	100.0
Europe	12,000	39.5
Asia	11,800	38.8
Africa	2,100	6.9
Latin America	4,200	13.8
Northern America	200	0.7
Language Spoken at Home		
Population 5 years and over	78,100	100.0
English only	39,600	50.7
Language other than English	38,600	49.4
Household Income		
Median household income (dollars)	44,600	—

BEDFORD-STUYVESANT

	Number	Percentage
Total Population	200,200	100.0
Age		
Under 18 years	61,900	30.9
65 years and over	19,000	9.5
Median age (years)	30.7	—
Mutually Exclusive Race and Hispanic Origin		
White, Non-Hispanic	2,100	1.0
Black or African American, Non-Hispanic	158,500	79.2
Asian and Pacific Islander, Non-Hispanic	2,100	1.0
Some other race, Non-Hispanic	800	0.4
Two or more races, Non-Hispanic	4,800	2.4
Hispanic (of any race)	31,500	15.7
Marital Status		
Population 15 years and over	147,600	100.0
Never married	69,300	47.0
Now married, except separated	43,100	29.2
Separated, widowed or divorced	35,200	23.8
Housing		
Occupied units	72,300	100.0
Owner-occupied	13,100	18.1
Renter-occupied	59,200	81.9
Education		
Population 25 years and over	117,200	100.0
High school graduate or higher	73,300	62.5
Bachelors degree or higher	12,500	10.7
Region of Birth of Foreign Born		
Total foreign born	40,800	100.0
Europe	800	2.0
Asia	2,100	5.1
Africa	2,600	6.4
Latin America	35,000	85.8
Northern America	200	0.5
Language Spoken at Home		
Population 5 years and over	183,700	100.0
English only	145,300	79.1
Language other than English	38,400	20.9
Household Income		
Median household income (dollars)	23,600	—

BENSONHURST

	Number	Percentage
Total Population	80,300	100.0
Age		
Under 18 years	16,900	21.0
65 years and over	13,000	16.2
Median age (years)	37.5	—
Mutually Exclusive Race and Hispanic Origin		
White, Non-Hispanic	51,300	63.9
Black or African American, Non-Hispanic	200	0.2
Asian and Pacific Islander, Non-Hispanic	18,800	23.4
Some other race, Non-Hispanic	400	0.5
Two or more races, Non-Hispanic	2,100	2.6
Hispanic (of any race)	7,200	9.0
Marital Status		
Population 15 years and over	66,100	100.0
Never married	17,900	27.1
Now married, except separated	37,000	56.0
Separated, widowed or divorced	11,200	16.9
Housing		
Occupied units	29,900	100.0
Owner-occupied	8,700	29.1
Renter-occupied	21,200	70.9
Education		
Population 25 years and over	55,900	100.0
High school graduate or higher	37,300	66.7
Bachelors degree or higher	10,800	19.3
Region of Birth of Foreign Born		
Total foreign born	42,100	100.0
Europe	20,900	49.6
Asia	16,800	39.9
Africa	600	1.4
Latin America	3,700	8.8
Northern America	200	0.5
Language Spoken at Home		
Population 5 years and over	75,800	100.0
English only	24,400	32.2
Language other than English	51,400	67.8
Household Income		
Median household income (dollars)	32,600	—

BERGEN BEACH		
	Number	*Percentage*
Total Population	12,500	100.0
Age		
Under 18 years	2,600	20.8
65 years and over	1,800	14.4
Median age (years)	39.6	—
Mutually Exclusive Race and Hispanic Origin		
White, Non-Hispanic	11,300	90.4
Black or African American, Non-Hispanic	300	2.4
Asian and Pacific Islander, Non-Hispanic	300	2.4
Some other race, Non-Hispanic	0	0.0
Two or more races, Non-Hispanic	100	0.8
Hispanic (of any race)	500	4.0
Marital Status		
Population 15 years and over	10,300	100.0
Never married	2,600	25.2
Now married, except separated	6,000	58.3
Separated, widowed or divorced	1,700	16.5
Housing		
Occupied units	4,700	100.0
Owner-occupied	2,800	59.6
Renter-occupied	1,900	40.4
Education		
Population 25 years and over	8,900	100.0
High school graduate or higher	7,500	84.3
Bachelors degree or higher	2,300	25.8
Region of Birth of Foreign Born		
Total foreign born	3,000	100.0
Europe	2,100	70.0
Asia	600	20.0
Africa	0	0.0
Latin America	300	10.0
Northern America	0	0.0
Language Spoken at Home		
Population 5 years and over	11,800	100.0
English only	7,700	65.3
Language other than English	4,100	34.7
Household Income		
Median household income (dollars)	53,500	—

BOERUM HILL		
	Number	*Percentage*
Total Population	11,700	100.0
Age		
Under 18 years	1,600	13.7
65 years and over	1,000	8.5
Median age (years)	34.4	—
Mutually Exclusive Race and Hispanic Origin		
White, Non-Hispanic	6,100	52.1
Black or African American, Non-Hispanic	1,700	14.5
Asian and Pacific Islander, Non-Hispanic	600	5.1
Some other race, Non-Hispanic	100	0.9
Two or more races, Non-Hispanic	500	4.3
Hispanic (of any race)	2,700	23.1
Marital Status		
Population 15 years and over	10,400	100.0
Never married	5,000	48.1
Now married, except separated	4,000	38.5
Separated, widowed or divorced	1,400	13.5
Housing		
Occupied units	4,900	100.0
Owner-occupied	1,100	22.4
Renter-occupied	3,800	77.6
Education		
Population 25 years and over	9,000	100.0
High school graduate or higher	7,200	80.0
Bachelors degree or higher	4,700	52.2
Region of Birth of Foreign Born		
Total foreign born	1,900	100.0
Europe	500	26.3
Asia	500	26.3
Africa	100	5.3
Latin America	800	42.1
Northern America	100	5.3
Language Spoken at Home		
Population 5 years and over	11,200	100.0
English only	7,300	65.2
Language other than English	3,900	34.8
Household Income		
Median household income (dollars)	54,000	—

	Number	Percentage
Total Population	155,900	100.0
Age		
Under 18 years	50,300	32.3
65 years and over	19,100	12.3
Median age (years)	28.8	—
Mutually Exclusive Race and Hispanic Origin		
White, Non-Hispanic	93,200	59.8
Black or African American, Non-Hispanic	1,600	1.0
Asian and Pacific Islander, Non-Hispanic	32,300	20.7
Some other race, Non-Hispanic	1,600	1.0
Two or more races, Non-Hispanic	4,400	2.8
Hispanic (of any race)	23,500	15.1
Marital Status		
Population 15 years and over	113,900	100.0
Never married	32,600	28.6
Now married, except separated	65,300	57.3
Separated, widowed or divorced	16,000	14.0
Housing		
Occupied units	46,800	100.0
Owner-occupied	13,000	27.8
Renter-occupied	33,800	72.2
Education		
Population 25 years and over	88,700	100.0
High school graduate or higher	52,700	59.4
Bachelors degree or higher	3,400	15.1
Region of Birth of Foreign Born		
Total foreign born	67,700	100.0
Europe	24,200	35.7
Asia	30,300	44.8
Africa	1,000	1.5
Latin America	11,600	17.1
Northern America	500	0.7
Language Spoken at Home		
Population 5 years and over	141,200	100.0
English only	34,100	24.2
Language other than English	107,100	75.8
Household Income		
Median household income (dollars)	28,300	—

	Number	Percentage
Total Population	31,200	100.0
Age		
Under 18 years	5,500	17.6
65 years and over	7,600	24.4
Median age (years)	44.6	—
Mutually Exclusive Race and Hispanic Origin		
White, Non-Hispanic	20,200	64.7
Black or African American, Non-Hispanic	500	1.6
Asian and Pacific Islander, Non-Hispanic	4,000	12.8
Some other race, Non-Hispanic	300	1.0
Two or more races, Non-Hispanic	1,200	3.8
Hispanic (of any race)	4,700	15.1
Marital Status		
Population 15 years and over	26,600	100.0
Never married	5,900	22.2
Now married, except separated	13,800	51.9
Separated, widowed or divorced	6,900	25.9
Housing		
Occupied units	13,200	100.0
Owner-occupied	2,200	16.7
Renter-occupied	11,000	83.3
Education		
Population 25 years and over	22,900	100.0
High school graduate or higher	16,500	72.1
Bachelors degree or higher	6,500	28.4
Region of Birth of Foreign Born		
Total foreign born	22,400	100.0
Europe	13,800	61.6
Asia	5,000	22.3
Africa	100	0.4
Latin America	3,500	15.6
Northern America	0	0.0
Language Spoken at Home		
Population 5 years and over	29,500	100.0
English only	5,200	17.6
Language other than English	24,300	82.4
Household Income		
Median household income (dollars)	20,400	—

BROOKLYN HEIGHTS

	Number	Percentage
Total Population	20,100	100.0
Age		
Under 18 years	2,100	10.4
65 years and over	2,600	12.9
Median age (years)	37.5	—
Mutually Exclusive Race and Hispanic Origin		
White, Non-Hispanic	15,700	78.1
Black or African American, Non-Hispanic	1,400	7.0
Asian and Pacific Islander, Non-Hispanic	1,100	5.5
Some other race, Non-Hispanic	100	0.5
Two or more races, Non-Hispanic	300	1.5
Hispanic (of any race)	1,500	7.5
Marital Status		
Population 15 years and over	18,100	100.0
Never married	7,900	43.6
Now married, except separated	8,000	44.2
Separated, widowed or divorced	2,200	12.2
Housing		
Occupied units	10,400	100.0
Owner-occupied	4,300	41.3
Renter-occupied	6,100	58.7
Education		
Population 25 years and over	16,300	100.0
High school graduate or higher	15,300	93.9
Bachelors degree or higher	11,500	70.6
Region of Birth of Foreign Born		
Total foreign born	2,800	100.0
Europe	1,300	46.4
Asia	900	32.1
Africa	0	0.0
Latin America	400	14.3
Northern America	100	3.6
Language Spoken at Home		
Population 5 years and over	19,100	100.0
English only	15,500	81.2
Language other than English	3,600	18.8
Household Income		
Median household income (dollars)	69,200	—

BROWNSVILLE

	Number	Percentage
Total Population	82,900	100.0
Age		
Under 18 years	29,600	35.7
65 years and over	6,400	7.7
Median age (years)	27.4	—
Mutually Exclusive Race and Hispanic Origin		
White, Non-Hispanic	600	0.7
Black or African American, Non-Hispanic	64,900	78.3
Asian and Pacific Islander, Non-Hispanic	800	1.0
Some other race, Non-Hispanic	300	0.4
Two or more races, Non-Hispanic	2,100	2.5
Hispanic (of any race)	14,300	17.2
Marital Status		
Population 15 years and over	58,500	100.0
Never married	28,200	48.2
Now married, except separated	16,800	28.7
Separated, widowed or divorced	13,500	23.1
Housing		
Occupied units	27,600	100.0
Owner-occupied	3,800	13.8
Renter-occupied	23,800	86.2
Education		
Population 25 years and over	44,600	100.0
High school graduate or higher	26,400	59.2
Bachelors degree or higher	3,100	7.0
Region of Birth of Foreign Born		
Total foreign born	20,800	100.0
Europe	500	2.4
Asia	700	3.4
Africa	900	4.3
Latin America	18,700	89.9
Northern America	0	0.0
Language Spoken at Home		
Population 5 years and over	75,600	100.0
English only	59,500	78.7
Language other than English	16,000	21.2
Household Income		
Median household income (dollars)	19,800	—

	Number	Percentage
Total Population	104,400	100.0
Age		
Under 18 years	35,100	33.6
65 years and over	6,700	6.4
Median age (years)	27.4	—
Mutually Exclusive Race and Hispanic Origin		
White, Non-Hispanic	2,800	2.7
Black or African American, Non-Hispanic	24,600	23.6
Asian and Pacific Islander, Non-Hispanic	3,400	3.3
Some other race, Non-Hispanic	800	0.8
Two or more races, Non-Hispanic	2,400	2.3
Hispanic (of any race)	70,000	67.0
Marital Status		
Population 15 years and over	74,400	100.0
Never married	31,600	42.5
Now married, except separated	28,800	37.6
Separated, widowed or divorced	14,800	19.9
Housing		
Occupied units	31,100	100.0
Owner-occupied	4,800	15.4
Renter-occupied	26,300	84.6
Education		
Population 25 years and over	56,400	100.0
High school graduate or higher	26,500	47.0
Bachelors degree or higher	4,000	7.1
Region of Birth of Foreign Born		
Total foreign born	36,200	100.0
Europe	700	1.9
Asia	2,800	7.7
Africa	400	1.1
Latin America	32,200	89.0
Northern America	0	0.0
Language Spoken at Home		
Population 5 years and over	94,200	100.0
English only	29,800	31.6
Language other than English	64,300	68.3
Household Income		
Median household income (dollars)	22,100	—

	Number	Percentage
Total Population	89,400	100.0
Age		
Under 18 years	26,100	29.2
65 years and over	8,600	9.6
Median age (years)	32.9	—
Mutually Exclusive Race and Hispanic Origin		
White, Non-Hispanic	14,200	15.9
Black or African American, Non-Hispanic	60,300	67.4
Asian and Pacific Islander, Non-Hispanic	3,400	3.8
Some other race, Non-Hispanic	400	0.4
Two or more races, Non-Hispanic	2,200	2.5
Hispanic (of any race)	8,700	9.7
Marital Status		
Population 15 years and over	67,600	100.0
Never married	25,100	37.1
Now married, except separated	29,900	44.2
Separated, widowed or divorced	12,600	18.6
Housing		
Occupied units	29,400	100.0
Owner-occupied	13,100	44.6
Renter-occupied	16,300	55.4
Education		
Population 25 years and over	54,500	100.0
High school graduate or higher	39,800	73.0
Bachelors degree or higher	10,400	19.1
Region of Birth of Foreign Born		
Total foreign born	37,300	100.0
Europe	2,900	7.8
Asia	2,900	7.8
Africa	1,300	3.5
Latin America	30,100	80.7
Northern America	100	0.3
Language Spoken at Home		
Population 5 years and over	82,900	100.0
English only	56,300	67.9
Language other than English	26,600	32.1
Household Income		
Median household income (dollars)	43,900	—

CARROLL GARDENS

	Number	Percentage
Total Population	18,800	100.0
Age		
Under 18 years	2,700	14.4
65 years and over	2,200	11.7
Median age (years)	35.3	—
Mutually Exclusive Race and Hispanic Origin		
White, Non-Hispanic	14,200	75.5
Black or African American, Non-Hispanic	600	3.2
Asian and Pacific Islander, Non-Hispanic	600	3.2
Some other race, Non-Hispanic	100	0.5
Two or more races, Non-Hispanic	700	3.7
Hispanic (of any race)	2,500	13.3
Marital Status		
Population 15 years and over	16,400	100.0
Never married	6,500	39.6
Now married, except separated	7,100	43.3
Separated, widowed or divorced	2,800	17.1
Housing		
Occupied units	9,200	100.0
Owner-occupied	2,500	27.2
Renter-occupied	6,700	72.8
Education		
Population 25 years and over	14,800	100.0
High school graduate or higher	12,700	85.8
Bachelors degree or higher	8,500	57.4
Region of Birth of Foreign Born		
Total foreign born	2,800	100.0
Europe	1,400	50.0
Asia	500	17.9
Africa	0	0.0
Latin America	800	28.6
Northern America	0	0.0
Language Spoken at Home		
Population 5 years and over	17,900	100.0
English only	13,400	74.9
Language other than English	4,600	25.7
Household Income		
Median household income (dollars)	61,400	—

CLINTON HILL

	Number	Percentage
Total Population	24,800	100.0
Age		
Under 18 years	4,300	17.3
65 years and over	2,500	10.1
Median age (years)	32.3	—
Mutually Exclusive Race and Hispanic Origin		
White, Non-Hispanic	5,200	21.0
Black or African American, Non-Hispanic	14,400	58.1
Asian and Pacific Islander, Non-Hispanic	1,300	5.2
Some other race, Non-Hispanic	300	1.2
Two or more races, Non-Hispanic	800	3.2
Hispanic (of any race)	3,500	14.1
Marital Status		
Population 15 years and over	21,800	100.0
Never married	10,300	47.2
Now married, except separated	7,300	33.5
Separated, widowed or divorced	4,200	19.3
Housing		
Occupied units	11,000	100.0
Owner-occupied	3,000	27.3
Renter-occupied	8,000	72.7
Education		
Population 25 years and over	17,500	100.0
High school graduate or higher	14,700	84.0
Bachelors degree or higher	7,000	40.0
Region of Birth of Foreign Born		
Total foreign born	4,700	100.0
Europe	400	8.5
Asia	900	19.1
Africa	300	6.4
Latin America	3,000	63.8
Northern America	100	2.1
Language Spoken at Home		
Population 5 years and over	23,900	100.0
English only	18,400	77.0
Language other than English	5,600	23.4
Household Income		
Median household income (dollars)	41,100	—

	Number	Percentage
Total Population	6,000	100.0
Age		
Under 18 years	800	13.3
65 years and over	900	15.0
Median age (years)	36.3	—
Mutually Exclusive Race and Hispanic Origin		
White, Non-Hispanic	4,400	73.3
Black or African American, Non-Hispanic	300	5.0
Asian and Pacific Islander, Non-Hispanic	500	8.3
Some other race, Non-Hispanic	0	0.0
Two or more races, Non-Hispanic	100	1.7
Hispanic (of any race)	600	10.0
Marital Status		
Population 15 years and over	5,200	100.0
Never married	1,900	36.5
Now married, except separated	2,500	48.1
Separated, widowed or divorced	800	15.4
Housing		
Occupied units	2,800	100.0
Owner-occupied	900	32.1
Renter-occupied	1,900	67.9
Education		
Population 25 years and over	4,900	100.0
High school graduate or higher	4,200	85.7
Bachelors degree or higher	3,300	67.3
Region of Birth of Foreign Born		
Total foreign born	1,000	100.0
Europe	200	20.0
Asia	500	50.0
Africa	0	0.0
Latin America	200	20.0
Northern America	0	0.0
Language Spoken at Home		
Population 5 years and over	5,800	100.0
English only	4,400	75.9
Language other than English	1,300	22.4
Household Income		
Median household income (dollars)	66,100	—

	Number	Percentage
Total Population	3,500	100.0
Age		
Under 18 years	600	17.1
65 years and over	200	5.7
Median age (years)	33.6	—
Mutually Exclusive Race and Hispanic Origin		
White, Non-Hispanic	1,800	51.4
Black or African American, Non-Hispanic	400	11.4
Asian and Pacific Islander, Non-Hispanic	200	5.7
Some other race, Non-Hispanic	0	0.0
Two or more races, Non-Hispanic	200	5.7
Hispanic (of any race)	900	25.7
Marital Status		
Population 15 years and over	3,100	100.0
Never married	1,400	45.2
Now married, except separated	1,300	41.9
Separated, widowed or divorced	400	12.9
Housing		
Occupied units	1,600	100.0
Owner-occupied	500	31.3
Renter-occupied	1,100	68.8
Education		
Population 25 years and over	2,600	100.0
High school graduate or higher	2,100	80.8
Bachelors degree or higher	1,300	50.0
Region of Birth of Foreign Born		
Total foreign born	800	100.0
Europe	100	12.5
Asia	300	37.5
Africa	0	0.0
Latin America	300	37.5
Northern America	0	0.0
Language Spoken at Home		
Population 5 years and over	3,300	100.0
English only	1,900	57.6
Language other than English	1,400	42.4
Household Income		
Median household income (dollars)	55,500	—

CONEY ISLAND

	Number	Percentage
Total Population	46,400	100.0
Age		
Under 18 years	11,400	24.6
65 years and over	9,800	21.1
Median age (years)	40.3	—
Mutually Exclusive Race and Hispanic Origin		
White, Non-Hispanic	21,400	46.1
Black or African American, Non-Hispanic	13,400	28.9
Asian and Pacific Islander, Non-Hispanic	1,800	3.9
Some other race, Non-Hispanic	100	0.2
Two or more races, Non-Hispanic	900	1.9
Hispanic (of any race)	8,600	18.5
Marital Status		
Population 15 years and over	36,900	100.0
Never married	12,300	33.3
Now married, except separated	15,100	40.9
Separated, widowed or divorced	9,500	25.7
Housing		
Occupied units	18,400	100.0
Owner-occupied	3,500	19.0
Renter-occupied	14,900	81.0
Education		
Population 25 years and over	31,300	100.0
High school graduate or higher	21,600	69.0
Bachelors degree or higher	6,200	19.8
Region of Birth of Foreign Born		
Total foreign born	16,900	100.0
Europe	11,500	68.0
Asia	1,700	10.1
Africa	500	3.0
Latin America	3,000	17.8
Northern America	0	0.0
Language Spoken at Home		
Population 5 years and over	43,700	100.0
English only	21,700	49.7
Language other than English	22,000	50.3
Household Income		
Median household income (dollars)	21,600	—

CROWN HEIGHTS

	Number	Percentage
Total Population	86,400	100.0
Age		
Under 18 years	26,200	30.3
65 years and over	7,700	8.9
Median age (years)	30.2	—
Mutually Exclusive Race and Hispanic Origin		
White, Non-Hispanic	10,200	11.8
Black or African American, Non-Hispanic	64,900	75.1
Asian and Pacific Islander, Non-Hispanic	700	0.8
Some other race, Non-Hispanic	800	0.9
Two or more races, Non-Hispanic	2,300	2.7
Hispanic (of any race)	7,800	9.0
Marital Status		
Population 15 years and over	64,800	100.0
Never married	29,300	45.2
Now married, except separated	21,900	33.8
Separated, widowed or divorced	13,600	21.0
Housing		
Occupied units	30,000	100.0
Owner-occupied	4,000	13.3
Renter-occupied	26,000	86.7
Education		
Population 25 years and over	50,400	100.0
High school graduate or higher	34,200	67.9
Bachelors degree or higher	7,700	15.3
Region of Birth of Foreign Born		
Total foreign born	36,300	100.0
Europe	1,900	5.2
Asia	1,100	3.0
Africa	1,300	3.6
Latin America	31,900	87.9
Northern America	200	0.6
Language Spoken at Home		
Population 5 years and over	79,700	100.0
English only	57,400	72.0
Language other than English	22,300	28.0
Household Income		
Median household income (dollars)	28,800	—

	Number	*Percentage*
Total Population	55,900	100.0
Age		
Under 18 years	18,300	32.7
65 years and over	3,500	6.3
Median age (years)	28.4	—
Mutually Exclusive Race and Hispanic Origin		
White, Non-Hispanic	2,700	4.8
Black or African American, Non-Hispanic	10,700	19.1
Asian and Pacific Islander, Non-Hispanic	4,500	8.1
Some other race, Non-Hispanic	1,900	3.4
Two or more races, Non-Hispanic	2,300	4.1
Hispanic (of any race)	33,800	60.5
Marital Status		
Population 15 years and over	40,300	100.0
Never married	15,200	37.7
Now married, except separated	18,100	44.9
Separated, widowed or divorced	7,000	17.4
Housing		
Occupied units	15,500	100.0
Owner-occupied	5,100	32.9
Renter-occupied	10,400	67.1
Education		
Population 25 years and over	31,000	100.0
High school graduate or higher	16,600	53.5
Bachelors degree or higher	2,700	8.7
Region of Birth of Foreign Born		
Total foreign born	24,200	100.0
Europe	500	2.1
Asia	2,500	10.3
Africa	100	0.4
Latin America	21,100	87.2
Northern America	0	0.0
Language Spoken at Home		
Population 5 years and over	51,000	100.0
English only	17,700	34.7
Language other than English	33,200	65.1
Household Income		
Median household income (dollars)	30,400	—

	Number	*Percentage*
Total Population	13,400	100.0
Age		
Under 18 years	2,900	21.6
65 years and over	1,000	7.5
Median age (years)	32.3	—
Mutually Exclusive Race and Hispanic Origin		
White, Non-Hispanic	4,100	30.6
Black or African American, Non-Hispanic	5,100	38.1
Asian and Pacific Islander, Non-Hispanic	1,100	8.2
Some other race, Non-Hispanic	100	0.7
Two or more races, Non-Hispanic	300	2.2
Hispanic (of any race)	2,800	20.9
Marital Status		
Population 15 years and over	11,100	100.0
Never married	5,600	50.5
Now married, except separated	3,400	30.6
Separated, widowed or divorced	2,100	18.9
Housing		
Occupied units	5,400	100.0
Owner-occupied	1,500	27.8
Renter-occupied	3,900	72.2
Education		
Population 25 years and over	9,400	100.0
High school graduate or higher	7,000	74.5
Bachelors degree or higher	3,500	37.2
Region of Birth of Foreign Born		
Total foreign born	2,200	100.0
Europe	300	13.6
Asia	900	40.9
Africa	100	4.5
Latin America	900	40.9
Northern America	0	0.0
Language Spoken at Home		
Population 5 years and over	12,700	100.0
English only	8,700	68.5
Language other than English	4,100	32.3
Household Income		
Median household income (dollars)	43,600	—

DYKER HEIGHTS

	Number	Percentage
Total Population	33,500	100.0
Age		
Under 18 years	6,900	20.6
65 years and over	5,700	17.0
Median age (years)	38.3	—
Mutually Exclusive Race and Hispanic Origin		
White, Non-Hispanic	23,600	70.4
Black or African American, Non-Hispanic	100	0.3
Asian and Pacific Islander, Non-Hispanic	5,300	15.8
Some other race, Non-Hispanic	100	0.3
Two or more races, Non-Hispanic	1,300	3.9
Hispanic (of any race)	2,500	7.5
Marital Status		
Population 15 years and over	27,300	100.0
Never married	7,700	28.2
Now married, except separated	15,100	55.3
Separated, widowed or divorced	4,500	16.5
Housing		
Occupied units	12,800	100.0
Owner-occupied	5,900	46.1
Renter-occupied	6,900	53.9
Education		
Population 25 years and over	23,300	100.0
High school graduate or higher	17,100	73.4
Bachelors degree or higher	5,300	22.7
Region of Birth of Foreign Born		
Total foreign born	11,300	100.0
Europe	5,000	44.2
Asia	4,800	42.5
Africa	500	4.4
Latin America	900	8.0
Northern America	0	0.0
Language Spoken at Home		
Population 5 years and over	31,000	100.0
English only	15,200	49.0
Language other than English	15,700	50.6
Household Income		
Median household income (dollars)	43,500	—

EAST FLATBUSH

	Number	Percentage
Total Population	181,300	100.0
Age		
Under 18 years	48,600	26.8
65 years and over	16,800	9.3
Median age (years)	33.6	—
Mutually Exclusive Race and Hispanic Origin		
White, Non-Hispanic	3,400	1.9
Black or African American, Non-Hispanic	158,300	87.3
Asian and Pacific Islander, Non-Hispanic	2,200	1.2
Some other race, Non-Hispanic	1,400	0.8
Two or more races, Non-Hispanic	5,400	3.0
Hispanic (of any race)	10,600	5.8
Marital Status		
Population 15 years and over	141,400	100.0
Never married	59,500	42.1
Now married, except separated	52,100	36.8
Separated, widowed or divorced	29,800	21.1
Housing		
Occupied units	61,300	100.0
Owner-occupied	18,700	30.5
Renter-occupied	42,600	69.5
Education		
Population 25 years and over	113,400	100.0
High school graduate or higher	79,900	70.5
Bachelors degree or higher	16,900	14.9
Region of Birth of Foreign Born		
Total foreign born	98,700	100.0
Europe	1,500	1.5
Asia	1,900	1.9
Africa	2,000	2.0
Latin America	93,200	94.4
Northern America	200	0.2
Language Spoken at Home		
Population 5 years and over	168,600	100.0
English only	126,700	75.1
Language other than English	41,900	24.9
Household Income		
Median household income (dollars)	35,300	—

	Number	Percentage
Total Population	116,800	100.0
Age		
Under 18 years	38,300	32.8
65 years and over	10,300	8.8
Median age (years)	29.9	—
Mutually Exclusive Race and Hispanic Origin		
White, Non-Hispanic	6,300	5.4
Black or African American, Non-Hispanic	73,800	63.2
Asian and Pacific Islander, Non-Hispanic	1,700	1.5
Some other race, Non-Hispanic	900	0.8
Two or more races, Non-Hispanic	2,800	2.4
Hispanic (of any race)	31,600	27.1
Marital Status		
Population 15 years and over	85,100	100.0
Never married	37,700	44.3
Now married, except separated	29,100	34.2
Separated, widowed or divorced	18,300	21.5
Housing		
Occupied units	39,500	100.0
Owner-occupied	7,600	19.2
Renter-occupied	31,900	80.8
Education		
Population 25 years and over	66,300	100.0
High school graduate or higher	40,600	61.2
Bachelors degree or higher	6,500	9.8
Region of Birth of Foreign Born		
Total foreign born	32,900	100.0
Europe	2,900	8.8
Asia	2,000	6.1
Africa	1,300	4.0
Latin America	26,600	80.9
Northern America	100	0.3
Language Spoken at Home		
Population 5 years and over	107,500	100.0
English only	70,900	66.0
Language other than English	36,600	34.0
Household Income		
Median household income (dollars)	23,600	—

	Number	Percentage
Total Population	98,800	100.0
Age		
Under 18 years	29,500	29.9
65 years and over	6,800	6.9
Median age (years)	30.9	—
Mutually Exclusive Race and Hispanic Origin		
White, Non-Hispanic	10,600	10.7
Black or African American, Non-Hispanic	60,700	61.4
Asian and Pacific Islander, Non-Hispanic	4,900	5.0
Some other race, Non-Hispanic	700	0.7
Two or more races, Non-Hispanic	4,800	4.9
Hispanic (of any race)	17,100	17.3
Marital Status		
Population 15 years and over	74,300	100.0
Never married	30,700	41.3
Now married, except separated	29,300	39.4
Separated, widowed or divorced	14,300	19.2
Housing		
Occupied units	33,100	100.0
Owner-occupied	3,900	11.8
Renter-occupied	29,200	88.2
Education		
Population 25 years and over	58,800	100.0
High school graduate or higher	39,800	67.7
Bachelors degree or higher	10,200	17.3
Region of Birth of Foreign Born		
Total foreign born	51,200	100.0
Europe	3,000	5.9
Asia	4,900	9.6
Africa	1,600	3.1
Latin America	41,500	81.1
Northern America	200	0.4
Language Spoken at Home		
Population 5 years and over	90,900	100.0
English only	48,800	53.7
Language other than English	42,100	46.3
Household Income		
Median household income (dollars)	32,200	—

FLATLANDS

	Number	Percentage
Total Population	58,600	100.0
Age		
Under 18 years	16,000	27.3
65 years and over	6,200	10.6
Median age (years)	34.5	—
Mutually Exclusive Race and Hispanic Origin		
White, Non-Hispanic	16,200	27.6
Black or African American, Non-Hispanic	33,600	57.3
Asian and Pacific Islander, Non-Hispanic	1,700	2.9
Some other race, Non-Hispanic	400	0.7
Two or more races, Non-Hispanic	1,800	3.1
Hispanic (of any race)	4,700	8.1
Marital Status		
Population 15 years and over	45,400	100.0
Never married	16,000	35.2
Now married, except separated	21,200	46.7
Separated, widowed or divorced	8,200	18.1
Housing		
Occupied units	19,400	100.0
Owner-occupied	11,100	57.2
Renter-occupied	8,300	42.8
Education		
Population 25 years and over	37,000	100.0
High school graduate or higher	29,400	79.5
Bachelors degree or higher	8,300	22.4
Region of Birth of Foreign Born		
Total foreign born	23,400	100.0
Europe	2,200	9.4
Asia	1,500	6.4
Africa	700	3.0
Latin America	18,900	80.8
Northern America	100	0.4
Language Spoken at Home		
Population 5 years and over	54,500	100.0
English only	37,200	68.3
Language other than English	17,200	31.6
Household Income		
Median household income (dollars)	49,100	—

FORT GREENE

	Number	Percentage
Total Population	28,300	100.0
Age		
Under 18 years	7,000	24.7
65 years and over	2,700	9.5
Median age (years)	30.9	—
Mutually Exclusive Race and Hispanic Origin		
White, Non-Hispanic	4,100	14.5
Black or African American, Non-Hispanic	16,000	56.5
Asian and Pacific Islander, Non-Hispanic	900	3.2
Some other race, Non-Hispanic	100	0.4
Two or more races, Non-Hispanic	1,100	3.9
Hispanic (of any race)	6,200	21.9
Marital Status		
Population 15 years and over	22,600	100.0
Never married	11,900	52.7
Now married, except separated	5,700	25.2
Separated, widowed or divorced	5,000	22.1
Housing		
Occupied units	11,100	100.0
Owner-occupied	2,000	18.0
Renter-occupied	9,100	82.0
Education		
Population 25 years and over	18,300	100.0
High school graduate or higher	13,000	71.0
Bachelors degree or higher	5,900	32.2
Region of Birth of Foreign Born		
Total foreign born	4,400	100.0
Europe	400	9.1
Asia	600	13.6
Africa	300	6.8
Latin America	2,900	65.9
Northern America	100	2.3
Language Spoken at Home		
Population 5 years and over	26,300	100.0
English only	19,000	72.2
Language other than English	7,300	27.8
Household Income		
Median household income (dollars)	34,600	—

GERRITSEN BEACH

	Number	Percentage
Total Population	6,900	100.0
Age		
Under 18 years	1,500	21.7
65 years and over	1,100	15.9
Median age (years)	40.6	—
Mutually Exclusive Race and Hispanic Origin		
White, Non-Hispanic	6,400	92.8
Black or African American, Non-Hispanic	0	0.0
Asian and Pacific Islander, Non-Hispanic	200	2.9
Some other race, Non-Hispanic	0	0.0
Two or more races, Non-Hispanic	100	1.4
Hispanic (of any race)	200	2.9
Marital Status		
Population 15 years and over	5,600	100.0
Never married	1,400	25.0
Now married, except separated	3,200	57.1
Separated, widowed or divorced	1,000	17.9
Housing		
Occupied units	2,600	100.0
Owner-occupied	2,100	80.8
Renter-occupied	500	19.2
Education		
Population 25 years and over	4,800	100.0
High school graduate or higher	4,000	83.3
Bachelors degree or higher	800	16.7
Region of Birth of Foreign Born		
Total foreign born	400	100.0
Europe	200	50.0
Asia	100	25.0
Africa	0	0.0
Latin America	100	25.0
Northern America	0	0.0
Language Spoken at Home		
Population 5 years and over	6,500	100.0
English only	6,000	92.3
Language other than English	500	7.7
Household Income		
Median household income (dollars)	55,900	—

GOWANUS

	Number	Percentage
Total Population	14,200	100.0
Age		
Under 18 years	3,600	25.4
65 years and over	1,300	9.2
Median age (years)	31.3	—
Mutually Exclusive Race and Hispanic Origin		
White, Non-Hispanic	2,800	19.7
Black or African American, Non-Hispanic	3,500	24.6
Asian and Pacific Islander, Non-Hispanic	400	2.8
Some other race, Non-Hispanic	200	1.4
Two or more races, Non-Hispanic	500	3.5
Hispanic (of any race)	6,600	46.5
Marital Status		
Population 15 years and over	11,100	100.0
Never married	5,200	46.8
Now married, except separated	3,600	32.4
Separated, widowed or divorced	2,300	20.7
Housing		
Occupied units	5,300	100.0
Owner-occupied	900	17.0
Renter-occupied	4,400	83.0
Education		
Population 25 years and over	8,800	100.0
High school graduate or higher	5,500	62.5
Bachelors degree or higher	1,700	19.3
Region of Birth of Foreign Born		
Total foreign born	2,700	100.0
Europe	200	7.4
Asia	300	11.1
Africa	100	3.7
Latin America	2,000	74.1
Northern America	0	0.0
Language Spoken at Home		
Population 5 years and over	13,100	100.0
English only	6,800	51.9
Language other than English	6,300	48.1
Household Income		
Median household income (dollars)	25,700	—

GRAVESEND

	Number	Percentage
Total Population	93,600	100.0
Age		
Under 18 years	19,700	21.0
65 years and over	16,500	17.6
Median age (years)	38.5	—
Mutually Exclusive Race and Hispanic Origin		
White, Non-Hispanic	62,000	66.2
Black or African American, Non-Hispanic	2,800	3.0
Asian and Pacific Islander, Non-Hispanic	17,000	18.2
Some other race, Non-Hispanic	400	0.4
Two or more races, Non-Hispanic	2,300	2.5
Hispanic (of any race)	9,200	9.8
Marital Status		
Population 15 years and over	77,200	100.0
Never married	20,800	26.9
Now married, except separated	41,900	54.3
Separated, widowed or divorced	14,500	18.8
Housing		
Occupied units	35,200	100.0
Owner-occupied	11,500	32.7
Renter-occupied	23,700	67.3
Education		
Population 25 years and over	65,500	100.0
High school graduate or higher	45,700	69.8
Bachelors degree or higher	13,600	20.8
Region of Birth of Foreign Born		
Total foreign born	43,200	100.0
Europe	21,800	50.5
Asia	16,300	37.7
Africa	600	1.4
Latin America	4,300	10.0
Northern America	100	0.2
Language Spoken at Home		
Population 5 years and over	88,100	100.0
English only	34,400	39.0
Language other than English	53,700	61.0
Household Income		
Median household income (dollars)	33,900	—

GREENPOINT

	Number	Percentage
Total Population	40,900	100.0
Age		
Under 18 years	7,100	17.4
65 years and over	4,600	11.2
Median age (years)	36.6	—
Mutually Exclusive Race and Hispanic Origin		
White, Non-Hispanic	29,100	71.1
Black or African American, Non-Hispanic	600	1.5
Asian and Pacific Islander, Non-Hispanic	1,700	4.2
Some other race, Non-Hispanic	200	0.5
Two or more races, Non-Hispanic	1,100	2.7
Hispanic (of any race)	8,200	20.0
Marital Status		
Population 15 years and over	34,800	100.0
Never married	12,300	35.3
Now married, except separated	16,000	46.0
Separated, widowed or divorced	6,500	18.7
Housing		
Occupied units	16,600	100.0
Owner-occupied	3,100	18.7
Renter-occupied	13,500	81.3
Education		
Population 25 years and over	29,100	100.0
High school graduate or higher	20,600	70.8
Bachelors degree or higher	6,500	22.3
Region of Birth of Foreign Born		
Total foreign born	20,700	100.0
Europe	15,500	74.9
Asia	1,500	7.2
Africa	100	0.5
Latin America	3,500	16.9
Northern America	100	0.5
Language Spoken at Home		
Population 5 years and over	38,800	100.0
English only	13,400	34.5
Language other than English	25,400	65.5
Household Income		
Median household income (dollars)	34,800	—

	Number	Percentage
Total Population	45,700	100.0
Age		
Under 18 years	12,300	26.9
65 years and over	5,700	12.5
Median age (years)	33.8	—
Mutually Exclusive Race and Hispanic Origin		
White, Non-Hispanic	22,900	50.1
Black or African American, Non-Hispanic	4,100	9.0
Asian and Pacific Islander, Non-Hispanic	8,200	17.9
Some other race, Non-Hispanic	600	1.3
Two or more races, Non-Hispanic	2,600	5.7
Hispanic (of any race)	7,100	15.5
Marital Status		
Population 15 years and over	35,000	100.0
Never married	10,300	29.4
Now married, except separated	18,900	54.0
Separated, widowed or divorced	5,800	16.6
Housing		
Occupied units	15,500	100.0
Owner-occupied	3,400	21.9
Renter-occupied	12,100	78.1
Education		
Population 25 years and over	29,000	100.0
High school graduate or higher	20,700	71.4
Bachelors degree or higher	7,400	25.5
Region of Birth of Foreign Born		
Total foreign born	25,400	100.0
Europe	9,400	37.0
Asia	9,400	37.0
Africa	500	2.0
Latin America	5,900	23.2
Northern America	100	0.4
Language Spoken at Home		
Population 5 years and over	42,100	100.0
English only	12,700	30.2
Language other than English	29,400	69.8
Household Income		
Median household income (dollars)	30,400	—

	Number	Percentage
Total Population	4,500	100.0
Age		
Under 18 years	900	20.0
65 years and over	1,000	22.2
Median age (years)	46.6	—
Mutually Exclusive Race and Hispanic Origin		
White, Non-Hispanic	4,300	95.6
Black or African American, Non-Hispanic	0	0.0
Asian and Pacific Islander, Non-Hispanic	100	2.2
Some other race, Non-Hispanic	0	0.0
Two or more races, Non-Hispanic	0	0.0
Hispanic (of any race)	100	2.2
Marital Status		
Population 15 years and over	3,900	100.0
Never married	800	20.5
Now married, except separated	2,400	61.5
Separated, widowed or divorced	700	17.9
Housing		
Occupied units	1,600	100.0
Owner-occupied	1,100	68.8
Renter-occupied	500	31.3
Education		
Population 25 years and over	3,300	100.0
High school graduate or higher	2,900	87.9
Bachelors degree or higher	1,700	51.5
Region of Birth of Foreign Born		
Total foreign born	1,600	100.0
Europe	1,300	81.3
Asia	200	12.5
Africa	0	0.0
Latin America	0	0.0
Northern America	0	0.0
Language Spoken at Home		
Population 5 years and over	4,300	100.0
English only	2,400	55.8
Language other than English	1,800	41.9
Household Income		
Median household income (dollars)	70,600	—

MARINE PARK

	Number	Percentage
Total Population	20,100	100.0
Age		
Under 18 years	4,800	23.9
65 years and over	2,900	14.4
Median age (years)	38.6	—
Mutually Exclusive Race and Hispanic Origin		
White, Non-Hispanic	16,700	83.1
Black or African American, Non-Hispanic	500	2.5
Asian and Pacific Islander, Non-Hispanic	1,100	5.5
Some other race, Non-Hispanic	100	0.5
Two or more races, Non-Hispanic	400	2.0
Hispanic (of any race)	1,500	7.5
Marital Status		
Population 15 years and over	16,000	100.0
Never married	4,000	25.0
Now married, except separated	9,800	61.3
Separated, widowed or divorced	2,200	13.8
Housing		
Occupied units	7,300	100.0
Owner-occupied	5,600	76.7
Renter-occupied	1,700	23.3
Education		
Population 25 years and over	13,900	100.0
High school graduate or higher	11,800	84.9
Bachelors degree or higher	3,700	26.6
Region of Birth of Foreign Born		
Total foreign born	3,400	100.0
Europe	2,000	58.8
Asia	700	20.6
Africa	0	0.0
Latin America	700	20.6
Northern America	0	0.0
Language Spoken at Home		
Population 5 years and over	18,900	100.0
English only	14,200	75.1
Language other than English	4,700	24.9
Household Income		
Median household income (dollars)	60,500	—

MIDWOOD

	Number	Percentage
Total Population	81,500	100.0
Age		
Under 18 years	23,100	28.3
65 years and over	13,100	16.1
Median age (years)	34.2	—
Mutually Exclusive Race and Hispanic Origin		
White, Non-Hispanic	65,000	79.8
Black or African American, Non-Hispanic	2,600	3.2
Asian and Pacific Islander, Non-Hispanic	7,600	9.3
Some other race, Non-Hispanic	400	0.5
Two or more races, Non-Hispanic	1,700	2.1
Hispanic (of any race)	4,500	5.5
Marital Status		
Population 15 years and over	62,400	100.0
Never married	16,200	26.0
Now married, except separated	35,600	57.1
Separated, widowed or divorced	10,600	17.0
Housing		
Occupied units	28,600	100.0
Owner-occupied	9,500	33.2
Renter-occupied	19,100	66.8
Education		
Population 25 years and over	50,800	100.0
High school graduate or higher	40,600	79.9
Bachelors degree or higher	17,300	34.1
Region of Birth of Foreign Born		
Total foreign born	34,000	100.0
Europe	18,700	55.0
Asia	10,200	30.0
Africa	900	2.6
Latin America	3,900	11.5
Northern America	300	0.9
Language Spoken at Home		
Population 5 years and over	75,400	100.0
English only	34,500	45.8
Language other than English	40,900	54.2
Household Income		
Median household income (dollars)	37,500	—

	Number	Percentage
Total Population	11,800	100.0
Age		
Under 18 years	2,300	19.5
65 years and over	2,300	19.5
Median age (years)	42.3	—
Mutually Exclusive Race and Hispanic Origin		
White, Non-Hispanic	10,100	85.6
Black or African American, Non-Hispanic	700	5.9
Asian and Pacific Islander, Non-Hispanic	500	4.2
Some other race, Non-Hispanic	0	0.0
Two or more races, Non-Hispanic	100	0.8
Hispanic (of any race)	400	3.4
Marital Status		
Population 15 years and over	9,900	100.0
Never married	2,500	25.3
Now married, except separated	5,700	57.6
Separated, widowed or divorced	1,700	17.2
Housing		
Occupied units	4,600	100.0
Owner-occupied	3,200	69.6
Renter-occupied	1,400	30.4
Education		
Population 25 years and over	8,700	100.0
High school graduate or higher	7,400	85.1
Bachelors degree or higher	2,800	32.2
Region of Birth of Foreign Born		
Total foreign born	3,100	100.0
Europe	1,900	61.3
Asia	600	19.4
Africa	100	3.2
Latin America	600	19.4
Northern America	0	0.0
Language Spoken at Home		
Population 5 years and over	11,200	100.0
English only	7,500	67.0
Language other than English	3,700	33.0
Household Income		
Median household income (dollars)	61,000	—

	Number	Percentage
Total Population	57,400	100.0
Age		
Under 18 years	10,200	17.8
65 years and over	4,100	7.1
Median age (years)	34.2	—
Mutually Exclusive Race and Hispanic Origin		
White, Non-Hispanic	35,500	61.8
Black or African American, Non-Hispanic	5,600	9.8
Asian and Pacific Islander, Non-Hispanic	2,700	4.7
Some other race, Non-Hispanic	500	0.9
Two or more races, Non-Hispanic	2,000	3.5
Hispanic (of any race)	11,100	19.3
Marital Status		
Population 15 years and over	48,700	100.0
Never married	22,000	45.2
Now married, except separated	20,200	41.5
Separated, widowed or divorced	6,500	13.3
Housing		
Occupied units	26,300	100.0
Owner-occupied	8,600	32.7
Renter-occupied	17,700	67.3
Education		
Population 25 years and over	42,700	100.0
High school graduate or higher	37,600	88.1
Bachelors degree or higher	26,200	61.4
Region of Birth of Foreign Born		
Total foreign born	10,100	100.0
Europe	2,200	21.8
Asia	2,200	21.8
Africa	300	3.0
Latin America	4,900	48.5
Northern America	400	4.0
Language Spoken at Home		
Population 5 years and over	54,300	100.0
English only	39,600	72.9
Language other than English	14,700	27.1
Household Income		
Median household income (dollars)	60,000	—

PROSPECT HEIGHTS

	Number	Percentage
Total Population	19,700	100.0
Age		
Under 18 years	3,700	18.8
65 years and over	1,500	7.6
Median age (years)	33.0	—
Mutually Exclusive Race and Hispanic Origin		
White, Non-Hispanic	5,400	27.4
Black or African American, Non-Hispanic	9,800	49.7
Asian and Pacific Islander, Non-Hispanic	800	4.1
Some other race, Non-Hispanic	200	1.0
Two or more races, Non-Hispanic	600	3.0
Hispanic (of any race)	2,700	13.7
Marital Status		
Population 15 years and over	16,500	100.0
Never married	8,400	50.9
Now married, except separated	5,600	33.9
Separated, widowed or divorced	2,500	15.2
Housing		
Occupied units	8,800	100.0
Owner-occupied	2,100	23.9
Renter-occupied	6,700	76.1
Education		
Population 25 years and over	13,600	100.0
High school graduate or higher	11,200	82.4
Bachelors degree or higher	6,700	49.3
Region of Birth of Foreign Born		
Total foreign born	4,900	100.0
Europe	500	10.2
Asia	700	14.3
Africa	300	6.1
Latin America	3,200	65.3
Northern America	100	2.0
Language Spoken at Home		
Population 5 years and over	18,400	100.0
English only	13,700	74.5
Language other than English	4,700	25.5
Household Income		
Median household income (dollars)	49,500	—

PROSPECT-LEFFERTS GARDENS

	Number	Percentage
Total Population	30,900	100.0
Age		
Under 18 years	8,100	26.2
65 years and over	3,000	9.7
Median age (years)	33.8	—
Mutually Exclusive Race and Hispanic Origin		
White, Non-Hispanic	1,500	4.9
Black or African American, Non-Hispanic	25,000	80.9
Asian and Pacific Islander, Non-Hispanic	300	1.0
Some other race, Non-Hispanic	300	1.0
Two or more races, Non-Hispanic	1,200	3.9
Hispanic (of any race)	2,800	9.1
Marital Status		
Population 15 years and over	24,300	100.0
Never married	10,800	44.4
Now married, except separated	8,500	35.0
Separated, widowed or divorced	5,000	20.6
Housing		
Occupied units	11,500	100.0
Owner-occupied	2,000	17.4
Renter-occupied	9,500	82.6
Education		
Population 25 years and over	19,700	100.0
High school graduate or higher	4,100	71.6
Bachelors degree or higher	3,100	15.7
Region of Birth of Foreign Born		
Total foreign born	15,200	100.0
Europe	300	2.0
Asia	300	2.0
Africa	600	3.9
Latin America	13,900	91.4
Northern America	0	0.0
Language Spoken at Home		
Population 5 years and over	28,900	100.0
English only	20,700	71.6
Language other than English	8,200	28.4
Household Income		
Median household income (dollars)	31,200	—

	Number	Percentage
Total Population	10,200	100.0
Age		
Under 18 years	3,600	35.3
65 years and over	900	8.8
Median age (years)	27.8	—
Mutually Exclusive Race and Hispanic Origin		
White, Non-Hispanic	700	6.9
Black or African American, Non-Hispanic	4,300	42.2
Asian and Pacific Islander, Non-Hispanic	0	0.0
Some other race, Non-Hispanic	200	2.0
Two or more races, Non-Hispanic	200	2.0
Hispanic (of any race)	4,700	46.1
Marital Status		
Population 15 years and over	7,000	100.0
Never married	3,500	50.0
Now married, except separated	1,800	25.7
Separated, widowed or divorced	1,700	24.3
Housing		
Occupied units	3,900	100.0
Owner-occupied	300	7.7
Renter-occupied	3,600	92.3
Education		
Population 25 years and over	5,500	100.0
High school graduate or higher	2,800	50.9
Bachelors degree or higher	500	9.1
Region of Birth of Foreign Born		
Total foreign born	900	100.0
Europe	0	0.0
Asia	100	11.1
Africa	100	11.1
Latin America	700	77.8
Northern America	0	0.0
Language Spoken at Home		
Population 5 years and over	9,200	100.0
English only	5,200	56.5
Language other than English	4,000	43.5
Household Income		
Median household income (dollars)	16,400	—

	Number	Percentage
Total Population	5,200	100.0
Age		
Under 18 years	1,400	26.9
65 years and over	700	13.5
Median age (years)	37.5	—
Mutually Exclusive Race and Hispanic Origin		
White, Non-Hispanic	4,000	76.9
Black or African American, Non-Hispanic	400	7.7
Asian and Pacific Islander, Non-Hispanic	100	1.9
Some other race, Non-Hispanic	100	1.9
Two or more races, Non-Hispanic	300	5.8
Hispanic (of any race)	500	9.6
Marital Status		
Population 15 years and over	4,200	100.0
Never married	1,400	33.3
Now married, except separated	1,900	45.2
Separated, widowed or divorced	900	21.4
Housing		
Occupied units	1,900	100.0
Owner-occupied	800	42.1
Renter-occupied	1,100	57.9
Education		
Population 25 years and over	3,300	100.0
High school graduate or higher	2,600	78.8
Bachelors degree or higher	900	27.3
Region of Birth of Foreign Born		
Total foreign born	1,800	100.0
Europe	1,200	66.7
Asia	400	22.2
Africa	0	0.0
Latin America	200	11.1
Northern America	0	0.0
Language Spoken at Home		
Population 5 years and over	5,000	100.0
English only	2,100	42.0
Language other than English	2,900	58.0
Household Income		
Median household income (dollars)	33,400	—

SHEEPSHEAD BAY

	Number	Percentage
Total Population	127,800	100.0
Age		
Under 18 years	27,900	21.8
65 years and over	23,000	18.0
Median age (years)	39.6	—
Mutually Exclusive Race and Hispanic Origin		
White, Non-Hispanic	93,600	73.2
Black or African American, Non-Hispanic	4,900	3.8
Asian and Pacific Islander, Non-Hispanic	18,000	14.1
Some other race, Non-Hispanic	500	0.4
Two or more races, Non-Hispanic	2,300	1.8
Hispanic (of any race)	8,400	6.6
Marital Status		
Population 15 years and over	105,000	100.0
Never married	27,300	26.0
Now married, except separated	57,100	54.4
Separated, widowed or divorced	20,600	19.6
Housing		
Occupied units	49,100	100.0
Owner-occupied	19,300	39.3
Renter-occupied	29,800	60.7
Education		
Population 25 years and over	88,900	100.0
High school graduate or higher	69,500	78.2
Bachelors degree or higher	26,300	29.6
Region of Birth of Foreign Born		
Total foreign born	61,300	100.0
Europe	34,100	55.6
Asia	20,800	33.9
Africa	900	1.5
Latin America	5,100	8.3
Northern America	200	0.3
Language Spoken at Home		
Population 5 years and over	120,800	100.0
English only	49,700	41.1
Language other than English	71,100	58.9
Household Income		
Median household income (dollars)	37,400	—

SUNSET PARK

	Number	Percentage
Total Population	82,600	100.0
Age		
Under 18 years	22,600	27.4
65 years and over	6,300	7.6
Median age (years)	30.1	—
Mutually Exclusive Race and Hispanic Origin		
White, Non-Hispanic	11,700	14.2
Black or African American, Non-Hispanic	2,500	3.0
Asian and Pacific Islander, Non-Hispanic	11,800	14.3
Some other race, Non-Hispanic	800	1.0
Two or more races, Non-Hispanic	2,400	2.9
Hispanic (of any race)	53,600	64.9
Marital Status		
Population 15 years and over	63,400	100.0
Never married	23,300	36.8
Now married, except separated	29,100	45.9
Separated, widowed or divorced	11,000	17.4
Housing		
Occupied units	25,000	100.0
Owner-occupied	5,800	23.2
Renter-occupied	19,200	76.8
Education		
Population 25 years and over	49,600	100.0
High school graduate or higher	25,500	51.4
Bachelors degree or higher	5,700	11.5
Region of Birth of Foreign Born		
Total foreign born	36,800	100.0
Europe	2,100	5.7
Asia	10,600	28.8
Africa	300	0.8
Latin America	23,700	64.4
Northern America	100	0.3
Language Spoken at Home		
Population 5 years and over	76,200	100.0
English only	16,400	21.5
Language other than English	59,700	78.3
Household Income		
Median household income (dollars)	30,200	—

WILLIAMSBURG	Number	Percentage
Total Population	119,400	100.0
Age		
Under 18 years	39,400	33.0
65 years and over	10,900	9.1
Median age (years)	27.0	—
Mutually Exclusive Race and Hispanic Origin		
White, Non-Hispanic	47,700	39.9
Black or African American, Non-Hispanic	8,200	6.9
Asian and Pacific Islander, Non-Hispanic	3,800	3.2
Some other race, Non-Hispanic	3,400	2.8
Two or more races, Non-Hispanic	3,400	2.8
Hispanic (of any race)	53,100	44.5
Marital Status		
Population 15 years and over	86,500	100.0
Never married	33,900	39.2
Now married, except separated	37,300	43.1
Separated, widowed or divorced	15,300	17.7
Housing		
Occupied units	39,100	100.0
Owner-occupied	4,500	11.5
Renter-occupied	34,600	88.5
Education		
Population 25 years and over	65,400	100.0
High school graduate or higher	33,800	51.7
Bachelors degree or higher	9,800	15.0
Region of Birth of Foreign Born		
Total foreign born	31,400	100.0
Europe	7,200	22.9
Asia	4,000	12.7
Africa	100	0.3
Latin America	19,600	62.4
Northern America	400	1.3
Language Spoken at Home		
Population 5 years and over	108,100	100.0
English only	28,500	26.4
Language other than English	79,600	73.6
Household Income		
Median household income (dollars)	24,000	—

WINDSOR TERRACE	Number	Percentage
Total Population	20,500	100.0
Age		
Under 18 years	3,800	18.5
65 years and over	3,000	14.6
Median age (years)	37.3	—
Mutually Exclusive Race and Hispanic Origin		
White, Non-Hispanic	13,100	63.9
Black or African American, Non-Hispanic	1,500	7.3
Asian and Pacific Islander, Non-Hispanic	1,800	8.8
Some other race, Non-Hispanic	200	1.0
Two or more races, Non-Hispanic	600	2.9
Hispanic (of any race)	3,400	16.6
Marital Status		
Population 15 years and over	17,300	100.0
Never married	6,400	37.0
Now married, except separated	7,800	45.1
Separated, widowed or divorced	3,100	17.9
Housing		
Occupied units	9,000	100.0
Owner-occupied	3,200	35.6
Renter-occupied	5,800	64.4
Education		
Population 25 years and over	15,100	100.0
High school graduate or higher	12,300	81.5
Bachelors degree or higher	6,100	40.4
Region of Birth of Foreign Born		
Total foreign born	5,800	100.0
Europe	2,100	36.2
Asia	1,700	29.3
Africa	100	1.7
Latin America	1,700	29.3
Northern America	100	1.7
Language Spoken at Home		
Population 5 years and over	19,400	100.0
English only	12,100	62.4
Language other than English	7,300	37.6
Household Income		
Median household income (dollars)	48,500	—

Bibliography

In addition to the sources listed below, see the Brooklyn Neighborhoods website: http://webhost.brooklyn.lib.ny.us/world/neighborhoods and the regular *New York Times* feature "If You're Thinking of Living in . . ."

Abel, Allen J. *Flatbush Odyssey: A Journey Through the Heart of Brooklyn*. Toronto: McClelland and Steward, 1995.

Alleman, Richard. *The Movie Lovers' Guide to New York*. New York: Perennial Library, 1988.

Anderson, Will. *The Breweries of Brooklyn*. CrotonMall, N.Y.: Will Anderson, 1976.

Armbruster, Eugene L. *Brooklyn's Eastern District*. Brooklyn: n.p., 1942.

———. *Coney Island*. New York: n.p., 1924.

Berman, John S. *Museum of the City of New York: Portraits of America, Coney Island*. New York: Barnes and Noble, 2003.

Berner, Tom. *Brooklyn Navy Yard*. Charleston, S.C.: Acadia, 1999.

Blair, Gwenda. *The Trumps: Three Generations That Built an Empire*. New York: Simon and Schuster, 2000.

Bolton, Reginald Pelham. *Indian Life of Long Ago in the City of New York*. 1934. Enlarged ed. New York: Harmony, 1972.

———. *New York City in Indian Possession*. 1920. New York: Museum of the American Indian, 1975.

Braid, Bernice, "Public Spaces, Private Places: Images of Brooklyn," in *The Long Island Historical Journal* 3, no. 1 (Fall 1990): 109–21.

Brooklyn Chamber of Commerce. *Official Brooklyn Guide*. Brooklyn: Herrin, 1939.

Brooklyn Chamber of Commerce and Stephen Van Dam. *Brooklyn@tlas*. New York: VanDam, 1998.

Brooklyn Eagle Almanac. Brooklyn: Brooklyn Eagle Press.

Brooklyn Historical Society. *Brooklyn's Hispanic Communities*. Brooklyn: Brooklyn Historical Society, 1989.

Brooklyn Rediscovery. *Brooklyn Almanac: Illustrations, Facts, Figures, People, Buildings, Books*. Margaret Latimer, ed. Brooklyn: Educational and Cultural Alliance, 1984.

———. *Brooklyn on Film*. John Manbeck and Mary Donovan, eds. Brooklyn: Educational and Cultural Alliance, 1979.

Brown, Joshua, and David Ment. *Factories, Foundries and Refineries: A History of Five Brooklyn Industries*. Brooklyn: Brooklyn Educational and Cultural Alliance, 1980.

Burrows, Edwin G., and Mike Wallace. *Gotham: A History of New York City to 1898*. New York: Oxford University Press, 1998.

Capote, Truman. *A House on the Heights*. Introduction by George Plimpton. New York: Little Bookroom, 2002.

Cohen, Rich. *Tough Jews*. New York: Simon and Schuster, 1998.

Comstock, Sarah. *Old Roads from the Heart of New York: Journeys Today by Ways of Yesterday Within Thirty Miles Around the Battery*. New York: Putnam, 1917.

Conklin, William J., and Jeffrey Simpson. *Brooklyn's City Hall*. New York: City of New York, Department of General Services, 1983.

Connally, Harold X. *Blacks in Brooklyn from 1900 to 1960*. New York: New York University Press, 1972.

———. *A Ghetto Grows in Brooklyn*. New York: New York University Press, 1977.

Cudahy, Brian J. *How We Got to Coney Island: The Development of Mass Transportation in Brooklyn and Kings County*. New York: Fordham University Press, 2002.

———. *The Malbone Street Wreck*. New York: Fordham University Press, 2000.

Denson, Charles. *Coney Island: Lost and Found*. Berkeley, Calif.: Ten Speed Press, 2002.

Department of Church Planning and Research, Protestant Council of the City of New York. *The Heart of Flatbush, Brooklyn: A Community Study*. Chicago: National Lutheran Council, 1954.

DiFazio, William. *Longshoremen: Community and Resistance on the Brooklyn Waterfront*. South Hadley, Mass.: Bergin and Garvy, 1985.

Disturnell, John, ed. *New York As It Was and As It Is: Giving an Account of the City from its Settlement to the Present Time; Forming a Complete Guide to the Great Metropolis of the Nation Including the City of Brooklyn and the Surrounding Cities and Villages*. New York: Van Nostrand, 1876.

Dolkart, Andrew S. *This Is Brooklyn: A Guide to the Borough's Historic Districts and Landmarks*. New York: Fund for the Borough of Brooklyn, 1990.

Edwards, Richard. *An Historical and Descriptive Review of the City of Brooklyn 1883*. Brooklyn: Boro Book Store, 1883.

Federal Writers Project of the Works Progress Administration in New York City. *New York City Guide*. 1939. New York: Random House, 1982.

Fisher, Edmund D. *Flatbush Past and Present*. Brooklyn: Midwood Club, 1902.

Freeman, Joshua. *Working-Class New York*. New York: New Press, 2000.

Freudenheim, Ellen, with Daniel P. Wiener. *Brooklyn: Where to Go, What to Do, How to Get There*. New York: St. Martin's, 1991.

Furman, Gabriel. *Notes Geographical and Historical Relating to the Town of Brooklyn in Kings County on Long Island*. 1824. Brooklyn: Renaissance, 1968.

Gallagher, John J. *The Battle of Brooklyn, 1776*. New York: Sarpedon, 1995.

Glen, Grace A. *Old Bay Ridge*. Brooklyn: Library Association of Brooklyn College, 1962.

Glueck, Grace, and Paul Gardner. *Brooklyn: People and Places, Past and Present*. New York: Abrams, 1991.

Goodwin, Doris Kearns. *Wait Till Next Year: A Memoir*. New York: Simon and Schuster, 1997.

Groce, Nancy. *New York: Songs of the City*. New York: Billboard/Watson-Guptill, 1990.

Habenstrat, Barbara. *Fort Greene, USA*. New York: Bobbs-Merrill, 1974.

Hall, Alice J. "Brooklyn: The Other Side of the Bridge." *National Geographic*, May 1983.

Historic and Beautiful Brooklyn: Flatlands, Flatbush, Brooklyn, Bushwick, New Utrecht, Gravesend. Brooklyn: Brooklyn Eagle Press, 1946.

Historic Brooklyn. Brooklyn: Brooklyn Trust, 1941.

Hoffman, Jerome. *The Bay Ridge Chronicles*. New York: Bay Ridge Centennial Committee of [Community] Planning Board 10, 1976.

Hotaling, Edward. *The Great Black Jockeys: The Lives and Times of the Men Who Dominated America's First National Sport*. Rocklin, Calif.: Forum, Prima Publishing, 1999.

Howard, Henry B., ed. *The Eagle and Brooklyn: The Record of the Progress of The Brooklyn Daily Eagle issued in commemoration of its Semi-Centennial and Occupancy of Its New Building; Together with the History of the City of Brooklyn from Its Settlement to the Present Time*. 2 vols. Brooklyn: Brooklyn Daily Eagle, 1893.

Ierardi, Eric J. *Gravesend, Brooklyn: Coney Island and Sheepshead Bay*. Dover, N.H.: Arcadia, 1996.

——. *Gravesend: The Home of Coney Island*. New York: Vantage, 1975.

Ierardi, Eric J., and the Gravesend Historical Society. *Guidemap to Historical Sites in Gravesend, Brooklyn*. 1996.

Immerso, Michael. *Coney Island: The People's Playground*. New Brunswick, N.J.: Rutgers University Press, 2002.

Jackson, Kenneth T. *Crabgrass Frontier: The Suburbanization of the United States*. New York: Oxford University Press, 1985.

Jackson, Kenneth T., ed. *The Encyclopedia of New York City*. New Haven: Yale University Press, 1995.

Kasson, John. *Amusing the Million: Coney Island at the Turn of the Century*. New York: Hill and Wang, 1978.

Kazin, Alfred. *A Walker in the City*. New York: Harcourt, Brace, 1951.

Kessner, Thomas. *The Golden Door: Italian and Jewish Immigrant Mobility in New York City*. New York: Oxford University Press, 1977.

Lancaster, Clay. *Old Brooklyn Heights: New York's First Suburb, Including Detailed Analysis of 61 Century-Old Houses*. Rutland, Ver.: Charles E. Tuttle, 1961.

———. *Prospect Park Handbook*. New York: Long Island University Press, 1972.

Landesman, Alter F. *Brownsville: The Birth, Development and Passing of a Jewish Community in New York*. New York: Bloch, 1969.

———. *A History of New Lots, Brooklyn, to 1887, Including the Villages of East New York, Cypress Hills, and Brownsville*. Port Washington, N.Y.: Kennekat, 1977.

Leeds, Mark. *Ethnic New York: A Complete Guide to the Many Faces and Cultures of New York*. Lincolnwood: Passport, 1996.

Linder, Marc, and Lawrence S. Zacharais. *Of Cabbages and Kings County: Agriculture and the Formation of Modern Brooklyn*. Iowa City: University of Iowa Press, 1997.

Lines, Ruth. *The Story of Sheepshead Bay, Manhattan Beach and the Sheepshead Bay Library*. Brooklyn: Brooklyn Public Library, 1949.

McCullough, David G. *The Great Bridge*. New York: Simon and Schuster, 1972.

McCullough, David W. *Brooklyn . . . And How It Got That Way*. New York: Dial, 1983.

McCullough, Edo. *Good Old Coney Island: A Sentimental Journey into the Past*. New York: Scribner's, 1957.

Manbeck, John B. *Coney Island Kaleidoscope*. Wilsonville, Ore.: Beautiful America, 1991.

Manbeck, John B., with Zella Jones. *The Brooklyn Century*. Brooklyn: Office of the Brooklyn Borough President, 2001.

Manbeck, John B., and Robert Singer. *The Brooklyn Film: Essays in the History of Filmmaking*. Foreword by Pete Hamill. Jefferson, N.C.: McFarland, 2003.

Maynard, Joan, and Gwen Cottman. *Weeksville: Then and Now*. Brooklyn: Society for the Preservation of Weeksville and Bedford-Stuyvesant History, 1983.

Ment, David. *The Shaping of a City: A Brief History of Brooklyn*. Brooklyn: Brooklyn Educational and Cultural Alliance, 1979.

Ment, David, and Mary Donovan. *The People of Brooklyn: A History of Two Neighborhoods*. Brooklyn: Brooklyn Educational and Cultural Alliance, 1980.

Ment, David, Anthony Robins, and David Framberger. *Building Blocks of Brooklyn: A Study of Urban Growth*. Brooklyn: Brooklyn Educational and Cultural Alliance, 1979.

Merlis, Brian, Lee Rosenzweig, and I. Stephen Miller. *Brooklyn's Gold Coast: The Sheepshead Bay Communities*. New York: Sheepshead Bay Historical Society with Israelowitz Publishing and Brooklyn Editions, 1997.

Miller, Ruth Seiden, ed. *Brooklyn USA: The Fourth Largest City in America*. Brooklyn: Brooklyn College Press, 1979.

Morrone, Francis. *An Architectural Guidebook to Brooklyn*. Salt Lake City: Gibbs-Smith, 2001.

Murphy, Robert. *Brooklyn Union: A Centennial History*. Brooklyn: Brooklyn Union Gas, 1995.

New York City Landmarks Preservation Commission, *Guide to New York City Landmarks*. Entries written by Andrew S. Dolkart. 2d ed. New York: John Wiley and Sons, 1998.

New York Public Library American History Desk Reference. New York: Stonesong, 1997.

Onderonk, Henry, Jr. *Revolutionary Incidents of Suffolk and Kings Counties; With an Account of the Battle of Long Island and British Prison Ships at New York*. Port Washington, N.Y.: Kennekat, 1949.

Ostrander, Stephen M. *A History of the City of Brooklyn and Kings County*. 2 vols. Brooklyn: n.p., 1894.

Palone, Anne Marie Barba. *East Flatbush: A Neighborhood History*. Brooklyn: Neighborhood Housing Services of East Flatbush, 1994.

Pelha, Reginald. *Indian Life of Long Ago in the City of New York*. Bolton, N.Y.: Harmony, 1972.

Pritchett, Wendell E. *Historical Studies of Urban America. Brownsville, Brooklyn: Blacks, Jews, and the Changing Face of the Ghetto*. Chicago: University of Chicago Press, 2002.

Rainone, Nanette, and Harriet Lyons, eds. *Brooklyn Fact and Trivia Book*. Brooklyn: Fund for the Borough of Brooklyn, 1986.

Rainone, Nanette, ed. *The Brooklyn Neighborhood Book*. New York: Fund for the Borough of Brooklyn, 1985.

Register, Woody. *The Kid of Coney Island: Fred Thompson and the Rise of American Amusements*. New York: Oxford University Press, 2001.

Reiss, Marcia. *Brooklyn Then and Now*. San Diego, Calif.: Thunder Bay Press, 2002.

Reiss, Marcia, ed. *Neighborhood History Guides*. Brooklyn: Brooklyn Historical Society, 2001, 2002, 2003.

Richman, Jeffrey I. *Brooklyn's Green-Wood Cemetery: New York's Buried Treasure*. Brooklyn: Green-Wood Cemetery, 1998.

Richmond, John. *Brooklyn, USA*. Layout and design by Abril Lamarque. New York: Creative Age, 1946.

Rieder, Jonathan. *Canarsie: The Jews and Italians of Brooklyn Against Liberalism*. Cambridge: Harvard University Press, 1985.

Robbins, Michael. W, ed. *Brooklyn, a State of Mind*. New York: Workman, 2001.

Roff, Sandra Shoiock, Anthony M. Cucchiara, and Barbara J. Dunlap. *From the Free Academy to CUNY: Illustrating Public Higher Education in New York City, 1847–1997*. New York: Fordham University Press, 2000.

Rosen, Marvin, and Walter Rosen, with Beth Allen. *Welcome to Junior's! Remembering Brooklyn with Recipes and Memories from Its Favorite Restaurant*. New York: William Morrow, 1999.

Ross, Peter. *A History of Long Island, from its Earliest Settlement to the Present Time*. New York: Lewis, 1902.

Schiavelli, Vincent. *Bruculinu, America: Remembrances of Sicilian-American Brooklyn Told in Stories and Recipes*. Boston: Houghton Miflin, 1998.

Schuchman, Joseph Fedele. "Cypress Hills: To Build a Future; A Development History and Historic Preservation Analysis of a Brooklyn Neighborhood." M.A. thesis, Cornell University, 1981.

Seitz, Sharon, and Stuart Miller. *The Other Islands of New York City: A Historical Companion*. Woodstock, Ver.: Countryman, 1996.

Seyfried, Vincent F. *The Long Island Rail Road: A Comparative History*. Parts 1–4. Garden City, N.Y.: Seyfried, 1961–66.

Shapiro, Michael. *The Last Good Season: Brooklyn, the Dodgers and Their Final Pennant Race Together*. New York: Doubleday, 2003.

Simon, Donald, "A Plan for All Seasons: The Design of Brooklyn's Prospect Park," *Long Island Historical Journal* 3, no. 1 (Fall 1990): 121–35.

Slide, Anthony. *The Big V: History of the Vitagraph Company*. Metuchen, N.J.: Scarecrow, 1976.

Smith, Albert E., with Phil A. Koury. *Two Reels and a Crank: From Nickelodeon to Picture Palaces*. Garden City, N.Y.: Doubleday, 1952.

Snow, Richard. *Coney Island: A Postcard Journey to the City of Fire*. New York: Brightwaters, 1984.

Snyder-Grenier, Ellen M. *Brooklyn! An Illustrated History*. Philadelphia: Temple University Press, 1996.

Stiles, Henry, ed. *The Civil, Political, Professional and Ecclesiastical History, and Commercial and Industrial Record of the County of Kings and the City of Brooklyn, New York, 1683–1884*. 2 vols. New York: W. W. Munsell, 1884.

———. *A History of the City of Brooklyn, Including the Old Town and Village of Brooklyn, the Town of Bushwick and the Village and City of Williamsburgh*. 3 vols. Brooklyn: Privately published, 1867, 1870.

Sutherland, Cara A. *Museum of the City of New York: Portraits of America, Bridges of New York City*. New York: Barnes and Noble, 2003.

Sutton, Joseph A. D. *Magic Carpet: Aleppo-in-Flatbush; The Story of a Unique Ethnic Jewish Community*. New York: Thayer-Jacoby, 1979.

Syrett, Harold Coffin. *The City of Brooklyn, 1865–1898: A Political History*. New York: Columbia University Press, 1944.

Talese, Gay. *The Bridge*. New York: Harper and Row, 1964.

Taylor, Clarence. *The Black Churches of Brooklyn*. New York: Columbia University Press, 1995.

Valerio, Anthony. *The Mediterranean Runs Through Brooklyn*. New York: H. B. Davis, 1982.

Vanderbilt, Gertrude Lefferts. *The Social History of Flatbush and Manners and Customs of the Dutch Settlers*. New York: Appleton, 1881.

Weld, Ralph Foster. *Brooklyn Is America*. New York: Columbia University Press, 1950.

———. *Brooklyn Village: 1816–1834*. New York: Columbia University Press, 1938.

White, Norval, and Elliot Willensky. *American Institute of Architects Guide to New York City*. 4th ed. New York: Crown, 2000.

Wilder, Craig. *A Covenant with Color: Race and Social Power in Brooklyn*. New York: Columbia University Press, 2000.

Willensky, Elliot. *When Brooklyn Was the World: 1920–1957*. New York: Harmony, 1986.

Witteman, Adolph. *U.S. Navy Yard, Brooklyn*. New York: Albertype, 1904.

Wolfe, Gerald R. *New York: A Guide to the Metropolis*. New York: New York University Press, 1994.

———. *New York, a Guide to the Metropolis: Walking Tours of Architecture and History*. New York: McGraw-Hill, 1994.

Younger, William Lee. *Old Brooklyn in Early Photographs 1865–1929: 157 Prints from the Collection of the Long Island [Brooklyn] Historical Society*. New York: Dover, 1978.

Index

Page numbers in *italics* indicate photographs.